Preface

This book is mainly targeted for BCA exam of Intranet Administration. It has been introduced in market after seeing the huge demand of ready to grasp material for exams with high level of quality, and its un-availability in market. We the GullyBaba Publishing House took a step ahead to publish the quality material focusing on exams at the same time giving you indepth knowledge about the subject.

GPH Book is the pioneer effort that provides a unique methodology so as to perform better in exams. If your goal is to attain higher grade use this powerful study tool independently or along with your text.

*On the Web : **www.gullybaba.com** is the vital resource for your exams acting as catalyst to boost up your preparation. Gullybaba.com has been Listed **no.1** in www.google.com and www.yahoo.com when you search "IGNOU MCA BCA MBA". Now you can access us on the net through **www.doctorignou.com, www.doeacconline.com, www.gphindia.com, and www.gullybabapublishinghouse.com.***

***Feedback about the book can be sent at* cs75writers@gullybaba.com.**

Acknowledgments :

We appreciate the staff and facility support provided by GullyBaba Publishing House. In particular, we appreciate the encouragement and professional advises received from Mr. Ajay Saini, Mr. Tarun Sharma, B. K. Krishna and many more.

Also we would like to thank typesetting and designing team Mrs. Bhawna Verma, Mr. Shravan Vats, Mr. Parveen Kumar, and Mr. Mukesh.

We gratefully acknowledges the significant contributions of Mr. Mahesh Chand, Mrs. Bimla Devi, Mrs. Bhawna Verma and our experts in bringing out this publication.

New Delhi ***Publisher***

INTRANET ADMINISTRATION

CS-75

For

Bachelor of Computer Applications [BCA]

By

S.ROY
MCA,B.SC.,DECM,DCPA,DECOM
Academic Counsellor - ARSD College,Delhi University
Guest Lecturer - Delhi College,Delhi University
Visiting Faculty - Punjab Technical University
Dinesh Verma
MCA, BCA, 'A' & 'O' Level, SCJP(USA), JP

Useful For

IGNOU, Nalanda University, Kurushetra University, Lalit Narayan Mithila University, Andhra University, Pt. Sunderlal Sharma (Open) University (Bilaspur), Annamalai University, Bangalore University, Bharathiar University, Bharathidasan University, HP University, Jamia Millia Islamia, Kakatiya University (Andhra Pradesh), KSOU (Karnataka), KOU (Rajasthan), MPBOU (MP), MDU (Haryana), Punjab University, Tamilnadu Open University, Sri Padmavati Mahila Visvavidyalayam (Andhra Pradesh), Sri Venkateswara University (Andhra Pradesh), UCSDE (Kerala), University of Jammu, YCMOU, Rajasthan University, UPRTOU (UP) and all other Indian Universities.

GULLYBABA PUBLISHING HOUSE (P) LTD.
AN ISO 9001:2008 CERTIFIED CO.

Developed and Produced by:

GullyBaba Publishing House (P) Ltd.

Regd. Office:
2525/193, 1st Floor,
Onkar Nagar-A, Tri Nagar,
New Delhi-110035
Landmark: Kanhaiya Nagar Metro Station

Branch Office:
1A/2A, 20, Hari Sadan,
Ansari Road, Daryaganj,
New Delhi-110002

E-mail: info@gullybaba.com, Website: GullyBaba.com

Edition: 2013

ISBN: 978-81-89086-31-2

Contents

Question Papers

CHAPTER 1

FUNDAMENTALS OF INTRANET

- *Introduction*
- *Objectives*
- *The Intranet*
- *Advantages of the Intranet*
- *Types of Intranet*
- *Software and Hardware Requirement for Intranet*
- *Application Areas*
- *Future of the Intranet*
- *Key Intranet Terms*

Many of these are using the Internet as a source of information and reference material, browsing the World Wide Web (WWW) and Newsgroups for the latest gossip or sharing/knowing facts on a whole range of issues ranging from life style to technology and spirituality to current affairs. Others use the Internet for transfer of information through the use of messages and data files via e-mail, File Transfer Protocol (FTP) or Gopher sites.

The latest has been the Web commerce that is currently making big news, and many businesses are setting up electronic shops on the Internet in anticipation of safe/ secure payment techniques poised to become widely available is being followed. This shall undoubtedly result in an increase in consumer confidence and in turn the customer would look forward for better, reliable and quality service.

Some of those businesses are also using Internet technologies, such as Web browsers and Web servers, in order to provide easy and widespread access to company's information to internal users only. Such networks have been termed as "private Internets", could be considered as sometimes having no connection at all to the outside world, were later became popular as "intranets". Despite the fact that intranets are for internal use only, the challenges for its use and maintenance are no different to those that can be found with the Internet itself. Indeed, building intranets and connecting corporate networks to the Internet is not a simple task.

Companies are turning to the Internet as an established, easily available, yet cost-effective resource that will allow them to gain a competitive edge over other players in the field. The benefits of adopting Internet technology range from lower communications costs (since transporting data across the Internet can cost much less than using a private network) to greatly improved communication speeds. However, it would be notable that there are many different risks involved in having an Intranet in place.

Q1. What is Intranet? Explain with the help of an example.

ANS : The literal meaning of the term Intranet as given in various dictionaries is as follows :

1. A network connecting an affiliated set of clients using standard internet protocols, especially TCP/IP and HTTP.

2. AN IP-based network of nodes behind a firewall, or behind several firewalls connected by secure, possibly virtual, networks.

An Intranet is the use of Internet technologies within an organization (or company) to achieve better results than the conventional means of data access and transfer. Intranet helps in cutting costs, easy and fast accessibility of day-to-day information. It could refer to a collection of networks at different locations, but catering to the requirements of the same organization.

Q2. How Intranet Works? Describe with the help of a diagram.

ANS : An Intranet can be defined as a private network, which uses Internet tools. The principal tool is the Web browser, but there are other Internet tools such as ftp and telnet that are useful. The resources defined as private may be protected physically (with a firewall or a separate physical network), geographically (by restricting access to computers with a network address on the local network), or personally (by username and password).

Typically, resources will be private either because they are confidential to the organization (for example, an internal telephone directory), or because they are covered by restrictive licenses (for example, if the Library subscribes to a bibliography whose license restricts its use to members of the University).

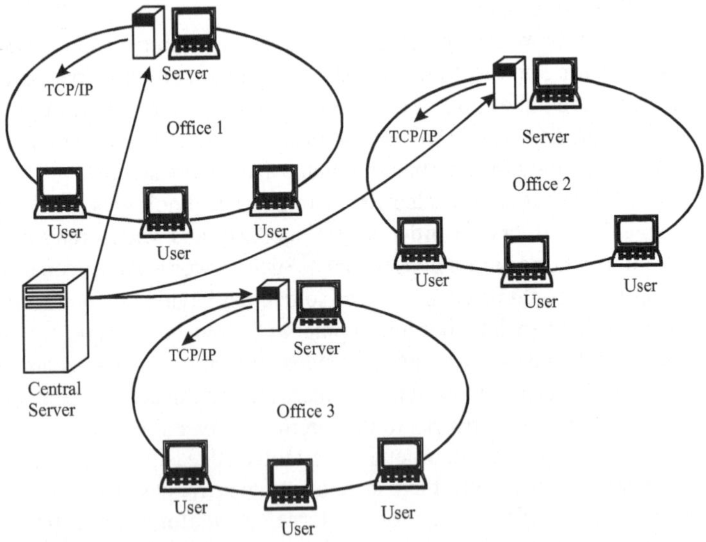

Figure : Intranet is more than a LAN but less than Internet

For an Intranet to work, all computers connected together in a network must speak and understand the same language, or protocol. The language used is Hypertext Mark-up Language (HTML) and the protocol that both intranets and the Internet uses are called Transmission Control Protocol/Internet Protocol or TCP/IP. A network server supports all the activities of an intranet. On the clients' side, is software known as a browser is used, usually Netscape Navigator or Internet Explorer.

The browser when invoked seeks a server computer through the communication medium that has the first or Home Page of the Intranet, which is usually seen in the folders as 'index.htm'. This is the default page for accessing the intranet from any computer attached to an internal network. This is what automatically appears on the screen when a user logs in and clicks on the browser icon on the desktop for accessing Internet also. The hyperlinks to specific files or databases requests for files send the control from anywhere on the network to the browser. The server accesses the file and sends back a copy of what it contains to the computer or client that has requested for it.

It is the simplicity of TCP/IP that makes Intranets so easy to set-up. Web browsers can be used to connect to virtually any information source, from Structured Query Language (SQL) databases to highly proprietary information systems.

Q3. How big can an Intranet be? Explain with the help of a suitable example.

ANS : As a big as a community of interest. Scale is an important factor in web implementation, but it has no bearing on the logical association of clients that make up an intranet. *For example*, a workgroup with one web server, a company with several hundred web-servers, and a professional organization with ten thousand web servers can each be considered an intranet.

While nothing constrains these webs to be "inside" or bounded in any physical sense, size is a significant from a network design perspective.

Q4. Differentiate between Intranet and Internet?

#: Is it Intranet or Internet that is right for your business? How will you decide it? [JUN03;Q1(b)]

ANS : Generally an Intranet is different from an Internet in the following ways:

(i). Intranet is a network within the organization whereas Internet is a worldwide network.

(ii). Intranet has access to Internet but not vice- versa.

Once the difference has been defined, the immediate possible question in everyone's mind would be: Is an intranet faster than getting data over the internet? The answer to this would be mix of features of local area network (LAN) as well as that of Internet. Clear answer depends on the possible ways of connecting the client to the network that could be as follows:

If the network is totally contained within a LAN, then it will get LAN speeds. I.e. the web server is connected via LAN to the client computer. Following are some factors that must be considered whenever the organization needs to decide on internet or intranet.

(a) When you are trying to create a system that will be used for internal communication within the organization, intranet is best for that situation. This will allows only internal peoples to access and share information with each other. External peoples cannot access anything from your intranet. But, it requires security settings on your intranet server so that outsider cannot enter your network.
(b) If you are planning to provide up-to-date product information to all of you business branches only, then also intranet is good for your organization. Since only your authorized branches can access your intranet, they are safe too.
(c) If your business required more interactions with your customers, then internet is good option here. Doing so will enable customers to access your web site from internet and can show whatever you offer to them anytime, anywhere .
(d) If you want to improve interaction and communication between departments of your organization, you need to set up an intranet. But, if you want to get customer advice and feedback, you need internet to serve better for your purpose.
(e) If you are developing or creating some products and want to advertise about the m, then internet is certainly the solution. Because public can only access your public web site not the private intranet.
(f) If you need a paperless office, so that every work of your office flow in electronic form, you need and intranet for the private intranet.
At last, we can conclude that anything that an organization wants to make accessible to public must be put on the internet. While anything that is going to be used by the persons of organization must be kept on the intranet.

Q5. Compare between Intranet, Internet & LAN. **[JUN01;Q1(c)]**
ANS :

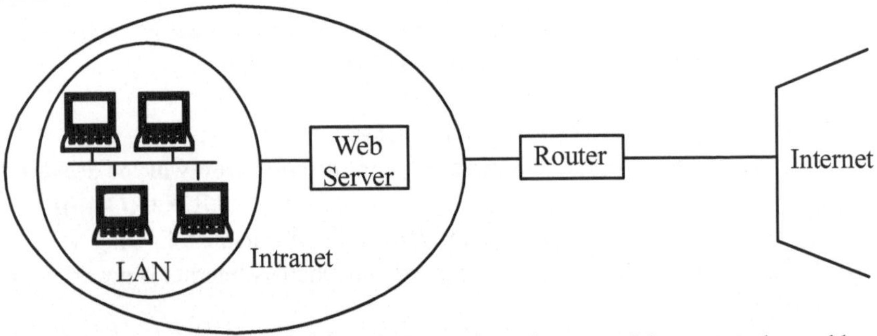

Intranet is defined as a network (LAN), which makes use of the protocols used by the Internet. In other words, it can be defined as a network, which makes use of TCP/IP protocol Stack.
Internet is simply a network made up of various protocols and various applications at each layer of OSI and TCP/IP reference model. Local Network is a group of computers connected together. No matter which protocols are used or even which reference model is implemented.

- LAN is a network, which is based upon some topology.
- Intranet is limited to a corporate. Internet is a global term, which can be used by anybody all over the world.

- Intranet includes a Web Server, a Network Server, client software and other hardware is same as LAN.
- Intranet includes a Web Server on which thousands of web sites are hosted, many name servers (DNS Servers) to Resolve host name to IP address. Many routers and switches which acts as a part of the Internet.
- LAN includes network server and client software.
- Internet may be just a LAN standard or sometimes a LAN-WAN combination Internet is a LAN-WAN-MAN combination. LAN is restricted to a single physical location.
- Intranet is easy to configure and a bit complex. Internet is very complex. LAN is very simple compare to Internet.

Q6. What are the advantages of the Intranet? Explain in detail the terms flexibility, versatility and cost effectiveness in context of Intranet. Give one example of successful intranet application.

#: List and explain various functions of an Intranet. **[JUN03;Q4(a)]**

ANS : Functions of an Intranet:

Various functions performed by the intranet in an organization are:

1) Communication
2) Database
3) Email
4) Information
5) Interaction
6) Doc management
7) Bulletin Boards
8) Publishing
9) Discussion
10) Scheduling
11) Desktop conferencing

Communication : Better communication is achieved. Communicating with both the public and staff can change the way people see the company and the product. Employees generally complain about communication, but now cannot. Using the Intranet, they share information in very easily.

Database : All the records of an organization can be kept in the form of database. It makes the querying, selecting very easy, fast and effective. A lot of filework is reduced. And hence saving of money, time and labor.

E-mail : Once Intranet is up and running, emails and comments will start coming. This will help to update the site with the help of suggestions. And increase the information of the employees if they mail any information regarding any difficulty. This will help to increase the communication between the employees and hence better working environment, healthy atmosphere.

Information : Intranet is a source of information for the employees of an organization regarding the organizations. Employees of one department can have knowledge regarding the other departments with the help of intranet. Suppose an employee of the accounts department want to know recent details of the production now he won't be needing to go to the production department and get details from there instead he has to just get connected to the intranet and get details from there. Information regarding the company seminars, entertainment programmes, and announcements all are available on intranet.

Interaction : Where there are means of communication between the members of the company interaction becomes very easy. Hence the flow of information and responses are the loveliest thing present on the intranet.

There can be a section on intranet where different employees will place their poems, stories, jokes and funny things which can be read by all just bringing the talent of the employees to the notice of others and making everybody gain something from it.

Discussion, scheduling, bulletin boards, desktop conferencing, doc management are few of the other benefits which are provided by the intranet.

Q7. What are the advantages of using Intranet? **[JUN02;Q1(c)]**

ANS : The most easily noticeable difference between an Internet server and a "collaborative" computing solution such as Lotus Notes (also called groupware, could be used for Intranet server) is the design philosophy. The Lotus Notes has been designed as a proprietary system for areas lacking proper connectivity, it uses a proprietary database structure, which replicates data and does not provide quick access to remote databases.

The real-world benefits and applications of intranets can be many in number. One major benefit of intranets is that it could be used to enhance communication, which in turn could lead to improved linkages within the organization. This communication could happen between various workgroups, departments, or even within entire organization, simply by hosting the contents on the intranet server.

Intranet can largely eliminate paper-based documents, which otherwise become outdated over passage of time. Increased communication will also lead to tremendous reduction in expenditure for numerous publishing services such as creating, printing, and distributing information for internal use. Besides these benefits, Web and conferencing technologies can be easily provided to improve synergy amongst the employees; still further, collaboration can be enhanced by use of internal newsgroups and mailing lists. Information posted to the newsgroups and distributed via mailing lists can be made available to selected groups within the organization and archived as a repository of information.

Using Internet technologies on an intranet means that organizations can deploy integrated applications that connect public and private networks using the same applications and data. Hence, straightaway standardization of activities or process will find its place. It could be possible that all users have to use the same environment in such an event thereby causing a fear for loss of freedom or creativity, but it has its own advantages.

Examples of successful intranet applications

Bharat Petroleum Corporation Limited (BPCL), a major oil company of India (http://www.bharatpetroleum.com/) uses an intranet to provide their employees with an efficient way to share the internal company information and let a number of workgroups to share and work on various projects. However, using the Internet, they also distribute financial data and news announcements to customers, shareholders, and others outside the company. The BPCL Web site also offers prospective customers an opportunity to conveniently apply for its Petrol credit cards and to purchase merchandise offered in their Web-based catalog.

The product development teams at Maruti Udyog Limited, India's leading car manufacturer (http://www.marutiudyog.com/) use the company's intranet to get their products to market conveniently and faster. The intranet also facilitates communications between sales, service, and remote field teams around the world, allowing the company to capitalize on areas of expertise in various locations. As with BPCL, the MUL employs Internet technologies in addition to the intranet solutions to educate customers and their worldwide sales force about new products. Prospective customers can easily find product information including photographs, datasheets, comparison of various models and success stories, as well as check on the availability of the latest car releases. Back in the server room, the intranet runs safely behind their firewall, the company connects its dealers and vendors to use the benefits of intranet for minute-to-minute update of inventory levels for maintaining a balance of supply-demand chain. The company publishes an electronic sales guide with important information their sales network can use to sell their products.

Broadly speaking, the benefits can be enumerated as follows:

Cheaper : Use of client browsers with one standard Window interface, offers easy integration with a number of other applications, such as electronic mail, faxes, videoconferencing, calendaring, and linkages within messages. As a single interface to a variety of information sources, the browser is cost-effective, highly efficient, uses minimal resources, and very easy to use.

Versatile : An Intranet server eliminates the need to replicate database by providing users with easy access to source data. A single WWW server platform can support both internal and external applications for both internal information - sharing and external marketing on the Internet. In contrast, the Lotus Notes application is costlier and purely an internal application.

Flexible : The Intranet provides the users with access to centralized information resources on a single point-and-click basis through the browser, which is available on a variety of client platforms (Windows, Mac, Unix, etc.), at any location. With Notes, data distribution is in real-time, on an as-requested basis, over a public (or private) network.

Intranets obviously have many advantages to both the organisation and its personnel.

The most obvious advantage is that everyone with access to a computer terminal can obtain the entire store of information that can be easily updated at regular intervals. It is essential to note that even a simple database like an organization telephone directory gets outdated quickly, sometimes even before it is printed on paper whereas an on-line directory can be updated immediatcly whenever there is a change needed.

Intranets encourage integration of applications; such as the simple word-processing application could be easily linked with e-mail services, and as such this redefining of the ways and possibilities could be used more efficiently and effectively.

Intranets provide access to electronic databases, documents, electronic training manuals, office circulars, internal job vacancies, etc. Any type of information the company feels is informative and useful can be hosted on the central server or databases, which can be extracted by browsers when needed without the employees having to leave their work area. This features provides a further benefit, i.e., freedom from the work area. The employee is free to travel anywhere without having to worry about what are lying on his desktop, since every information required is available on the Intranet site which could be easily hooked up from his laptop computer and a mobile modem.

The ease of use of the end user would be the most noticeable because of the similarity of intranets to the Internet. Since the intranet technology is based purely upon the user-friendly atmosphere of the World Wide Web (WWW), the system is very easy to use. It does not matter that users do not necessarily understand the intricacies of how the information flows up and down to their workstation or to the centralized server; it is the ease of obtaining required right information at right time, which matters the most.

Several other factors contribute to increasing the profitability of a business. For companies that are highly dynamic and rapid in action, the primary factors among those are:

Increased market share

Increased product margins

Cutting expenses

Utilizing existing resources more efficiently

Increasing market share and product margins leave to the Marketing and Purchasing personnel. The cost cutting however can of help to the central office or headquarters. The last factor is crucial to the company's Planning department since profitability the company's most crucial and bottom line consideration. Most companies today are suffering with inefficiencies, redundant operations, and unproductive tasks. Many of these can be greatly reduced or eliminated with a well-designed Intranet.

The following activities can help the companies for building up a well-designed Intranet site for themselves that will improve the overall profitability:

Improved and more efficient employee training

Decreased orientation time before new employees become productive

Improved employee and departmental morale

Better project management

Increased inter-departmental communication channels

Faster and improved dissemination of information to all departments

Inter-department collaborative efforts

Decreased production costs if currently publish information for internal use

Q8. What are the different types/Categories of Intranet?

ANS : Intranets have been broadly classified into three types based on their functionality, viz., the Bulletin board, database management and information access.

Bulletin board : This type of Intranet allows everyone in an organization the capability to review or update information that would normally be placed on an organization bulletin board, such as, a calendar of events, a status board, pictures of events or employees, policy changes, etc. It just acts like a broadcast system or notice board of the company in which updates may be or may not be frequent.

Database management : This type of Intranet allows everyone in an organization with the capability to maintain a "real-time" interactive database. The database can be used to support the tracking of products, inventories, bidding, or provide information on a particular subject any time of day, from any location. The information is kept updated as quickly as possible since time and information is money for the organization.

Information Access : This type of Intranet is the type commonly found on the World Wide Web. The static web page may include information on any subject. The static page can then be accessed from a simple search engine provided free as part of the Internet.

This "free service" networks are now-a-days making good money through advertisements, even major newspaper companies and news agencies have started using this type of intranets of late for proper organization of news items and finally hosting of entire content to the internet with a click of the mouse button. Information access is the key to making the Intranet commercially feasible. While individuals within an organization may have secure access to particular parts of an Intranet, the marketing and promotion of an organization is the accepted norm. By advertising on the Internet the organization is available to a broader customer base, via the global structure of the Internet.

Some experts have taken a lead and have categorized intranet into four different types based on their application or usage as well as its architecture. They are as follows:

The Communications Intranet : Intranets of this type tend to feature in geographically dispersed organizations. The motivation for its implementation is greater efficiency and cost saving, through the reduction of fax and telephone calls. This intranet is common with franchises or organizations that have a large number of salespeople or agents in the field. Example, Maruti Udyog.

The Integrating Intranet : These intranets are designed to replace the complexity of in-house communications and processing systems that in large organisations often use. Different interfaces commonly lack means of interconnection. Such intranets offer organisations a common interface (through browser) that can link-up its different divisions through hypertext links. It follows that standardisation is paramount in an integrating intranet. Example, IGNOU.

The Catalogue Intranet : Intranets of this type are often more accurately described as extranets. They are designed to give access to a large catalogue of information, like a multimedia catalogue. Example, a news agency or companies offering search engines like the Yahoo.

Q9. What are the various steps involved in the design of Intranet's structure? Explain each step with example. **[DEC02;Q4(b)]**

#: What is the process of Designing Intranet? **[DEC01;Q3(a)]**

#: Write a short note on planning and content of an Intranet.

[JUN01;Q3][JUN02;Q3]

ANS : The four basic steps of the Intranet project are Planning, Constructing (Content), Implementing and Maintaining. Each step is followed by the other.

Following parameters are to be considered when planning your own Intranet:

- **What is the purpose :** One need to make sure that why I want to have an Intranet?
- **Advantages :** What advantages I am going to get if I am replacing my LAN with the Intranet?
- **Save Money :** Does an Intranet save money for me?
- **Security :** What sort of security I need to implement for my Intranet?
- **Software required :** What software do I required to build Intranet I want.
- Hardware should not be forgotten.
- What is going to be on my Intranet? That is content. Content is again a crucial issue.

The purpose of the Internet is simple. It is to corporate all the advantages of the Internet protocols and technologies which are not possible with LAN.

One need to make sure the security level required and the budget which can be spend for implementing security. Both the things need to be balanced in order to get proper security model for Intranet.

The software required depends upon the field of the company. There is variety of software available which can be used or which is supported by the Intranet protocol stack (TCP/IP protocol Stack). To get started with the Intranet, following softwares are required:

- Web Server Software
- HTML authoring Tool
- Browser
- TCP/IP based network

Selection of Hardware is to be done again with the Software being used and Software requirement. For example, an Internet with 1000 clients requires 256 MB of memory and the same server uses Oracle as Back-End tool, which requires additional 256 MB of RAM. Memory requirements increase as number of hosts of the Intranet increase.

Content of the Intranet : The content that is going to be put on Intranet must serve purpose. One needs to make sure that whatever is going to be put on Intranet is worth or not.

Moreover, good design of the content includes structure as well as appearance. The design, which is created, should reflect the mission defined while planning the Intranet.

Creating each page : Once content is available, it is time to convert the material to a form suitable for display.

It is needed to decide what percentage of existing material can be used and who will be responsible for converting that information.

Testing : Once the content is formatted, test your pages and then test them again!!!! It is a sort of feedback of content. That whatever is worked out really works nicely or not.

Part of content plan should include a test plan detailing:

- What should be tested?
- Who will perform the tests?
- What to do if there are problems?
- When to do retest?

Tracking results and taking feedback: Once Intranet is up and running, emails and comments will start coming. We have to get ready to deal with these comments in an effective manner.

A typical Intranet site may include following Heads as content:

- News
- Organizations under us
- References, Tools & Utilities
- Feedback
- About Us
- Contact Us
- Search
- Go to Home on each
- Go to specific page (when required)

Then cover the implementation for this two aspects are covered one is software and another is hardware. According to the requirements of the client, various software and hardware is purchased. Intranet is established within the organisation. At last maintenance comes which is the most important part often implementation as without maintenance. Important availability cannot be ascertained i.e., frequent failure may result due to stop which further results in less to the organisation.

Q10. How will you ensure security of your Intranet? [JUN02;Q1(a)]

#. List various security concerns and threats for an Intranet. List the various encryption and decryption methods.

#. What are the different security techniques available for establishing effective security measures? Explain them. [JUN03;Q3(b)]

ANS : The Intranet requires security because of :

- Hardware causes
- Software causes
- Information

Hardware can be stolen, tampered by frustrated employee, destruction of the resources. Whereas software causes include deletion or theft of a program, corruption of a program, change in program code and thus making it malfunctioning, bugs in the software or virus attack.

Third component of the system liable to be attacked in data which is so important and crucial for an organization/company.

Security should be provided in order to make an Intranet functioning successfully and reliably. There are many ways through which Intranet can be made secured and reliable. Those are :

(1) Certificates
(2) Firewalls
(3) Encryption/Decryption methods
(4) Multiple Level Security
(5) SOCKS

Certificates : Digital Certificates or Digital Signatures are used for securing e-mails, money transactions. Certificates includes a Public Key which is assigned to the users and is required to be sent when user wants to make any transaction. The certificate acts as an evidence of the user's digital identity.

Digital certificates provide excellent means of controlling and monitoring access to the Intranet. The certificate itself acts as a token for access control. The certificate could contain a series of digits and alphabets combined together.

Firewalls : Firewalls provide security by following:

(1) Packet Filtering
(2) Application Gateways for restricting applications
(3) Proxy Servers

Proxy servers are used to isolate IP address range from the Internet. One interface of the Proxy Server is connected to the Internet, whose IP address is known to the Internet (Outside World). This IP address is also called Live IP address.

Whereas other interface is connected to the Intranet where all hosts are assigned unique IP addresses which are independent of the Internet (hidden to the Internet). Firewalls can also be implemented on the proxy server either to give access or deny access based upon Applications or IP addresses.

Encryption :

Public Key Solutions : The Public Key Solutions involves a third party provider which provides key and checks for the authentication based upon the key.

The Architecture is shown in the figure below:

Third Party

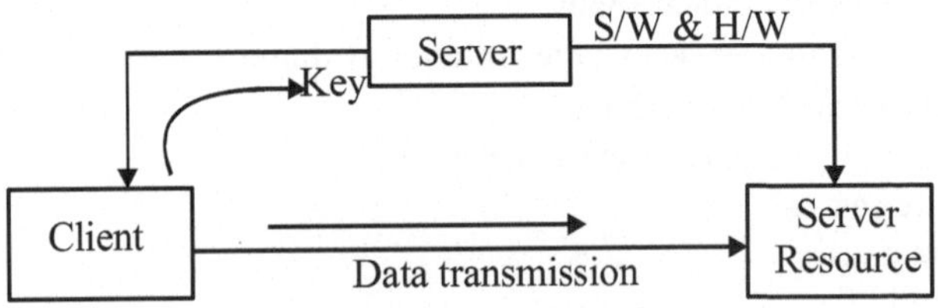

(-Public Key Authentication)

As soon as the third party server authenticates the key, data transmission takes place between the stations on the physical path.

Secured Sockets Layer (SSL) : It is used to secure the web server for authentication of the Users who want to access the resource. Resource requested may be

HTTP or FTP or any other protocol supported by the Web Server.
Today, almost all commercial web sites are using SSL to ensure the authenticity of the server and integrity of the data delivered to web site users.
Virtual private Network (VPN) : If an Intranet is extended between two geographically separated locations, VPN is used to secure Intranet data.

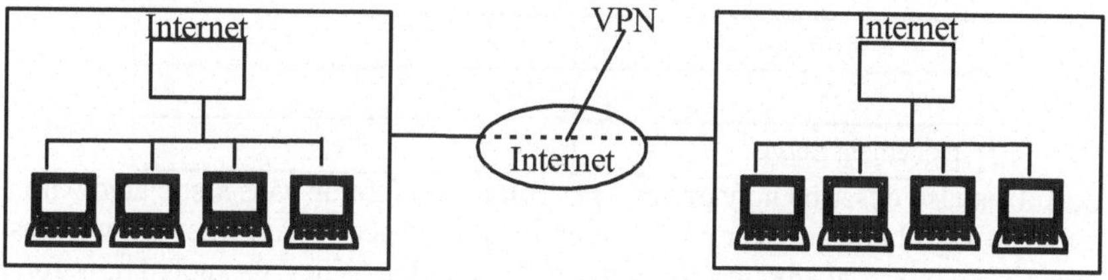

As shown in the diagram, when two geographically separated Intranets are connected using the Internet, VPN is established between the two to secure data of the Intranets. VPN uses IP addresses to differentiate between Internet and Intranet users.
Multiple Level Security : Multiple level security involves more than one type of security mechanisms implemented to secure data. It can be combination of any two described above.
SOCKS : Different types of security can be implemented to secure data. Now these different types of security works at different layers of OSI reference model.
SOCKS works at Transport Layer of OSI and it allows TCP application to access firewalls in a secured and controlled manner.
There are number of products based on SOCKS specifications, latest version is SOCKS 5.

SOCKS implementation requires a change to all existing client-server based software so that all of them use the SOCKS library. This process is known as "socksifying".

Q11. What are the software and hardware requirement for the intranet?
#: What are the hardware and software requirements for setting up an Intranet? How do these requirements differ for each organization?
[DEC02;Q1(a)][JUN01;Q1(a)]
ANS : Hardware: An Intranet is simply a standard Wide Area Network (WAN). The use of the term Intranet recently to describe using software developed for the Internet on the company's WAN. Web servers are an example.
To setup a WAN, one will need to have some type of communications between the different sites. National ISDN, Very Small Aperture Terminal (VSAT) connectivity or a long distance Frame Relay could be the best choice. It will be essential to install a router at each site. Each router would connect back to a central site over dedicated phone lines. Note that the hardware should be configured for the following protocols/ services.

Protocol/Service	To be installed on
IP	Network
HTTP	Server
SMTP/POP3/IMAP4	Server
LDAP	Server
X509 Certificate	Server
Java	ORB
Document Server	Server

Scientists also describe how optimal performance of intranets is associated with a number of key hardware factors. In order to optimise performance, servers with fast processors and large amounts of memory are essential. They also noted how good multi-tasking and multi-threading ability is which is also crucial for most of the Web applications. In addition, sufficient memory and disk capacity at the user workstation would improve performance through increased caching. The limitation of large image files can also be considered important to improve performance, but images may be equally important to expand and illustrate data, and pages of text can be discouraging, especially in an educational context. Finally, the database itself, which forms the foundations of almost every intranet, can have a significant effect on performance.

Operating System for Server and Clients

On the Server : Since 1994, when the original pair of web servers — **NCSA HTTPd** and **CERN HTTPd**, dozens of commercial and shareware programs have been developed. While the Netscape Enterprise Server defines the commercial high end, the other is Microsoft's Internet Information Server (IIS) Netscape Enterprise Server and lightweight Fast Track Server.

On the Clients : All of the clients running popular operating systems such as Microsoft Windows, MacOS, UNIX, etc. could be used to function as backbone software for the Intranets.

Only one software is sufficient for working with the Intranet viz., the browser software that should be loaded on all the clients. This software serves as a single interface to both the Intranet as well as the Internet. At present, Microsoft Internet Explorer and Netscape Navigator both remain the top web browsers available. Apart for these, various other web browsers are also available to access the information such as NCSA Mosaic.

Language support : Intranet works on the basis of scripts written in any of the following languages, viz., SGML, HTML, DHTML, XML, ASP, CGI, Perl, UML, VRML, etc. Though almost all are variants of the basic markup language or development over it, all provide flexibility to program the needs of the organizations. It is essential to test minutely how the output looks when published on the central server, by using different browsers on different operating systems.

Some organisations need to connect various offices through their Intranet. Those organisations need to have additional hardware device like router to connect to different locations. If organisation has great security issue, they also need to implement powerful firewall. This firewall can be software based or hardware based, depends on level of security, cost and efficiency.

The Intranet Software and Hardware equipments are a variable. As an organisation grows, we might want to add a search engine to help user find out informations quickly.

Some advanced features like Database support, logging, controlling access, Security etc. requires additional software to manage large Intranets.

If an organisation wants to provide several hundred to thousands of users getting connected to the Internet server and running applications, use remote login to connect, e-mail distribution software, or serve multimedia - video and audio, then hardware will need to be sophisticated and powerful enough to meet the peak-time demands that will put on the system.

Q12. Discuss the various application areas of Intranet. [JUNE04, Q1(a)]

ANS : The uses of an Intranet are only limited by imagination. Some of the larger sectors where Intranet can be easily and successfully implemented are as follows:

Education Sector
- Universities
- Colleges
- Institutes

Industry Sector
- Small and large scale manufacturing
- Automation and control

Service Sector
- Hotel
- Tourism
- Travel
- Transportation
- Communication

Research & Development
- Laboratories
- Organizations
- Space

Govt. Sector
- Ministries
- Departments
- States
- Law & order

The following is a partial list of many potential uses of the Intranet, both commonly used and not so commonly used.

Company Documents
- Manuals
- Building Maps
- Airport Directions to other Company locations
- Approved Vendors list

- Procedures library
- Product Manuals
- Daily Bulletins
- History graphs
- Knowledge Base
- Competition products, news and web sites

Customer related

- Controlled Responses
- Feedback Forum
- Company Bulletin Boards
- Company Store
- News Flashes
- Supplies Ordering
- Database queries

General Administration and Management

- Department Budgets
- Departmental FAQs (Frequently Asked Questions)
- Employee Attendance
- VIntercompany chatting
- Internal postings
- Employee Orientation
- Online Collaboration Projects
- Organizational Charts
- Security Policies
- Trend Graphs
- Equipment checkouts

Training

- Employee Proficiency Training
- Training Materials
- Video Training

Coordination and control

- Form routing
- Forms Library
- Help Desk submission forms

Meetings related

- Meeting minutes
- Meeting schedules
- Online Meetings
- Meeting Room schedules

Q13. What is the future of the internet? Explain.

ANS : At present, the world of information technology is guided by the C^3 paradigm that stands for command, control and communication, which is normally used for military applications and strategies. These techniques are poised to become obsolete with the advent of Intranets and shall no longer remain the driving forces in companies.

The talk of the day start with another C^3 paradigm that stands for coordination, cooperation and collaboration. And this is what available in store for the future. It emphasizes better support and interaction towards common goal between various activities within an organization.

And this is possible through the Intranet technologies, which is helping in redefining the whole new world of computing thereby making integration a buzzword for everyone.

As stated by experts that it is 'because the browser has evolved far beyond its original uses, it may well become the universal interface to all information resources in the future.' As Internet technology expands, then it follows that intranets must necessarily benefit from these advances since the technology is shared. 'The result will be the increased integration of corporate data-access systems with inter-corporate communication systems and corporate-customer communications.'

Q14. Explain few terms which are used in Intranet.

ANS : Following is list of most widely used terms, which come in way during study of Intranets:

Applets : Little programs that can make the Web pages more aesthetically beautiful by means of animations, text, and graphics moving across the screen.

Bits, Bitmap : Many tiny dots, which are put together to make a picture. Bits are combined to make a graphic image called a bitmap. GIF and JPEG files are the most popular kinds of bitmap files.

Bookmark : A list of pages a user likes to frequently visit. Netscape® Navigator and Explorer® have a "bookmark" menu item which allows users to add favorite sites via the Bookmark option. A term equivalent to the conventional bookmark used by readers to indicate position in a text book where they left it while reading it last time.

Browser : A program that allows the user to access and read information on the World Wide Web. Netscape® Navigator and Microsoft Explorer® are the best known browsers.

Counter : A software code that indicates how many times a site has been visited. It gets automatically updated and is usually represented by a small rectangle with numbers normally visible at the bottom of web pages, something like the odometer of a car.

Cyberspace : The conceptual or virtual area where pages, data, images, and all the rest are stored. It is the area from where requests are accepted and fulfilled from computer to computer, user to user.

FAQs : Stands for Frequently Asked Questions. Common questions and their answers that occur regularly within a user group. FAQs also appear as a hot link on many web sites and sometimes acts as reservoir of knowledge about the company or its products. FAQs are a time-saving feature for all kind of users.

Firewall : A protection of the internal company network against unauthorized access via the Internet.

Frame : A presentation format, which enables Web page designers and users to mark a part of the screen for links to other pages. Frames usually appear on the left side, top, and/or bottom of the screen. Frames contain icons and hot links.

FTP-File Transfer Protocol : A very common method of moving files between two Internet sites. FTP is a special way to log in to another Internet site for the purposes of retrieving and/or sending files. There are many Internet sites that have established publicly accessible repositories of material that can be obtained using FTP by logging in using the account name anonymous. Thus, these sites are called anonymous FTP servers.

GIF (Graphics Interchange Format) : A type of graphics file found frequently on the net. A picture of a vice-president, for example, may appear on the Intranet as a GIF.

Home Page : The primary Web page for an individual or organization. This page link to other related pages.

Hot Links : A connection from one Web page to another. A hypertext link. Hot links are frequently indicated by colored, underlined text and/or an icon. HTML-Hypertext markup language The language used in writing pages for the World Wide Web. No knowledge of HTML is necessary for using the Intranet, or for maintaining pages.

HTTP-Hypertext Transfer Protocol : The way Web pages are transferred over the internet or an Intranet.

Icon : A small picture or graphic used to represent a location in the inter- or Intranet (for example a flow-chart graphic to take the user to the departmental flow chart); an action (a mailbox as a place to send feedback); or a program (a W to indicate Microsoft Word).

Daemon : A daemon is a Unix background process that implements the server side of a protocol. Daemons are unique to Unix. For example, FTPd stands for the File Transfer Protocol daemon

HTTPd : It stands for HTTP *daemon*. HTTPd is the program run on a Unix platform to establish a web server. On other platforms, such as Microsoft Windows NT, the web server is a background process implemented as a system service.

ISDN : Stands for Integrated Services Digital Network. It is a way to move more data over existing regular phone lines. ISDN is rapidly becoming available to almost every country and every one who need it, at affordable charges and data transfer rates. In most countries it is available at a price comparable to standard analog phone line connectivity. It can provide speeds of roughly 128 kilobits per second over regular phone lines.

Java : A programming language that in particular, allows browsers to download and run applets (very small programs allowing animations and the like).

JPEG : Stands for Joint Photographic Experts Group. A standard format of storing digitized, color, or black-and-white photographs. JPEG files are smaller than corresponding GIF files.

LDAP : Stands for Lightweight Directory Access Protocol. LDAP is preferred for creating directories. LDAP provides a standard way for Internet clients, applications, and servers to access directory services using TCP/IP, regardless of the hardware/software platform.

Network : A number of computers connected together.

Internet : Lots of networks all over the world are connected to make the Internet.

Intranet : Lots of networks connected within an organization (locations could be geographically distant) such as a university or company.

Search Engine : Software used to find information on the Web. Examples are Google, Lycos and Yahoo.

Server : A computer with the capacity to provide connectivity (sharing) to multiple personal computers or clients.

Surfing : Going from page to page, link to link, via a browser. Surfing could can be called "clicking" for the mouse clicks that make the process possible, or "linking" from the program logic, which makes the process happen.

T-1: A leased-line connection capable of carrying data at 1,544,000 bits per second. Theoretically, a T-1 line could move a megabyte at maximum capacity in less than 10 seconds. This transfer rate is still not fast enough for full-screen, full-motion video, for which at least 10 Mega bits per second would be needed. T-1 is the fastest speed commonly used to connect networks to the Internet.

TCP/IP : Stands for Transmission Control Protocol/Internet Protocol. This is the group of protocols that define the Internet and communication method used by it. Originally designed for the UNIX operating system, TCP/IP software is now available for every major operating system. In order to be compatible to the Internet, the computer must have TCP/IP compatible software.

URL - Uniform Resource Locator : Address of location for accessing Web pages. Clicking on an icon or "hot text" is the most common means of accessing and using a URL. Typing the URL in the "Location" on Netscape® Navigator or Internet Explorer®, (for example, {INTRANET NAME}@[COMPANY NAME].com) is another way of getting to a Web page.

Web or Net : The World Wide Web (a server) consisting of a hypermedia system (linking sounds, text, pictures, video) that the computer (a client) can access.

Web Page : The basic unit of the World Wide Web. Information on a Web page can include graphics, audio, and video. A number of properly linked web pages make up an Intranet or internet.

Web Server : A host computer that stores Web pages and responds to requests for viewing. Web servers communicate with Web browsers (by HTTP).

Webmaster : The supervisor ensuring that the system is up and running; the coordinator of access; the administrator for communications between users and hosts to sites.

Q15. Write a short note on the cost factor involved in setting up an Intranet.
[JUNE04;Q6(b)] [DEC02;Q1(b)]

#. How Much Does an Intranet Cost?

#. How will you calculate the cost of setting up an Intranet? Explain with example.
[DEC01;Q3(b)]

ANS : The cost of the Intranet depends on many parameters, as well as there are many variables. Mainly cost depends on the requirement / facilities we want with out intranet. As the facilities / requirement increases the cost also increases. Requirement are of three types :

(1) Hardware Requirements.

(2) Software Requirements.

(3) Use Training Requirements, like how much efficient your hardware should be to handle the activities you want to perform. Software requirement also depends on the activities you want to run on the intranet. User training is also necessary to develop "feel good" factor among the employees of the organisation.

For example, if network is large, better hardware configuration is required, which results in high cost of Server itself.

With 100 clients running a small Intranet requires one server with 100 MHz, 16 MB of RAM and 2 GB of IDE Hard Disk.

But if Intranet is having 1000 clients, with Database Support, it requires 3 Servers of 200 MHz, 32 MB of RAM and 4.3 GB Hard Disk with Disk Mirroring implemented (it means 6 Hard Disks are required). 2 servers will be used to share the overall load of the Intranet and hence the cost of the Intranet increases in this regard.

Similarly, if your Intranet requires software for Database, for Server side Scripting (ASP, ISAPI or any other), all this counts in terms of high cost as well as high resources in terms of Hardware.

Following are some approximate prices for Intranet Tools:

Server (133 MHz Pentium, 32 MB RAM, two 2 GB Hard Drives – Rs.2 Lacs to 3 Lacs.
Network Server – Rs. 1 Lac
Communications Server – Rs. 50000
Editors – Rs.10000
Search Engine – Rs. 0
Database – Rs. 1 to 2 Lacs
Proxy Server – Rs. 50000
Other Software – Rs. 100000
Client Hardware – Rs. 25000 per terminal

So, if we calculate for an Enterprise Network, it requires approximately Rs. 7 lacs just for intranet.

Q16. How will you estimate your Intranet work requirements? [JUN03;Q2(a)]

ANS : An Intranet requirement estimate on the basis of its functions, load of traffic, the services provides by it to internal as well as external uses. Intranet reflects the working structure of its oganisation. To set up an Intranet smoothly and perfectly the requirement estimate on the following three points:

(1) Hardware Requirements.

(2) Software Requirements.

(3) Use Training Requirements.

After all formality we first decide which kind of hardware components are required for Server as well as Client. In this we identify the configuration of server and client PCs. This is very critical. Because any oganisation is not making frequently change in the hardware of PCs. It also depends upon which OS you are going to use within Intranet on Client side and on Server side. Some about each components of PCs like

(a) Speed of CPU.

(b) Capacity of RAM.

(c) Capacity of HDD.

(d) Other Secondary storage device or Backup Device Etc.

In the software requirements we decide about OS for Serve as well as for Client PCs. For an Intranet than we have must use Win NT or Win 2000 family OS. If use Linux, then this site not work properly because Linux does not support this. It also depend on hardware configuration so when selecting OS its obvious that you must aware with its minimum hardware requirements.

The User(s) training is plays major role in success of any Intranet. Because inefficient user(s) never avail the feature of Intranet. So it's must that you provide proper training to user(s).

Q17. "Intranet Planning is more than money." Do you agree with this statement? Explain your answer. **[DEC02;Q3(b)]**

ANS : Yes, when you start planning your intranet, the first question you'll probably hear is "How much will this cost?" While costs are a major factor in deciding both the scope of your intranet and even whether or not to have one, the bottom-line setup costs aren't as important as deciding your overall return from your intranet. Your overall return factors in several cost elements including:

Cost of setup, including hardware and software

Cost of converting existing information for use on your intranet

Cost of creating new information

Cost of designing and programming for intranet applications

Cost of training

And while that quickly add up to a significant sum, you'll see that costs are reduced in other areas including:

Printing : Material will still need to be printed, but users will have to print the relevant information as needed.

Communication : Communication is improved. The way an organization communicated its message is vital to the success of the organization. Communicating with both the public and staff can change the way people see your company and your product. Employees often complain about poor communication; they feel left out of the loop or like they're working on a project that has no focus or purpose. Using an intranet, people can share information in an easy-to-use format that removes many organization constraints.

Technology : Skills are enhanced. Your staff and organization benefit by keeping employee's current skills. Intranets are an easy way to teach new skills or upgrade existing skills. The Web and the Internet are hot topics in the newspaper and on television and your employees have a natural curiosity to see what the type is about. You can use this natural curiosity to encourage your users do some simple self-training.

As you plan your intranet, keep in mind the costs are only one aspect of the plan and that costs will change as you assess your audience, intranet goals, content requirements resources (hardware, software, and human), and security issues.

Q18. How will you select best browser for the Intranet of your organization? **[Jun2002;Q5(a)]**

ANS : The answers to these questions depend on how you use your intranet within your organization and the technical level of the people involved. If you use all the latest technology on your intranet, You'll be faced with people downloaded best versions, trying to run unstable software, not to mention the incompatibilities between systems and a host of other configuration problems. Surveys have shown that costs increase substantially when more than one browser is supported within an organization. Here's what you should do:

1. Evaluate the technical needs of your intranet.
2. Evaluate the technical knowledge of your users.
3. Evaluate those browsers that meet the technical needs of your intranet.
4. Choose the browser that best meets these needs.
5. Make that browser available, along with any necessary helper applications or plug-ins, to all your users.
6. Publish your policy on your intranet so your users will understand the reasons for the choice.
7. Go back to the beginning of this list of steps and repeat the process as often as necessary.

Q19. How can an Intranet save money for an organization? **[DEC01;Q1(a)]**

ANS : Costs are reduced in the areas of :

• **Printing :** by storing the information on the Intranet, we can quickly produce updated sections of material quickly and at much lower cost, while the employees want to print a document, they only print the page they need, all other information is readily available on the Intranet.

• **Communication :** Better communication is achieved. Communicating with both the public and staff can change the way people see the company and the product. Employees generally complain about communication, but now cannot. Using the Intranet, they share information in easy to use format.

• **Technology :** Skills are enhanced and advanced.

• **Database :** All the records of an organization can be kept in the form of database. It makes the querying, selecting very easy, fast and effective. A lot of filework is reduced. And hence saving of money, time and labor.

• **E-mail :** Once Intranet is up and running, emails and comments will start coming. This will help to update the site with the help of suggestions. And increase the information of the employees if they mail any information regarding any difficulty. This will help to increase the communication between the employees and hence better working environment, healthy atmosphere.

• **Information :** Intranet is a source of information for the employees of an organization regarding the organizations. Employees of one department can have knowledge regarding the other departments with the help of intranet. Suppose an employee of the accounts department want to know recent details of the production now he won't be needing to go to the production department and get details from there instead he has to just get connected to the intranet and get details from there. Information regarding the company seminars, entertainment programmes, and announcements all are available on intranet. Fast flow of information will further help in increasing the revenues to the company.

Interaction : Where there are means of communication between the members of the company interaction becomes very easy. Hence the flow of information and responses are the loveliest thing present on the intranet.

Discussion, scheduling, bulletin boards, desktop conferencing, doc management are few of the other benefits which are provided by the intranet and help in increasing the profitability of the organization directly or indirectly.

Q20. Write a short note on the creation of a realistic Intranet plan. [DEC01;Q1(b)]

#: What are various internal issues that have to be addressed while creating an Intranet business plan. Explain them. [DEC01;Q5]

ANS : You can now begin creating your intranet business plan. The business plan should include information on why you need an intranet, what your goals are, what resource you'll need, and how much it will cost. You'll also use the business plan to begin thinking about content and security.

A little planning now will smooth over problems later. You've heard it before, and now we're telling you again: intranets have a way of growing quickly in new, exciting ways, If you'll be able to harness the positive growth of your intranet.

If you haven't created a plan, your intranet will grow out of control without direction, potentially dragging down the processes you were hoping to improve.

Crafting Your Intranet Plan : An intranet is the perfect solution for any organization with anywhere from twenty to several thousand people who either all work at the corporate headquarters or are scattered over a wide geographical area and will access the system from a remote location. It's also an ideal fit for any situation in which a large amount of content and security is required.

A little planning now will smooth over problems later. You've heard it before, and now we're telling you again: intranets have a way of growing quickly in new, exciting ways. If you've done the planning up front, you'll be able to harness the positive growth of your intranet.

If you haven't created a plan, your intranet will grow out of control without direction, potentially dragging down the processes you were hoping to improve.

Most companies do not want to put documents on their intranet that are considered sensitive in either a competitive or a legal sense, and most companies avoid putting personnel files and payroll information on an intranet unless the effective security system is in place. As you can see, establishing the hardware and software stems for your intranet is the easy part; deciding on the content is much more difficult.

Don't worry about using a special planning tool, such as Microsoft project, to create your intranet plan. Because your project will include many different plan. Because your project will include many different aspects of your intranet, one tool may not be suitable for all the tasks you'll need to include in your plan.

Once your-group, department, or corporation has made the initial decision to implement an intranet, several important factors will determine whether the transition from a traditional host-based system to an intranet will be a smooth process or a violent upheaval. Many of these issues are not straightforward technical issues with one correct answer but thorny political issues that will take all your diplomatic skills to resolve.

Document your planning process. Keep notes from your meetings and e-mails from other members on the team. Your documentation will be helpful when you begin to write your intranet plan.

Q21. What are the differences between Intranets and a normal internet site?

ANS : The key difference is in the thought processes involved in developing an Intranet versus an external web site.

Public websites need to consider a broad array of users and elements such as branding and marketing strategies. While these elements exist to an extent when developing an Intranet, the influence is significantly muted. The focus for an Intranet lies more in creating efficiency and cost savings through sharing information and automating workflows. While somewhat lofty statements, these are actually quite down to earth. For example, many companies have a vacation notification form which employees fill in by hand and then turn into the appropriate HR representative. What if a web form were developed to submit this form automatically and also automate the appropriate approval process and announcement of the employee's absence? This system would eliminate steps in this process, improve the HR workflow and lessen the steps that the employee must take freeing more time for billable work. It is in these areas that we specialize.

Q22. What are the most frequently asked questions about Intranet? [DEC01;Q4(b)]

ANS : FAQ (Frequently Asked Questions) contains the most general questions that are asked commonly by the users about Intranet. Answer to these questions help users understand about the Intranet.·

Company announcements :

1. How do we gather all of the data scattered throughout our system?

Before design and development of Intranet tools can take place, a plan must be developed to gather this information, this may include:

- Integration of **legacy databases** into web-based front end
- **Inventory** of current web enabled tools
- Development of **publishing model**
- **Pooling** relevant documents

2. What departments can benefit from an Intranet?

In brief, **any department**:

- Human Resources
- Training
- Sales & Marketing
- Legal
- Finance & accounting
- Corporate Communications
- Research & Development
- Engineering
- Shipping & transportation
- Many others not listed

3. Can we hire Transmissions for developing parts of a system or does Transmissions only develop complete Intranets?

We are available to develop **according to your companies needs**:

- If you lack design expertise, we would be happy to **design an interface for your system**
- We can provide **search functionality**
- If you have the people in house to develop your systems but lack architectural direction, we can **develop functional specifications and technical documentation**
- We can provide **copywriting services** and **translation services**
- If your company wants to add a single application to its current intranet, we can develop **complete applications**
- We can perform a **system inventory**
- If your company lacks resources to host the intranet in house, we can provide **hosting services**
- We can develop **mapping applications and building floor plans.**
- If your company is looking for ways to **improve efficiency or usability**, Transmissions is available to study your company's processes and provide a list of areas which could be streamlined with suggestions for improvement

4. What are the sorts of intranet applications that can be developed?

- Content administration
- Search
- Timesheet system
- Software distribution
- Project status and support systems
- Data mining
- Corporate library management
- Product support databases
- Company news administration system
- Phone directories
- Newsletters
- Skill tracking systems
- Conference room scheduling
- Document sharing and collaborative development
- Company policies/procedures, form submissions
- Sales support applications

- Financial reporting
- Product catalogs
- Employee benefits programs
- Company announcements
- Calendars with company events

5. What is Intranet File Sharing for?

Intranet File Sharing is the right tool for through search of your files across your local network. Search for the necessary files on your neighbor computers in shared folders. You can find very quick and easy any files like multimedia files, Microsoft Office documents and others in your local network. Program allows you to organize more detailed scan using a great amount of parameters: files wildcard mask, file size, files containing any of all of specified words, searching only in active computers from your network and so on. With the big number of details you'll find every file you want in your network!

6. How Intranet File Sharing works?

Intranet File Sharing is a client-server solution. Searching local network with Intranet File Sharing is simpler as possible: just access the Intranet File Sharing server from within your web browser. Intranet File Sharing is divided into two big parts: the indexing section which scans, index and store, at a given period of time, data about files founded in shares (including hidden shares) from your network, IP subnet-works or just specified servers and the information retrieval part which process queries from clients, extract information and send the response back to the client.

7. What about the performances of Intranet File Sharing?

The major advantage of Intranet File Sharing is searching speed. Featuring an client-server architecture, Intranet File Sharing was developed to achieve the maximum of performance. You can use it on networks with many hundreds of computers. The speed of the application helped by the power of Microsoft SQL Server allows you to quickly search hundreds of thousands of files and even millions. Intranet File Sharing was tested several months on networks with hundred of computers, answering hundreds of thousands of queries.

8. What software requires Intranet File Sharing?

Intranet File Sharing requires Windows NT/2000/XP with Internet Information Server (IIS) and a database system based on the engine of Microsoft SQL Server: you can use either MSDE (Microsoft Data Engine) or Microsoft SQL Server 7.0 or Microsoft SQL Server 2000. For clients is required only a web browser to access Intranet File Sharing. We recommend you to use Microsoft Internet Explorer.

Microsoft SQL Server can be found here: http://www.microsoft.com/sql/ MSDE, the free database engine, can be found here: http://msdn.microsoft.com/vstudio/msde/

Q23. What is Gopher?

ANS : A system that pre-dates the World Wide Web for organizing and displaying files on Internet servers. A Gopher server presents its contents as a hierarchically structured list of files. With the ascendancy of the Web, most Gopher databases are being converted to Web sites which can be more easily accessed via Web search engines.

Gopher was developed at the University of Minnesota and named after the school's mascot. Two systems, *Veronica* and *Jughead*, let you search global indices of resources stored in Gopher systems. Used for Internet that offers a smooth, menu-driven way to traverse international "gopher space" – which these days literally means several hundred servers worldwide, offering text, computer programs, audio, still images, and even movie clips. It provides a seamless, "hidden programming" interface with which you can transfer files, browse databases, and telnet to sites around the globe, simply and easily.

Q24. What is Word Wide Web?

ANS : A system of Internet servers that support specially formatted documents. The documents are formatted in a script called HTML (*Hypertext Markup Language*) that supports links to other documents, as well as graphics, audio, and video files. This means you can jump from one document to another simply by clicking on hot spots (image links). Not all Internet servers are part of the World Wide Web.

World-Wide Web provides users on computer networks with a consistent means to access a variety of media in a simplified fashion. A popular software program to search the Web is called Mosaic; the Web project has modified that way people view and create information-it has created the first global hypermedia network.

There are several applications called Web browsers that make it easy to access the World Wide Web; Two of the most popular being Netscape Navigator and Microsoft's Internet Explorer.

Q25. What are different components of E-mail? Also write a short note on E-mail Addressing?

ANS : Short for *electronic **mail**,* the transmission of messages over communications networks. The messages can be notes entered from the keyboard or electronic files stored on disk. Most mainframes, minicomputers, and computer networks have an e-mail system. Some electronic-mail systems are confined to a single computer system or network, but others have gateways to other computer systems, enabling users to send electronic mail anywhere in the world. Companies that are fully computerized make extensive use of e-mail because it is fast, flexible, and reliable. Various components are described below:-

Now to send the email message, we do the following in the mail window that you have opened:

1. Enter the subject of your message into the "Subject" window. You don't have to put a subject, but it helps in keeping track of multiple messages to or from the same person. It is good practice to include one for all messages.

2. Enter the e-mail address(s) of the persons that you are sending the message to in the "Mail To:" field. For this example we are going to send a message to the Chief Minister of Delhi, so enter *cm@delhi.gov.*

Be sure to put the address exactly like this. The regular postal service may still deliver mail if you make a spelling mistake in the address, but most computers will reject email if even one character is wrong in the address.

3. Enter the email address(es) of any other persons that you wish to receive copies of the message. In this case, let's send a copy to the Health Minister (in case the Chief Minister doesn't have time to take care of your request!), and let's send a copy to ourselves so we will have a record of the message that we sent. So enter into the "CC:" field

healthminister@delhi.gov, your address

Where *your address* is whatever your personal email address is. ("CC:" stands for "Carbon Copy", from the old days when people used mechanical typewriters with carbon paper for copies and rode around in covered wagons!)

Notice that in this case we use commas to separate multiple addresses. Entries in the "CC:" field are optional (you don't *have* to send a copy to anyone), but you must enter an address in the "Mail To:" field, since it wouldn't make much sense to send a message without an address for the primary person the message is for! The distinction between the primary recipients and those receiving a CC: is for human sensibilities. In either case, the computer sends the email message to the address listed. The only difference is where the recipients address will be printed in the mail header when it is read.

4. Now type whatever you wish to say in the message into the main window frame. The lines will wrap automatically when you come to the edge of the field, and if you need more space, the window will scroll down automatically.

5. You may edit any of the fields in the mail window at any time before sending the message by using the mouse to position the cursor and inserting new text or erasing text with the "delete" key.

When you are happy with everything as typed into the Mail Window, click the "Send Now" button to send the message.

***Note on E-mail Addressing* :** As the Internet addresses are mostly on the different server, 'in the cases when sender and receiver are not on the same system need to be more elaborate.

To send a message to someone, you must type his or her e-mail address in the *to* section of your e-mail message. Generally, there are two parts to your e-mail address: your login identity and the identity of your ISP. These are separated by the symbol @. A typical e-mail address for someone who uses Hotmail, for example, looks like this: yourname@hotmail.com.

The extension—.com—indicates that Hotmail is a commercial establishment. Other common extensions are .gov for government users and .edu for educational users. E-mail addresses outside the United States may include letters that indicate the country e.g. .us of the user's ISP.

Once a message is assigned an address, it can be send to the destination via the interconnected Internet system. The e-mail handling system on the sender's computer (using any e-mail software) breaks the message into manageable pieces called "packets". Each packet is addressed to the final destination. These packets may flow different path to reach the destination. At the destination they are reassembled in the correct order by the destination e-mail machine.

Moreover, when we send e-mail, it goes to a name server. In order to deliver the e-mail, the Internet needs to know the numeric IP address, such as 163.52.128.2.

Domain Name Servers look up the alphabetic address and substitute the numeric IP address for it so the e-mail can be delivered properly.

Q26. What are the different types of Browsers? Give examples.

ANS : Types Of Web Browsers : To access the World Wide Web, you must use a Web browser. A browser is a software program that allows users to access and navigate the World Wide Web. The language of Web Browsers is generically termed *hypertext.* The name implies that hypertext is more than just text on a computer screen. It is much more than mere text. The most important feature of hypertext is the concept of a *link.*

There are two types of browsers:

☞ **Graphical :** Text, images, audio, and video are retrievable through a graphical software program such as Netscape Navigator and Internet Explorer. These browsers are available for both Windows-based and Macintosh computers. Navigation is accomplished by pointing and clicking with a mouse on highlighted words and graphics.

You can install a graphical browser such as Netscape Navigator in your Windows-based or Macintosh machine. To use these programs to access the Web, you need a connection to the Internet. This is accomplished through such means as an ethernet connection, a dialup connection known as a SLIP or PPP, or a cable modem. For example, with Internet Explorer version 5.0, you get additional Internet-related software.

Windows™ Media Player version 6.0
NetMeeting® conferencing software version 2.11
ActiveX® controls
Chat version 2.5
DirectShow® application programming interface
Subscriptions for automatic Web page update
Dynamic hypertext markup language (HTML)

☞**Text:** Lynx is a browser that provides access to the Web in text-only mode. Navigation is accomplished by highlighting emphasized words in the screen with the arrow up and down keys, and then pressing the forward arrow (or Enter) key to follow the link.

Extending the Browser - Plug-Ins : Software programs may be configured to a Web browser in order to enhance its capabilities. When the browser encounters a sound, image or video file, it hands off the data to other programs, called **plug-ins,** to run or display the file. Working in conjunction with plug-ins, browsers can offer a seamless multimedia experience. Many plug-ins are available for free.

File formats requiring plug-ins are known as **MIME types.** MIME stands for Multimedia Internet Mail Extension, and was originally developed to help e-mail software handle a variety of binary (non-ASCII) file attachments. The use of MIME has expanded to the Web. For example, basic MIME type handled by Web browsers is text/html associated with file extension .html.

Q27. What is meant by Downloading? Explain, stepwise the process of Downloading?

ANS : Downloading is the transmission of a file from one computer system to another, usually smaller computer system. From the Internet user's point-of-view, to download a file is to request it from another computer (or from a Web page on another computer) and to receive it.

Mastering the skill of downloading from the Internet is nothing today compared to the days BW (Before the Web). Now, downloading such things as plug-ins for your favorite browser or even computer programs is as easy as a mouse click.

Simply put, downloading from the Web is almost like copying a computer file or program from a floppy disk onto your computer's hard drive. Only, instead of using a floppy disk placed in the "A" drive, the file is "copied" to your PC from the Web. All those fancy graphics, sounds, and words displayed on your browser's window are all actually bits and bytes of computer code transmitted to you over the network. The Web has made many Internet tasks as easy to do as clicking on a link or graphic, and downloading files from the 'Net is among them. Today, Netscape Navigator or Internet Explorer include FTP protocol functions right out of the box. There's no need to use special FTP software or search FTP sites to get software for your computer. Just use your browser.

Besides having the ability to download right from the Web with your browser, most Web sites used for downloading also include detailed descriptions of each file it has available. This feature makes it easy for you to read about the file and decide right then and there whether or not you want to download it. You no longer need to mess with a large index file. You simple click on the "download now" button or other prompt and the process automatically executes.

Another plus — if you're downloading from the Web and you use Windows, you can either open another instance of your browser and continue surfing around, or open another program and continue working all while the download continues.

Software Categories : The software files you'll find available for downloading to your computer on the Web mostly fall into one of these three types.

☞ **Demoware :** A commercial product the manufacturer has made available to those who want to try the program out before they buy it. It usually is accompanied by a timing mechanism that prohibits the program from working after a set amount of time. Some demos will have important features locked out and unavailable for you to use, like the ability to save a file you create with the demo.

☞ **Shareware :** A fully functional software program the developer places on the Internet for you to download and use to see if you like it. If you find that you do indeed like the program, and you continue to use it past the trial period (usually 30 days) you are morally obligated to "buy" it. You purchase the program by submitting the registration fee imposed by the author.

☞ **Freeware :** A full-blown product the author is simply giving away. For instance, Internet Explorer, Microsoft's Web browser program is freeware — Microsoft lets anyone who wants it to download it free of charge.

Basic How-to : Thanks to the development of the World Wide Web and the browser software currently available, downloading from the Internet is a simple point-and-click process. There is no reason why anyone, no matter what experience they have on the 'Net, should not take advantage of it.

The whole process begins by selecting a file you wish to download. This may be the hardest part of downloading because of the sheer number of files available. Just as an example, let's use Microsoft's download site to download a copy of Internet Explorer (IE). This is Microsoft's free Web browser program.

Use your current browser to access Microsoft's IE site (www.microsoft.com/ie) where you'll find a complete description f the program as well as directions for downloading it. IE has several versions available — so decide which version you'll need. There are versions available for different computer operating systems, and versions with a variety of options. For our tutorial, choose the version that includes Microsoft mail and Microsoft news. This will give you the ability to read Internet newsgroups as well as send and receive email. It's a nice package to have.

After you select the version in the drop-down list you're sent to the download area to select a server from which the file will be sent to your computer. Pick the server closest to your location. (The server's location is mentioned in the list.) Click on your choice and the process will start.

Your computer will ask you where you want the downloaded file placed on your disk. You can elect to have it stored anywhere on your computer — just remember where you put it. You'll need to know this later on after the download is complete. Iset up a folder (subdirectory) on my hard disk labeled "Downloads" to store any files that I download. I recommend that you do the same. It keeps your downloaded files in one location where you can access them easily.

After you select the place to store the downloaded file on your computer, the download begins. While this is going on, you can elect to do something else. Some files are quite large and depending on the speed of your Internet connection, will take some time to complete. Windows tries to estimate the amount of time the process will take and displays the progress in a window on your screen.

When the download is complete the progress window will disappear. You're now free to log off and proceed with the installation of IE.

Q28. How does an organization choose the type of Internet connection it should have. Assume that an organization is having a LAN with 100 machines then what type of Internet connection is suitable for it and why?

ANS : ***Need for Speed* :** As we know "Speed costs money. How fast can you afford to go?" The same is true for Internet access.

Beyond 56k, higher speeds cost more money—in both equipment and the price of the access itself. With a little information, you'll be able to find a balance between what you want and what you can afford.

Knowing the options

As in our case the requirement of High Bandwidth / Speed is there, as we have to connect 100s of systems. If all the systems will connect simultaneously then speed requirement will be very high. As, Internet speed ratings are based on kilobits per second (kbps). Usually, kbps is abbreviated to “k.” So, 112k access is twice as fast as 56k, for example, meaning it will download or send twice as much data in the same amount of time. Here’s the rundown of what’s currently available:

56k : A 56k modem is currently standard equipment in most computers. If you have a computer manufactured before 1998, it’s possible that it has a slower modem (28.8k or 33.3k). Check your computer’s documentation to find out whether you’re behind the times for standard dial-up access before you look at even faster options.

Pros: If you don’t have a 56k modem, they’re fairly easy to install for the technically astute. They’re also inexpensive to have installed. This is the cheapest method of Internet access.

Cons: Not the fastest type of access. Also, if your ISP gets overburdened, you may have trouble dialing in.

ISDN : An ISDN (integrated services digital network) connection gives you two 64k lines. You can use one line as your voice or fax line and the other for data, or you can use both for data to give you connection speeds of up to 128k. ISDN lines need to be installed by your local telephone provider—for a fee.

Pros: They’re virtually everywhere.

Cons: A little expensive for what you get, if DSL or cable access is available in your area.

DSL : DSL (digital subscriber line) technology allows connection speeds of about 384k—nearly seven times faster than 56k access and three times faster than ISDN (even faster DSL access speeds are available, though price usually limits these options to business use.)

Pros: Since DSL uses telephone wiring that’s already in your home, many local telephone companies are attracting new customers with low prices—sometimes even free installation and a modem. A DSL line is always connected to the Internet. Your computer doesn’t need to dial in for access. It’s “always on.”

Cons: Not widely available. You need to be within a specified distance from a local telephone provider’s main office to receive DSL access. And if they’re not offering special prices, installation and monthly fees can be expensive.

Cable access : Usually offered by the same companies that provide cable television service, cable modem access uses the same data line as your television. In the places where it’s available, it can provide speeds of 2,000k and higher.

Pros: Cable access is extremely fast, and many people already have the necessary wiring in their homes because they subscribe to cable television.

Cons : Not widely available (even if you have cable, your local provider may not offer Internet access). Also, some cable modem access systems only use the television cable for “downstream” data (receiving email and downloading web pages, for example). In these systems, you still need a dial-up connection and modem to send “upstream” information (such as outgoing email).

Other, even speedier types of access are available, but price makes them prohibitive to most home users. These include T1, T2, T3, and business-class DSL. If you access the Internet from a workplace that employs one of these services, please bear in mind that you’re unlikely to attain the same speed at home.

As our application is in Business area : If we run a home-based business, your Internet access fees may well be a business expense. If faster access will help you be more productive and earn more, it's money well spent.

This type of connection is well suited in our case. As it provides good speed 2000k it means even when all 100 systems will access everyone will utilize Internet simultaneously 20k speed.

Q29(i). How does WWW work?

ANS : All the Web servers on the Internet are collectively referred to as the World Wide Web. The number of WWW servers grew from 100 to 7000. The growth will be exponential in the years to come and will probably be the force driving the technology and use of the Internet into every walk of life of human being.

To access the Web server, you use client software called a browser program. With a browser, you can choose an element on the Web page, which can then cross-link you to a computer animation, or play sounds, or display another Web page. Browsers can even contact another Web server located across the world.

(ii) What are the important features of WWW ?

ANS : WWW made it possible for a site to set up a number of pages of information containing text, pictures, sound and even video with embedded links to other pages. There are many features of WWW which are as follows :

Hypertext Information System : The idea behind hypertext is that instead of reading text in a rigid, linear structure (such as a book), you can skip easily from one point to another. You can get more information, go back, jump to other topics, and navigate through the text based on what interests you at the time.

Graphical and Easy to Navigate : One of the best parts of the Web is its ability to display both text and graphics ion full colour on the same page. Before the Web, using the Internet involved simple text-only connections.

The Web provides capabilities for graphics, sound, and video to be incorporated with the text.

Cross-Platform : Cross-platform means that you can access Web information equally well from any computer hardware running any operation system using and display.

The Web is distributed : The Web provides so much of information as a consumer of that information; go to that site to view the information.

The Web Is Dynamic : Because information on the web is contained on the site that published it, the people who published it in the first place can update it at any time. If you are browsing that information, you do not have to install a new version of the help system, buy another book, or call technical support to get updated information. Just bring up your browser and check out what is up there. For example, the development effort for a Web server called Apache. It is being developed and tested through a core of volunteers. It has many features of the larger commercial servers, and above all it is free. The Apache Web site at http://www.apache.org is the central location for information about the Apache software, documentation, and the server software itself. Because the site can be updated any time, new releases can be distributed quickly and easily. New information and news can be published almost immediately.

Accessing of Many Forms of Internet Information : There are dozens of different ways of getting at information on the Net namely, FTP, Gopher, Usenet new, WAIS databases, Telnet, and e-mail. Before the Web became as popular as it is now, to get to these different kinds of information you had to use different tools for each one, all of which had to be installed and all of which used different commands. The Web browsers namely Internet Explorer Version 4.0 and later versions have changed these. Although the Web itself is its own information system, with its own Internet protocol (HTTP), the HyperText Transfer Protocol. Web browsers can also read files from other Internet services and you can create links to information on those systems just as you would create links to information on Web pages.

To point your browser to different kinds of information on the Internet, you use different kinds of URLs. Most start with http; which indicates a file at the actual Web site.

Q30. List the differences between Netscape Navigator and Internet Explorer.

ANS : Following are the differences between Netscape Navigator and Internet Explorer.

S.No.	*Netscape Navigator*	*Internet Explorer*
1.Customizable automatic domain search in Address Bar.	NO	YES
2.Vendor Designed keyword mapping to URLs in Address Bar	YES	NO
3.User customizable keyword mapping to URLs in address bar.	NO	YES
4.Customizable Search Engines used in auto searching.	NO	YES
5.Thumbnail view of favorite sites.	NO	YES
6.Integrate mail, news, calendar and conference clients of choice.	NO	YES
In Dynamic HTML		
1.Object model(DOM)- W3C preliminary requirements for document object model (DOM)	NO	YES
2.XML support	NO	YES
3.Dynamic HTML styles and contents	NO	YES
4.Data binding and awareness	NO	YES
5.Dynamic Web Pages	NO	YES
6.Support for Visual Basic Development system scripting language.	NO	YES
7.Integration of objects and scripts.	NO	YES
8. Full event model for all tags; completely scriptable.	NO	YES
9.Scripting of Plug-Ins	YES	NO
Multimedia		
1.Multimedia controls and HTML transitions filters.	NO	YES
2. Interactive Music Control	NO	YES
3.Video Streaming Support	NO	YES
JAVA		
1.Advanced Abstract Windowing Toolkit(AWT)	YES	YES

2.Advanced Class Libraries and the J/Direct API	NO	YES
3.Automatic and bi-directional integration of ActiveX control and JavaBeans.	NO	YES
4.Dynamic HTML object model exposed to JAVA.	NO	YES
5.Multimedia class libraries with support for the Direct X API.	NO	YES
WEBCASTING		
1.Subscriptions (Basic notification and delivery of web content). Subscribe to any web site.	NO	YES
2.Notification of updates of sites via mail, desktop or subscription status folder.	NO	YES
3.Receive web site content in locally cached web pages, desktop web items on mail.	NO	YES
4.Easy optimized web cast of existing sites.	NO	YES
5.Proposed channel definition format (CDF) support.	NO	YES
6.Exclusive premium channels.	NO	YES
7.Full screen channel viewing.	NO	YES
8.Channel guide/finder.	NO	YES
9.Automatic software distribution via open software description (OSD) proposed standard.	NO	YES
Off Line Browsing Support		
1.Customize downloads of favorite web sites for offline viewing via automatic web site crawl.	NO	YES
2.Download control over page depth site crawl.	N/A	YES
3.Download control over images, applets, controls, audio and video.	N/A	YES
4.Support side passwords.	N/A	YES
Performance		
1.HTTP 1.1 performance enhancements.	NO	YES
2.Native shell integration.	NO	YES
3.Fast Cache.	NO	YES
Security and Privacy		
1.Security Zones	NO	YES
2.Cryptographic API (CAPI) enabling developers to integrate strong cryptography into their applications.	NO	YES
3.Centralized certificate management with administrative tools.	NO	YES
4.Platform for privacy preference (P3) working draft support.	NO	YES

From the above point of differences, there are also differences in surfing web site. Netscape has launched Internet Browser earlier then the Microsoft Internet Explorer. Due to marketing and above technical differences, Microsoft Internet Explorer is gradually capturing market of Netscape Communicator (Navigator).

Being Netscape Communicator is earlier launched than Microsoft Internet Explorer, the standard of all browsers has set according to Netscape Communicator. Due to this companies have both Microsoft Internet Explorer and Netscape Communicator. Almost every company supports both browsers. Here are some examples, which show advantage of Microsoft Internet Explorer and Netscape Communicator.

(a) *http://www.microsoft.com/ms.htm*

This site has folders which can be expanded by clicking + symbol but Netscape communicator can not open this site and redirect to http://www.microsoft.com/default.htm.

(b) *http://www.msdn.microsoft.com/default.htm*

This site has menus, which can be seen on Internet Explorer but not on Netscape Communication.

(c) *http://www.msn.com*

The border at "Today at MSN" boxes in last, can be viewed by Internet Explorer but no by Netscape Communicator.

(d) *http://www.microsoft.com/pffice/upgradecomparision/office97.htm*

When we place pointer on "Web Collaboration" it highlighted with different color and can only be viewed by Internet Explorer, not by the Netscape Communicator.

http://www.microsoft.com/exchange

When we place pointer on "Product Information", it appears as button in Internet Explorer. This does not happen in Netscape Communicator.

And there are many such examples available on the net.

Q31. What are the differences between saving a HTML page in .txt format and saving the same HTML page in .html format.

ANS : There are many differences between saving a HTML page in .txt format and saving the same HTML page in .html format. These are following:-

1. Saving .txt format only saves text visible on the site. No dynamic effects, pictures, sound will be saved.

2. No Background will be saved in .txt format. While .html page will preserve the background color or image as it is.

3.Hyperlinks will not work in .txt format while in .html page hyperlinks will work accordingly.

4. Format or Representation will not saved in .txt format while in .html format the formatting of the page and representation will remain as it is.

5. .txt format is not viewable from the browser. But .html can be viewed from the browser.

6. .html form containing the Text Boxes, Buttons. .txt format is not able to save all these Text Boxes, Buttons.

7. .txt format can never support hypertext (text having some extra facilities as compared to normal text), in .txt hypertext will behave like normal text.

8. All pictures or graphics displayed in .html file will not get save in .txt format.

Q32. What are the differences between a Home Page and a Web Page? List atleast 10 features of a Home Page. [DEC02;Q4(a)]

ANS : Many browsers have a Home button on their toolbars and this yet another meaning. to a web browser, "Home is that place to which you return when you get lost or tired of browsing – your browser Home page. It is a place to get your bearing before venturing out again.

A good Home page for your browser is one that loads quickly, contains information that you want to check regularly (such as headlines in your area of interest or a local weather forecast) and links to a wide variety of other pages. (So that you can quickly go where you want). Portals make good browser Home page and most let you customise the feature to display. By default, Internet Explorers Home button points to Microsoft portal site.

Web Page : Your browser's start page is the web page that the browser loads when you open the browser without requesting a specific page. Internet explorer automatically starts with the browser home page, but navigator allows the start page to be different from the browser Home page. You ISP's installation program may change your start page to the IPS's Home page on the web.

You can create a simple web page by using front page express, composer or any other web page editor Internet explorer provides many print options–

- Printing all documents linked to current page.
- Printing a list of links contained on current page.

Ten Features of Home Page

The ten features of Home Page are following:

1. Home page is the page you return to when you click home button on toolbar.

2. It is the page opens when you open Internet explorer.

3. "Home" is that place to which you return when you get lost or tired of browsing.

4. Home Page loads quickly and contains information that is of daily use.

5. The main (or starting) page of web site.

6. It is used to refer to a browser's start page.

7. It links to a wide variety of other pages.

8. Home Page is like magazine cover or the front page of newspaper.

9. It act as an introduction to the site, explaining its purpose and describing the information found on other pages throughout the site.

10. Home page act as the table of contents for the rest of the site.

CHAPTER 2

INTRANET'S SECURITY

- *Introduction*
- *Objectives*
- *Security concerns*
- *Threats*
- *Security solutions*
- *Advise from security experts*

Every company starts its operations with a genuine and honest thinking. As the time passes, based on the need of its employees as well as customers, a number of processes evolve automatically, which form the core of experience as well as strong standing of the company.

Through the security breaches, companies loose highly valuable information. What is the most valuable thing any company has with it? Truly, it is the ideology of how to implement its creativity in to the market and see that the experience and services reach customers properly so that both the customers as well as the company prosper simultaneously.

Imagine a situation when a company develops a major new product secretly using its Intranet. Hackers break the security and take away all the details or even cause certain damage to the software products. They can even sell the details to the competitors or blackmail the company.

Security has long been seen as a major threatening point in the implementation of Internet or intranet technology in any enterprise. As networks have grown and connected to the Internet, a huge variety of hackers have haunted the professionals responsible for both delivering information within the enterprise and to its partners, and protecting it from unauthorized outsiders.

A good security technology should be powerful enough to support the features administrators need, including rules validation to inform the administrator of potential security back doors, automatic incident reporting to inform administrators when a security breach has occurred, and secure management of the firewall itself so hackers cannot reconfigure the firewall and create security problems.

Q1. In what way security is concern with website?

ANS : The history of security concerns is not new to anyone. They have been of great concern to man and since many centuries man has been endeavoring to devise new techniques for strong security measures.

Every time the technology updates itself, new techniques evolve, but at the same time the thieves or intruders (in the information technology line, they are called "hackers") also get equivalently intelligent since they too must be using increasingly sophisticated tools. Hence, in order to prevent them from intrusion, the companies who manage Internet and intranet sites full of voluminous information and experience must do proper policing as well in addition to their existing day-to-day activities.

Even though the security capabilities of the latest Internet and intranet technologies have enabled the companies to control the availability of information and its authenticity in a much better manner than ever before, still many things have been left for completion. The increasing sophistication of both server and client software means that extremely strong levels of security has provided built-in without actually requiring users to undergo complex measures to control the access as well as even to hack them down.

In order to prevent the intruders to enter into the house, it is necessary for the house owner to look after the behaviour of internal and external people (usually who deal with the owner directly or indirectly). Similarly to prevent the data from the hackers, the Internal or External security concerns, possibility of attacks and their measures have to be carefully analyzed well before hand in order to avert any eventuality.

Access to the intranet site can be broken down into:

- Those who can enter the site
- The who can access the various secured areas
- Those who can update the site's content

Out of the above three, the first two could be considered safe whereas the users who fall under the third category could cause the company's professionals to have sleepless nights.

Q2. What are threats? Define internal and external threats.

#: What are various security threats to Intranet? How do you resolve them?

[JUN01;Q4(a)]

ANS : It must be clearly understood that the source of threat and the likely target could be many in number but all of them can be classified as either major or minor threats. Similarly, they can be organized into two groups viz., internal and external threats. Details of threats have been dealt within subsequent paragraphs.

Internal Threats : Internal security problems are probably the most common. One never knows what someone is going to do. Even the most loyal employees or workers can change their tune and turn malicious, wreaking havoc on the computing environment.

By thoroughly scrutinizing the workers' backgrounds, references, and previous employers carefully, and changing and auditing security methods, especially observation of the work pattern or behaviour of the employees (may be on day-today basis), it would be possible to know about the possibilities of internal threats before hand. Still further, this information would be useful to track down the line easily when any attack takes place.

External Threats : External security threats are the most problematic ones. Till date the greatest threat was the virus menace. Now, with the sophisticated technology, a number of new threats have also developed. It becomes difficult to know when an outsider will attempt to hack down the systems or who the intruder may be. There are a number of examples in the past, the recent being hacking of Indian government's servers by certain terrorists and foreign nationals.

Some people go to great extremes to gain access to the systems and information. If intranet is connected with outside world via the Internet, it will discover a whole new set of potential problems and subject to a number of attacks.

Complete and proper security configuration and administration is indeed a complex issue. One should think carefully about the security breaches before connecting to the Internet. One of the simplest and crudest methods could be that too many system administrators connect to the intranet first assuming that Internet should be treated as the potentially hostile environment and consider security at a later stage. This method could be highly useful in detecting possible loopholes in the system before hand.

Q3. Explain the different types of security solutions for a web site.

ANS : Though there are a number of security solutions available due to sophistication in technology, there are a number of risks and difficulties attached to them. The attacks could be momentary but the aftermath could be so much disgraceful that it may take many months or even years to get back to the normal. History is evident that many such attacks have led to total shutting down of the company itself.

The prime most could be the unwilling overhead in the form of huge investment on extra hardware and software. It is quite possible that while implementing various security measures, the company ends up with investment more than the actual cost of the hardware and software.

Additionally, sufficient training for concerned personnel would also have to be added up to the expenditure statement. Hence, keeping all these issues in view, the company has to plan in such a manner that the investment on providing basic computing infrastructure and that of its security are properly balanced.

Security models : The first and foremost thing one needs to do is to chalk out a security plan and policy based on any security model. The term security policy shall appear a number of times while dealing with different security measures since it forms the foundation for the measures.

It is essential to distinguish between public knowledge information and the more detailed pieces of information relating to specific groups, departments, or projects. Very obviously, there is no need at all to keep documents such as web site material, press releases, product information, etc. that can be found anywhere is public. They can be found in any newspaper or Website, care must be taken to review and protect the intellectual property.

A classical case study : *With due acknowledgments to a security exponent who proposed this theory.* He has carefully classified the security models by giving striking analogies to the real world in the form of following five generalized examples that happen to everyone during day-to-day activities:

The Open House : In this case, the front door and all the rooms are unlocked. Visitors will be free to move around anywhere from any room to any room. This resembles to an unprotected site where users do not require any special authentication to view the information.

The Owner : A case where the front door is locked but all the rooms are unlocked. The owner lives in the house and locks the front door in order to keep the neighbors out but once anyone gets into the house, they will be free to go into all other rooms. This is a useful security model if any company gets a lot of outsiders (i.e., customers, visitors, consultants, etc.) passing through but only want to have its employees access the site.

The Garden Party : An excellent case in which the front door is unlocked but certain rooms inside the house are locked. Anyone may wish to allow people to help themselves to the bar on the front lawn and get into the washrooms but not necessarily into the bedrooms where the owner has kept all of his personal things.

The Paying Guest : This is a must stringent measure than the above in which the front door is locked and certain rooms are locked. The guest has a key to enter the house and is able to get into his room only but the other rooms are off his limits. This model will verify whether or not a user should be allowed to enter the site. Once this user is authenticated, only then he or she may move freely throughout the other rooms as long as they have access to them.

The Fort : A locked massive iron gate with barbed wire, front door locked, all rooms also locked, and there is a watchman guarding the house. Simple, unless the users have the proper credentials or certificates or entry passes, they will not be allowed to get in.

Any one can select any of the above security model or a combination of them. While selecting it should be borne deep in mind that every model have its own cost factor and other considerations.

Q4. What are the common threats to the hardware, software and data?

ANS : The first component in the computer system vulnerable to attacks or threats and most important to be protected is the hardware. The following are some of the common threats to the hardware:

Theft of a computer, printer, or other resources.

Tampering by a disinterested or frustrated employee who takes every chance to manipulate with control switches, tampering the network or cuts the cable.

Destruction of resources by means that can cause terrific problem like fire, flood, or electrical power surges. Since some of them are natural attacks, they may or may not be in the control of the human alone, however, protection should be thought of well in advance.

Ordinary wear and tear

In order to implement solution to the above threats, it is advisable that the company should maintain proper password protected hardware wherever necessary, it should also consider keeping the other peripherals and networking components out of the reach of common users and employees. Further, the provision of keeping hardware backup (extra computers and servers, may be of lesser capacity) as standby when the one working generates trouble due to attack or wear and tear; it is likely that the company may find this option a costlier, it is strongly recommended to consider it seriously.

The cabling should be properly laid out in conduits and only few "trusted" personnel should be entrusted the work of overseeing the activities. It is also to be ensured that the passwords, firewalls, etc. measures are not handled by only one person and also that communication of confidential information such as change of passwords and documents do not fall into the hands of unauthorized personnel.

Software : *The second component vulnerable to the threats to the system is software. Threats to software may include but not limited to the following:*

✓ Deletion of a program, either by accident or by malicious intent.

✓ Theft of a program by the user.

✓ Corruption of a program, caused either by a hardware failure or by a virus. Usually, it has been observed that more of the attacks are due to virus attacks that cause terrible destruction in moments.

✓ Bugs in the software (intentional or unintentional).

✓ Virus attack.

The software developers have wide experience of tackling such issues. Students who develop software project spending days and nights struggling with software code to make things happen suddenly find that their files do not open or are missing. Reasons could be many, it could be disk drive media failure, virus attack, unintentional deletion, cross-linking of files, corrupted file allocation table, bad sectors, and many more.

Assume only one attack out of the above list i.e., the virus attack. Though the present anti-virus software solutions can detect and clean as many as 50000 viruses, it becomes extremely difficult to detect a new virus numbered 50001. The recent happenings of I Love You, Love Bug, Dinner Party with CEO, etc., viruses have virtually spread all over the world not leaving any type of system. As reported at many places, the casualty has been extremely high and the organizations could not come to a stable state till date. It would be notable that even for developing an antidote it would take many man-hours of research and testing before the things are set right, and in the mean while the virus would have done all the damage it can.

Numerous corporate offices do their day-to-day work on-line. A simple task like sending messages, circulars, interview, meeting, promotions, etc. all are dealt on the corporate intranet. The NIC, Indian Oil, Bharat Petroleum, VSNL and many more does work "electronically". Assume that a new virus enters the network passing through the stringent anti-viral tests successfully (and of course, undetected). The story starts then and ends in few more moments.

Information : *The third and major component of the system liable to be attacked is the data and data files used by the company. It is the most serious of all the threats. Threats to the hardware and software are considered negligible in* *comparison with the threats to information since it is this information that acts as the knowledge about the organization. Hardware can be replaced and software can be reinstalled, but information once lost cannot be obtained back. Threats to information can include:*

✓ Deletion of a file or files.

✓ Corruption, caused either by hardware problems or by a bug in the software.

✓ Theft of company data files.

A surge in electrical pulse can cause colossal damage to the data. Dishonesty and distrust as well as frustration have already been discussed in the beginning of this unit, which can be potential threats to the company's information base.

Making and testing backups regularly could be the simplest and easiest of all the security measures. But a new question will immediately arise – "how many backups and where". Clearly, it is possible that the backup could contain virus or there was a media failure or bad sector. Still a step further, the entire building collapses due to earthquake or fire. Solutions lie in terms of maintaining a number of backups, some put at a remote server or site (may be few thousand kilometers away from the location).

Such issues of security threats and management can be found separately as "Disaster Management".

Certification : *One solution for the protection of the computing infrastructure is to use digital certificate-based solutions. Users can be given access based on their possession of certificates signed or authorized for access by or on behalf of the server to which they intend to have access. There are a number of certification solutions available in the market today. In India, the Ministry of Communication and Information Technology has even set up a whole new organization to oversee various security related concerns and certification under the title Controller of Certification Authority.*

The certificate acts as an evidence of the user's digital identity. Certificates can also be combined with other access control mechanisms, such as emails, money transactions, tokens (a form of identification hardware carried by users) or only accepting visitors from certain controlled group or authenticated addresses.

At present, the certification is most easily implemented with a custom solution combined with a server called the certification authority (CA). It is an external or third party service, which can issue and revoke certificates and authenticate any certificates presented in order to gain access. This could be implemented by use of a simple public key infrastructure (PKI), a system that establishes a hierarchy of authority for the issuance and authentication of certificates and users presenting them.

Digital certificates provide excellent means of controlling and monitoring access to the intranets. The certificate itself acts as a token for access control. The user must present it in order to access the intranet or Internet site. The certificate could contain a series of digits and alphabets combined together. The best example can be the use of cash card or the prepaid mobile phone card. The customer pays for the required number of hours of mobile phone usage well in advance and scratches the card to obtain the "certificate". The customer then connects to the intranet site of the phone company by dialing it and then enters the "secret" code. Upon entering this code, the phone company updates the usage records and permits the customer to use the services for the extended period.

A similar service offered by the popular Internet service provider (ISP) of India called the Videsh Sanchar Nigam Limited (VSNL) offers email services for which the customers are handed over a card containing the secret code for the number of hours of usage. Those cards are available at many stores or shops. The customer has to log into the VSNL server and create a new account with the given code number and thereafter use it as long as it permits. Such services are available for ordinary telephone services where prepaid

While in many implementations this is done automatically, in many other implementations the certificate is stored on a separate database or token such as a smart card which the user has to present to the local client in order for it to pass it to the server to gain access. Some other implementations use a number of certificates (or multi-level certificates) to ensure proper security measures.

Q5. Explain the Firewalls and it's different types of architecture.

#: What is a Firewall? How will you configure it? **[DEC02;Q5(a)]**

ANS : For intranet developers, restricting access of unauthorized users to the web site has been the greatest challenge. In addition to preventing external users, a watchful eye on the users within the company may also have to be maintained. There are various tools to provide protection against unwanted intruders into the corporate wide networks, but the most popular amidst all security measures is the firewall.

The simplest way to restrict the users to peek inside the internals of the web site is to use firewalls, where the information cannot be seen or accessed from the Internet at large. Simple firewalls consist of software that prevents access to internal networks from the Internet. While general traffic such as email is allowed in to the mail server, programs such as FTP clients, telnet users or search engine queries cannot access machines beyond the safety premises of the firewall.

Firewalls also offer additional protection to local users who like to browse or surf out from the intranet to the Internet, by acting as proxy to obtain web pages so that the name and IP number of machines on the network are not revealed to other web sites that the users visit. Not revealing the IP address would help preventing hackers from knowing about the details of the structure of the intranet.

While firewall remains the basic foundation of Internet and intranet security, for many users getting into the corporate intranet would require increasing levels of technology. The intranet technology would need to be expanded beyond those physically present on the same intranet from time to time.

Though there exist a number of definitions of firewall, in simplest terms it can be defined as "a mechanism used to protect a trusted network from an entrusted network". It can also be defined as "A firewall is a system, or group of systems that enforce an access control policy between two networks, and thus should be viewed as an implementation of policy". From the above two definitions, it can be understood that a firewall is only as good as the security policy it supports.

It should be very clear right from the beginning that a firewall is not simply for protecting a corporate network from unauthorized external access via the Internet, but it can also be used internally to prevent unauthorized access to a particular subnet, workgroup or LAN within a corporate network.

Three broad categories of firewall configuration are:

Packet-filtering : Such low-level filters pass or drop packets based on their source or destination addresses or ports. Routers already provide this level of filtering. Such a firewall is easy and inexpensive to set up, but its capabilities are quite limited. A packet-filtering firewall can fail if its table of valid and invalid addresses is incorrect. Such a firewall is also susceptible to address spoofing (making a filter believe that a packet is coming from a different address).

Application-filtering : These higher levels filters screen traffic involving specific applications or services (for example ftp or e-mail). The advantage of such a filter is that it allows for more sophisticated evaluation and authentication measures. For example, such a firewall could be designed to protect against a gopher server moving a file onto a machine or to check for an attack entering with an application. The large number of possibilities-for example, an application calling another application-makes it very difficult to build in safeguards against every possible attack.

Circuit-level : Such a filter looks not only at source and destination addresses but also at the circuits (temporary paths) that have been established for a connection. Such circuits are established-for example, when using TCP (Transport Control Protocol)-during an initial handshaking session. Such a filter can detect address-spoofing, for example, because such a misleading packet would have no way of getting the circuit information that is set up during the handshaking. While very effective for certain protocols, circuit filters are of limited use with connectionless protocols (such as UDP), which may send packets over various paths.

Q6. What are the well known encryption /decryption methods?

ANS : One of the best method of ensuring security is to change the form of communication. Let the messages be encoded in such a pattern that it becomes almost impossible to decode for other while the actual user should be able to decode with the use of a simple certificate or key. There are three well known implementations of the encryption/decryption methods:

✓ Public key infrastructure solutions
✓ Web server security through SSL
✓ Virtual private networks

Even though there are a number of other solutions available, the encryption/decryption methods have remained most popular and economical in contrast to the others. Details about each of the security solution have been discussed in detail in the following paragraphs.

Public key infrastructure solutions : The use of public-key based security systems requires great attention and due care in design and management of security features. The security of entire system is dependent on the security of the key since it is the key that will be used for signing certificates of various messages and documents. This is done at the top of the public key infrastructure also commonly called the root. The encryption and decryption is done by specialized hardware.

Usually, all the keys used for accessing the server are held at a secret location in the primary memory of the server. This area or location is highly prone to attacks (for example, in a server core memory dump). It is obvious that a higher degree of protection is required for this target location.

Specialized hardware such as protected memory or cryptographic memory module for storing and protecting the keys proves to be a good solution. The keys are stored in a highly encrypted format. When loaded for signing, the keys are decrypted using complex encryption/decryption algorithms and loaded into the memory of the secure server, which then performs all the signing operations required on behalf of the server. It should be noted that the keys are never displayed in their unencrypted form to the server or any other user, so even if an intruder manages to access the network, the keys remains safe.

Physical security of the cryptographic modules is also built in order to provide total security of the whole system and protect from unauthorized tampering or any kind of manipulation. The physical security is ensured by use of advanced manufacturing technology wherein strong systems are fabricated to protect the sophisticated security hardware.

Since digital certificates are highly dependent on hardware computations, it is essential that mechanisms are evolved to increase the speed of computing by various means such as parallel processing, provision of additional processors, separate hardware for protection, etc. Assume that a number of users log on to the server, then in such an event it is sure to face a bottleneck at the security gate since it would take considerable time in processing encryption/decryption of the keys or certificates. Nowadays, in order to reduce this kind of difficulty, a separate server called firewall server is placed in front of the main server. Any one willing to access the main server has to get through this gate.

Web server security through SSL : As it is well known that the Intranets and extranets are purely based on use of powerful web servers to deliver information to the users, the username/ password authentication pair has been a highly popular method for preventing access to the web servers. Problem arises with use such pairs when these keys are sent in the form of character/text strings, which are prone to be intercepted, read and converted with simple tools.

A significant enhancement was achieved when communications between the user and the server was sent in encrypted form and later decrypted at the other end. The enhancement went step by step and today it has stood as one of the most secured and popular method of secured communication called the Secure Sockets Layer (SSL). Today, almost all commercial web sites are using SSL to ensure or guarantee the authenticity of the server and integrity of the data delivered to web site users. SSL has become fundamental to the spread of Internet community, and commerce and trade over Internet. Over years, the spread of its use for an increasing range of transactions across the Internet has gone manifold.

Finally, it should be noted that by default most SSL implementations on web servers do not support or authenticate the client web browser. Therefore, SSL is at present best suited to the largely anonymous requirements of retailing and definitely requires lot of enhancements to actually pickup worldwide.

Virtual private networks (VPN) : In order to encrypt/decrypt all the communication network traffic that passes through the Internet or intranet, a VPN uses software or hardware. This kind of implementation is considered the best when limited access to an intranet is needed, for example, when two branches of the same company want to use the same information, or suppliers and customers trying to hook up their supply chains. Best example is that of Maruti Udyog Limited that uses a similar kind of solution.

The greatest disadvantage of a VPN implementation is its non-flexibility to accept unknown locations. VPN works extremely well for two fixed known points, but less well suitable the needs of groups of users and situation becomes worse if they are from unknown locations.

Implementation using the combination of a public key infrastructure, secure web server and virtual private network technologies is considered the most powerful solution for data security. The addition of suitable physical security solutions such as cryptographic keys can further ensure that the security is perfect as well as robust.

Q7. "When planning for an Intranet, there is no need to plan an Intranet Security Policy in advance." Do you agree with this statement? Explain. [DEC02;Q2(b)]

ANS : "When planning for an Intranet, there is no need to plan an Intranet Security policy in advance." I am not agree with this statement.

As we know that anything done without planning is dangerous. No matter what we are doing. So, of you believe in above sentence, you are leaving yourself and your business on the luck! And nobody is going to leave his or her business on luck specially when it comes on security.

Security is one of the most critical issues that must be addressed before implementation. When you have implemented your Intranet without thinking of security, you will face strange problems. You will find that outsiders are trying and also gaining access to resources of your Intranet. It depends on you and your business that what contents are you publishing on your Intranet. If those contents are valuable for you, you can imagine the event when you will come to know that you valuable data has been stolen.

It is really foolishness to not to think about security. Even when organizations are planning and implementing maximum security that they can implement, they are not secure. They are always on the prying eyes of hackers, crackers and viruses. Then how will you ensure that your Intranet will be protected from these hackers, crackers and viruses? You will also face the problems from your employees as they might accidentally delete some documents, or maliciously destroy some or all your contents. And you have no way to identify the cause damage!

So, you must always think of security before implementing your Intranet.

Q8. What are the different levels in Internet Security?

ANS : Security requirements vary from organization to organization, and also vary based on the content organization's intends to place on its servers. While for certain intranets simple security solutions are enough, for many organizations solution could be in the form of implementing more than a firewall or multi-layered security architecture.

A company can implement a wide range of security models but the most useful ones are those that are organized in multiple levels. Implementation of a multi-layered or multi-tiered scheme is easier and flexible than using all or no security approach in which a user allows either total access or provides a total denial.

In addition to not just access, security methods also protect information from accidental or intentional modification, manipulation or destruction. Most security experts opine that a security breach is more likely to come from within a company's own staff rather than from outside. These may be frustrated employees, or enthusiasts who are after the thrill of breaking the code.

As one can see that in the physical world, there are many layers of security. For instance, a bank maintaining lockers has strong vaults, good locks, alter guards, and highly sensitive alarms, etc. Each security measure tries to compensate the limitations of others. Similarly, assuming information is cash, Intranets also follow the same suite and have a similar layered approach.

Most commercial servers use a powerful operating system as base that provides good methods of file-system security. Some servers require additional software to control access to server resources and files. The immediately next higher level is the software tool that monitors the system logs, serious looking out for any suspicious activity. When any intrusion is detected, the software generates an alert message. The response could be spontaneous and automatic, with an option to generate the alert message manually. The history recorded in the server logs is usually used to assess damage and for planning restoration from the damage.

Use of firewalls and proper alarm systems can act as complement to above security measures, which can be added to network routers to detect or block potential threats. There devises help in filtering, detecting and then permitting the user requests and have tendency to scan the IP packets for blocking suspicious behaviour or patterns. A proxy server also helps a lot since it hides the real IP addresses of users requesting resources outside the firewall.

Finally, software run outside the firewall tries all known security tricks of hackers, thus scanning for vulnerability points. The security implementation also should be supplemented with regular process audits by an independent security expert.

Q9. What are the precautions/advise you will take while making a website?

ANS : Several companies employee professionals as security specialists whose basic job is to detect and cover loopholes in the security systems of the company. It would be highly astonishing to ask why would a company pay someone to hack its intranet system. The answer would be obvious, that they intend to improve the security of its intranet as well as to identify where from the possible risks can crop in. It should be always remembered that majority of the threats come from inside the company

Good resources : Books such as "Intranet Security: Stories from the Trenches" by Linda McCarthy, which also happens to be her first book could prove to be a bible to the current day security specialists.

Qualifications of security professionals : For the security professionals, it is essential that they have too much power to check the security measures or enforce them and simultaneously they should know how to use it effectively. It is also essential that the personnel though being competent do not have a striking ego. Egoistic personalities can be very harmful to the security systems; the firewall experts, security managers, etc., all personnel should be bound by the sense of responsibility, trust, loyalty and above all cool nature in tackling complex security issues.

Firewall configuration makes all the difference : The greatest blunder any company does is to just install a firewall and to finally think that they have ensured perfect security. While firewalls protect from outside threats, it requires updating from time to time. Poor firewall configuration has been considered the cause of the biggest security breaches that took place until this date.

Motivation behind hackers to hack : Good security people are usually broad minded, for instance, even if there is a small loop way made in the fence, the security personnel will try level best to make a way out only through the loop even though one could easily walk a few meters to where the fence ends and go around. This means that the security personnel attempt to locate and isolate the loopholes rather than go around a big way to reengineer the problem. They also tend to be alert regarding such holes either in the fence or in the software. Hackers also work in the same fashion. Even though both are motivated by the challenge, the difference is that both have opposite goals, i.e. good vs. bad. The solution lies in asking a question to oneself "what causes someone to do a bank robbery? Why does one person grow up and become a police officer while another person with a similar personality and traits becomes a bank robber?" It is to be remembered that information has the same value as money. Until everyone start to think about it that way, data will continue to be at risk.

Lot of care required while programming : It is a common and well-known saying that many developers of "secure systems" leave a "back door" way for themselves so that they can get into the system bypassing the secure front door.

The big problem is that often the companies owning the web servers or intranets have so many contractors and newly recruited programmers writing critical code who do not know the intricacies of the system security. The code never being reviewed causes the greatest concern (may be due to ignorance).

Security risks present on the networks : Lots of risks are present everywhere on Internet as well as on intranet, if it is not known what is being done. Every day a number of servers get connected to the global community but it is less than one percent companies who serious thinks about the security issues. A study of security of web servers reveal that out of 2,000 high-profile web servers consisting of various kinds such as commerce servers, banks, industries, government and so on, only three companies noticed the breaches.

Routine security audits are essential : It is essential that regular security audits are conducted to find out physically which computer is connected and permits access to which networks. Also, the profiles, browser permissions, certification, passwords, location of the computer in the network layout plan, firewall configuration, etc. for each computer and user on the intranet has to be carefully studied during the audits. There are a number of other issues that cannot be dealt with directly such as integrity of the personnel. It is essential that the personnel be requested to fill up a questionnaire or they are interviewed briefly about the security measures using indirect questions.

Example of security audit as case study : Linda narrates one of her experience about a security audit. She was performing a spot audit where she was checking certain systems. It was noticed that there could be systems that was not even part of the audit. The exact location on the network layout plan was found out and it was noticed that it had an extra connection to it but she could not make out by the network map where the connection lead to. Consequently, she decided to audit that system and found that it was connected to the Internet, to that company's intranet as well as to a customer network. Still ahead, it was found that a hacker had broken into the system and replaced the system files and put them back in proper place. Nobody in the company even knew that system had been broken into and only two people knew that it was even connected to the Internet.

Q10. How will you ensure security from external threats to an Intranet.
[JUN02;Q4(a)]

ANS : External threat are most problematic because we never know when an outsider will attempt to gain access to the system and information.

To ensure security to the Internet, security goals has to be defined. Following points should be considered:

1. Decide what we are trying to protect - Software, Hardware, Confidential data or network operations.

2. Who do need to protect-current user, previous employees or intruders.

3. Determine likelihood of the threats.

4. Review your process and procedures continously and make further improvement.

Intranet threats can be secured from External Threats via following ways:

1. Using Authentication - Firewalls can be implemented on the routers to either give/deny access to specific hosts based upon their IP addresses.

2. Using Proxy Servers - Proxy Server helps in the following ways :- It blocks services on the Network

- Protects Intranet Services
- Provides logging and statistics
- Easy to configure
- Doesn't require use of valid Internet IP addresses, through increased Intranet Security
- Hides real IP address of the user

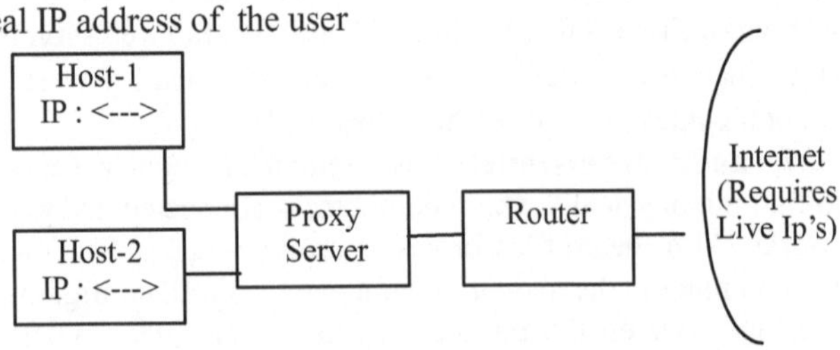

- As Shown in a diagram, all hosts as a part of the Intranet are assigned their own IP addresses which are no longer either as a part of the Internet or even known to the Internet.
- Whenever a user accesses the Internet, Proxy Server performs the address translation through NAT Software.NAT stands for Network Address Translation.

Also Refer Q-13 Page-52, For More Detail.

Q10. Explain the role of an Intranet Server. **[JUN02;Q4(b)]**

ANS : Web servers usually store text and graphics files, but they can also serve files of other types, including word-processing documents, audio, video, and animation.

Most of the traffic processed by the Web server is one way, from the browser to the server, although the increasing use of HTML elements, such as forms that send data back to the server for processing, is starting to change this. The number of two-way transactions is definitely on the rise.

A intranet or Web server can also run other programs, such as database-related applications or search engines, and several standard interfaces have emerged to manage these functions, including CGI (Common Gateway Interface), Microsoft's ISAPI (Internet Server API), and Netscape's NSAPI (Netscape Server API). Linking programs can be written in C or C++ or even in Visual Basic, and recently Sun Microsystems' Java programming Language has seen a huge wave of interest due to its platform independent nature. Java is also popular because it allows fairly sophisticated programs to be run on the client's CPU cycles rather than the server's Having said that a Web server is perfectly capable of running other programs, you should not come away from this section with the idea that you can use a Windows 95 system both as a Web server and as someone's personal workstation; that won't work. Users of an intranet set up in this way would see very poor performance, and the person whose workstation this is would never get any computer time to get any work done. Likewise, Windows 3.1 is only suitable as a browser platform for intranet use. Windows NT Workstation can turn a small to intermediate intranet without any difficulty, and NT Server can run large intranets with ease. And Windows 2000 is also emerging as popular server.

Q11. How will you protect your Internet from being accessed by unauthorised external people? **[DEC01;Q1(c)]**

#: What are the different ways of controlling access to Intranet? Explain them. **[JUN01;Q4(b)]**

ANS : Controlling Access to Your Intranet : You can control access to your Intranet in three ways, and you can use these methods to restrict access to a single intranet document or to directories containing a large number of documents:

By user authentication : This refers to authentication by username and password and is often provided by the operating system. Some operating systems, such as Windows NT, have robust security systems; some have relatively fragile security,

1 and Windows 3.1 has none to speak of.

IP address or domain name : Most servers let you exclude specific users or groups of users by their unique IP address.

By encryption : Using one of the popular encryption techniques is often recommended to ensure confidentiality of applications. Many popular servers support SSL, and some of them, including those from Microsoft and Netscape, include support for digital certificates. See the following sidebar for a more detailed look at encryption.

Q12. Write a short note on the following: [DEC01;Q6(a)]

ANS : (i) Servers and Security

Securing Intranet Server Configurations : You can securely configure your Intranet server in two major ways: One involves physically isolating the server, and the other isolates the webserver based on the networking protocol in use. Let's take a look.

Physical Isolation : Placing your Intranet server on a section of your network where unknown Internet users can't access it is always a great policy. This, in effect, eliminates most of the possibilities for intrusion from an outsider. A potential intruder would have to physically gain access to your premises in order to violate security and gain access to the intranet server. Physical access to your premises is something you can control, and it goes a long way toward securing your Web site.

Protocol Isolation : Protocol isolation techniques involve Web servers that do not use TCP/IP as the primary means of network communication. Some Web servers are capable of using other network protocols to communicate with Web clients needing access. For instance, you can opt to use Microsoft's NetBEUI protocol, or perhaps you can use IPX/SPX, which is more performance-oriented than NetBEUI. If your Web server has no way of talking to the rest of the Internet, logic dictates that a potential intruder wouldn't be able to talk to your Web server from across the Internet. Protocols are a very technical subject.

Q13. How do you establish your Intranet Security Policy? [JUN01;Q1(d)]

ANS : Once you've compiled a list of all the ways in which your network may be threatened, you can begin to formulate an intranet security policy. In many ways today's computing world is radically different from the computing environments of yesteryear. These days many intranets are in private offices and labs and are often managed by someone employed outside the traditional computer data center or IS department-someone who may have little or no understanding or interest in system administration and security-protection techniques.

A connection to the Internet is, of course, a two-way street. Once your intranet is connected to the Internet, you're giving outsiders the means they need to reach your internal networks. A major component in planning your intranet is the process of defining a set of reasonable security goals and then implementing a security policy based on those goals.

We use the word reasonable because it's extremely difficult to both service your normal users without inconveniencing them and keep out intruders at the same time. And never assume that your system is bulletproof. As soon as you do, you've let your guard down, and someone will surely break in, which could cost you your entire network, your sensitive data, or even your business. Read this section carefully before finalizing and implementing your security policy. Let's take a look.

Defining Security Goals : As you begin to formulate your security policy, consider the following:

Look at exactly what you are trying to protect-network hardware, software, company-confidential data, and network operations.

Look at who you need to protect it from-current users, previous employees, and outsiders trying to break into your system.

Look at what you need to protect it from-fire, smoke, floods, extremes of temperature and humidity, power outages, earthquakes, and theft.

Determine the likelihood of these potential threats.

Implement measures that will protect your assets in a way that you or your firm can afford.

Review your processes and procedures continuously, and improve them every time you find a weakness or a new security mechanism becomes available.

Your security policy should minimize all types of threats and ensure network compromise or security breaches are as infrequent as impossible. It should also minimize the affect of any security breach once it occurs.

As you develop your security policy, focus on the following goals:

- Preventing malicious damage to files and systems.
- Preventing accidental damage to files and systems.
- Limiting the results of any deletions or damage to files that do over.
- Protecting the integrity and confidentiality of data.
- Preventing unauthorized access to the system.
- Providing appropriate disaster-recovery systems so the server can be restored and be back online again quickly.

CHAPTER 3

CHOOSING INTRANET HARDWARE AND SOFTWARE

- *Introduction*
- *Objectives*
- *Selection of computing infrastructure*
- *Hardware*
- *Network environment*
- *Software*
- *Other aspects*

Intranets not only provide a secure environment for the companies, but also provide excellent working environment that is full of information and resources for the users as well as decision makers in the company's management. Intranets use a greater part of the system and networking resources. If the data is bulky and consisting of audio or video then they must have broader bandwidth as well as higher throughput for transmission of data. Whereas general messages and documents forming major part of textual information require less time and transmission speed, the multimedia files require more than 10,000 times the transmission bandwidth. This bottleneck must have been faced by almost everyone accessing the Internet via modem, and the difference it makes when accessing the Internet through ISDN or leased line connectivity. Evidently, the amount of time it can take from the moment a web page is requested, gets loaded along with all the graphics until the user actually sees the affect on the computer can be considerable.

Now that many organizations are demanding higher services (also called value added services) such as fixing, minimal cost call routing, connectivity to the corporate EPABX, chatting, video conferencing, IP telephony, etc. would on one side require heavy investments but on the other side assure value for money. These value added services though seems to be costly at the first instance, provides reduction in recurring expenditure of communication costs while enhancing productivity. Installation of such services requires one time high budget. The companies are realizing that video conferencing over an intranet can offer a highly cost-effective alternative to many face-to-face meetings, especially where the members or decision makers are located at far of places.

Just few years back, when analog audio and video conferencing systems were used, the procurement and installation was complex, less reliable as well as costly. With the advance of technology and reduction in communication costs, it has become possible to send and receive voluminous amount of information much quickly and at almost negligible costs.

Q1. What are the procedure for selection of computing infrastructure?

ANS : Since an Intranet can be defined as simply a standard WAN limited to an organization, powerful hardware should be made available for web server. The computing equipment must be selected in such a manner that they do not get obsolete very quickly or become too costly for the company.

It is also important that other points such as the following along with their specifications should essentially be considered and drawn carefully:

Communication medium/services that provide connectivity between different locations of the company should use technologies such as ISDN, leased line, etc.

Network equipment and connectivity should address various networking equipment such as routers, types of cables, as well as the topology behind the network

It is a must that the hardware should be configured for protocols such as IP, HTTP, SMTP, POP, X509 Certification, etc. in order to provide security to the intranet server.

For an intranet to work smoothly, the following tasks should be properly synchronized:

- All computers connected together in a network must communicate using the same language and protocol. Inability to do so may leave the users disconnected to the repository of information and resources
- It must be always remembered that the language used is Hyper Text Markup Language (HTML) and every thing that is developed for and intended to be hosted on the intranet must follow HTML invariably.
- The protocol suite applicable for both intranets and Internet are called Transmission Control Protocol/ Internet Protocol (TCP/IP) and every computer should be compatible to TCP/IP. Though, TCP/IP evolved initially on UNIX based computers, it became a standard for data communication and more recently for every type of communication across intranet and internet, especially supported by every major operating system in use.
- The intranet is driven by a network server that uses a browser, like Netscape Navigator or Internet Explorer.

Q2. What is the process of choosing Intranet Server Hardware? [JUN01;Q5(b)]

ANS : Hardware forms the greatest asset of the company, but it reaches the obsolescence rate very quickly. Normally, it is said that every six months technology in the electronics, telecommunication and computing discipline changes. With such rapid rate of obsolescence, it is very important how the professionals select hardware equipment including the server, clients, peripherals, etc. while maintaining a proper balance between cost and the obsolescence rate.

Care must be taken to ensure that proper spare parts are available even after about five years of commissioning. In addition to this it should also be ensured that proper and reliable service backup is available throughout for keeping the intranet at maximum uptime.

Whenever any component of the entire intranet system breaks down or any extra component of higher capacity is required to be added, proper compatible component must be selected.

Besides this one has to consider in mind that what type of activities our intranet is going to handle. According to that hardware is chosen.

Q3. Explain the concept of client-server.

ANS : ***Servers :*** *The success or usage of the intranet server is measured by the number of operations it handles per unit time. The selection of a good server depends on how many connections per hour it is expected to handle.*

While most of the parameters are too general, the most important checkpoints for selection of a server would be the type and speed of processor, its memory capacity (both primary and secondary), number of connections it can handle easily, etc. Typically, a mid range or high-end server with following specifications would be sufficient for a medium to large organization:

A Pentium III Xeon based server (dual processor recommended)

2 x 40 GB HDD (one extra recommended for backup)

128 MB RAM (256 MB recommended)

As it is, normally, there is absolutely no restriction or limits on number of nodes with in an Intranet; any organization with 10000 web servers can form an Intranet. Limits exist only on use of licensed software or on user restrictions on the network environment

Very powerful and mass store back-up devices help in ensuring recovery of data from hardware failures with minimum efforts.

Service Support must be considered as a strong point for hardware, especially for servers and should be available readily. Many branded products such as HP, Compaq or Dell servers come with good and strong network of support services. The hardware are usually bought with service contracts or warranties, which could be extended for further periods as needed.

It is obvious that the information can be retrieved faster if the processors are faster, RAM is bigger and hard disk drive access is faster.

The basic software required for the server should be capable of handling NCSA HTTP and CERN HTTP. Products such as Netscape Enterprise Server, MS IIS, FastTrack Server, etc. are well known products in this line. They are available (both free as well as commercial) for variety of OS such as UNIX, Windows NT, MacOS, etc.

Clients : *The most interesting thing is that almost every computer can be connected as client to the intranet server. The client could be based on any architecture whether Intel, AMD, Motorola or any other well known processor or operating system such as Unix, Windows NT, Mac OS, etc.*

In addition to the operating system, a client would require only a browser such as MS Internet Explorer, Netscape Navigator, NCSA Mosaic, Lynx, Emacs, Midas WWW, etc. to work comfortably with the intranet. It must be ensured that the browsers have the following:

- ✓ Browser is of latest version.
- ✓ It supports TCP/IP.
- ✓ It is compatible to Microsoft and Java technologies.

Q4. What are the Security systems in context of internet?

ANS : If the company intends to connect to the Internet, then it should pay great attention to the configuration of firewalls. Just as no one would leave the house unlocked at night, it is also expected that no one would leave the computer system or intranet open to various attacks from the outside.

Securing an intranet is not a simple task. Mere installation of firewall hardware and software would not help the intranet to protect itself. Proper configuration as well as updation from time to time is also as essential.

Some firewalls are available in form of ready-made hardware equipment whereas some are available as customizable program, but some firewalls are sold as features of hardware routers or combination of both hardware and software.

All units entering the intranet must be scrutinized to ensure that they are not coming from the unauthenticated sites or users. It also helps in checking whether someone of the company is not trying to go beyond the intranet system to access prohibited sites or competitors' system.

Proper programming of the ports of the company's web server through detection of IP addresses could be an excellent strategy or solution for preventing every unauthorized access.

For example, it is possible to set up a firewall policy that will exclude everything sent to port 80 (that is mostly used by hackers) except those sent to the public Web server. It may, however, be noted that this kind of filtering can only act as a good first level of security.

In addition to the above method, the company should install additional levels of security measures since it is possible for hackers to generate and send data with headers of the data looking like those send from authorized users. Difficulties start when the hackers or attackers obtain information regarding the server, certain hosts and subnets of the intranet.

The best method to protect the web servers or intranet servers is to use application gateways or simply "proxies". These gateways act as intermediaries between users' systems and external systems and handle identification or authentication at a higher level than at hardware level. Every request, whether from outside or from within the intranet system, would first be received by the proxy server, which scrutinizes the requests and prevents the undesirable and unknown ones.

Even the destination web site or user would not be able to know that the interaction being done was with the proxy or gateway server and not the actual server, thus sending and receiving data "on behalf of the user". This kind of proxy or gateway can be useful for providing secure services encompassing HTTP, FTP, Telnet, email, etc.

Another best methods to keep the attackers at bay is known as network address translator or NAT. The philosophy behind the design of NAT is that the more an attacker knows about the intranet, the easier it would be attack and cause damage to it. It is sufficient to know the IP addresses of a server to open it and destroy every important data posted on it.

There is a separate set of IP address for a company's internal use, more popularly known as "internal IP address" or subnet IP address. This IP address is never passed on to outside. It is useful for every communication within the organization. For dealing with external communication, the web server must have a static IP. Having a static IP could also be a problematic issue. As far as web servers generate dynamic IP addresses (those addresses assigned to users when they connect to the server and this changes every time they log into the intranet), the entire network is safe as the hacker or attacker would never be able to detect from where the request or information has actually originated. The NAT equipment serves as address translator from internal to external IP address and vice versa and routing them within these private addresses.

The firewalls available today do all the things like filter the data packets, provide proxy services and do stateful inspection of packets. Now-a-days, the firewalls are providing additional services like detection and cleaning known viruses, as well as prevent unwanted Java or ActiveX programs.

Q5. What is Local Area Network (LAN)?

ANS : LAN stands for **Local Area Network**. A LAN is an interconnection of computers and associated peripherals as well as to the communications system that allows users to access and share resources (computers, printers, servers) with other users.

Text, images, audio, full motion video, fax, and many other value-added services can now be shared over the LAN. They are great time and money saving electronic components for the companies to share resources and information. They are simple, inexpensive, and support a number of protocols. Though there a number of types of networks, the networks are designed in such a manner that one supports the other. The exact number of benefits accruable from networks cannot be enumerated easily in terms of monetary benefit.

In order to understand the LAN system, one must first become familiar with the basic terminology and concepts. The most common terms and concepts that are specific to LAN are as follows:

- ✓ LAN transmission media
- ✓ LAN technology and topology
- ✓ Network protocols
- ✓ Network management
- ✓ LAN applications
- ✓ LAN networking devices

Q6. What is Address Translation?

ANS : When a web site address or URL is typed in the web browser, email or other web related service, note that it is typed something as www.startv.com and not as series of numbers. It is essential for the server to know where exactly the data has to be sent to or received from, this address is mapped on to (or translated into) a series of numbers. The translation is called "domain name resolving", "host name resolving" or "name server lookup". For instance, the VSNL site address www.vsnl.net.in would translate to a group of four octets like 202.30.15.30. The translation is done on the whole name and not on each byte between the periods. The task of number translation is done solely by a domain name server (DNS) on the intranet server. Like all devices, it has its own IP address (e.g. 194.62.15.20). The router must have an IP address of the same network (194.62.15.x in this case) for the convenience of the entire network to use the services of the router. The NAT router also has a separate IP address that would be used for external communication through the Internet. Note that all IP addresses are unique and any duplication would result in collision. For example, a NAT router may have IP address of 194.62.15.2 for internal use and 202.63.10.15 for external or public (or internet or ISP) IP address.

If the request is for a computer outside the LAN, it is just sent to the router. A normal router would just route everything via the Internet to the server computer, however, a NAT router would replace the IP of the source compute with it's own IP address so that while receiving acknowledgment or any error response, NAT may handle it first and then permit it to the LAN.

Q7. Explain the Groupware with the help of suitable example.

ANS : Groupware are collection of software tools that encompass a broad range of applications. Even though groupware broadly consists of applications like calendars, project planning, sharing documents, emails, etc., it is many times costlier than Intranet e.g. a Lotus Notes application can cost over Rs. 8 crore for a big group whereas for same group corporate Intranet could be easily served with about Rs. 8 lakh. These application are many but not limited to the following:

✓ **Communication tools**
- Voice mail
- Email
- Fax
- Video conferencing applications

✓ **Project management**
- Project planners
- Project management
- Project scheduling

✓ **News and general services**
- Electronic bulletin board services
- Electronic calendar service
- News service
- Reminder services

✓ **General office management tools**
- Document management
- Office productivity tools
- Spreadsheets
- Word processors
- Graphical editors

✓ **Web tools**
- Authoring
- Publishing
- Content management
- Other graphical tools

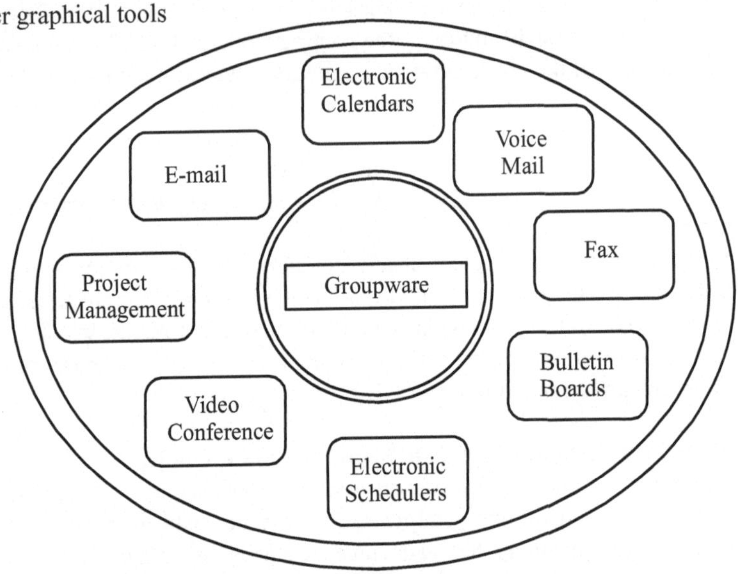

Figure: Contents of a groupware

With the use of groupware, users can easily do most of the office related management work, which otherwise would be extremely difficult. For instance, it would be possible to edit, analyze, share, store and retrieve document. Still further, they can be very comfortably translated, or published in no time. They help a lot in increasing the productivity of every user as well as of the organization as a whole.

The downside of groupware is that they are very costly and with the increase in complexity or additional features, the cost too increases proportionately.

However, since intranets work purely on inexpensive browsers as front-ends and actual applications on the web server as back-end, many-a-times the groupware proves to be cheaper, but such implementations are rare.

As long as same operating system and hardware were used, there were no problems, but maintenance and technical support cost was extremely high. Additionally, the software team has to learn every bit of things related to computers. Since different users work on different platforms and application, which in turn use different protocols and services, there was no coordination or collaboration between one another.

With the advent of intranet, users were free to use any platform they like on any computer architecture. In order to eliminate every kind of barrier, all they had to have is a HTML and Java support through browser that remains the only requirement. Now, the users do not have to learn everything and can comfortably concentrate on their line of working leaving the intrinsic details to the intranet software or groupware.

It may be noted that the most difficult part of any intranet is document management. Whereas document generation, delivery and distribution, etc. phases are relatively easier as compared to any earlier methods, the management of huge amount of day-to-day documents still remain a problematic issue. Not just storage but context based search also has been troubling the groupware developers.

Many developers have found solution to this problem through a specialized tool called the content management tool. These tools were initially developed for use of web site management, it found suitable place readily on the intranets as well and has now fast becoming the strong feature of all.

The latest technology in the line of intranet tools has been the Web-based Distributed Authoring and Versioning (WebDAV), which is an extension to the existing HTTP services. A number of functionalities have been added to the WebDAV thereby making it the ultimate for web authoring, publishing and collaboration. It is now like to evolve a new file system like NTFS, FAT, etc. called the web file system. WebDAV is one of the best-used server modules and many companies developing intranet software or groupware as well as various publishing and office management tools are going ahead to incorporate its support features to their products. For example, Dream weaver, Director and Flash support the intranet, enabling even more disciplined approach and association among the designers and developers who create powerful and massive web sites. A number of developers of service tools like the FTP, Telnet, etc. are also supporting the cause of intranet.

Q8. Explain the different types of Database Connectivity.

ANS : Basic connectivity : A number of database management systems are available today such as the Oracle, Sybase, Ingress, Gupta's SQL Base, etc.

Most of the databases that are used to store massive data for use through Internet deploy Relational Database Management System (RDBMS) designed for PC class hardware. They are also available in both server (workgroup) and local engine (stand-alone) configurations, and are usually bundled with the power of Structured Query Language (SQL), transaction processing, and distributed processing for building business applications. By supporting client/server architecture, these software achieve a higher level of scalability, which makes them suitable for a wide range of applications; from a stand-alone, single-user environment to a multi-user workgroup environment.

To build the client side of applications, developers use various tools. Some of the popular software development environments include Visual Basic, C/C++, Power Builder, Java, Delphi, etc. It must be ensured that the databases can connect to these programming languages, or in other words, these database management systems should support these languages by being backend support.

Middleware support : All the connectivity interfaces related tools come under the category of middleware. Middleware provides the link for data exchange between the different points of processing in a distributed application. In an intranet application, the points of processing are the database software, the server software and the client application.

Many of the popular databases also provide support of and to the middleware and consequently, the term middleware has become lesser known. Though software like the ASP, Perl, etc. have got wide popularity, a lot of work is being done to integrate a number of features of the traditional software made available in the middleware also.

During processing of any request, the client/server architecture is maintained and the database and client applications are processed separately even though running on the same platform or machine. For certain middleware, a connectivity interface is not required to support data exchange between the application and middleware or database.

Open Database Connectivity (ODBC) : It happens that in addition to conventional or most popular database management systems, many companies go for proprietary software creating problem for themselves as well as for the clients. It is strongly recommended that companies should use that particular DBMS software which is most popular and widely used.

If this is not followed, a number of difficulties arise with database connectivity and the company may have to shell out enormous amount of money on obtaining proper connectivity tools.

It must also be ensured that whenever any DBMS or middleware is procured, all relevant database connectivity tools are also bundled. Most important of all of the connectivity tools or drivers is the ODBC, which permits connectivity to any type of database from the client application.

Many developers provide not just a simple ODBC driver, but a complete industry standard ODBC database solution for a wide range of operating systems such as Windows, Unix, Linux, MacOS, Sun Solaris, etc.

Java Database Connectivity (JDBC)

With two different types of technologies available in the market today viz., the Windows and the Java technologies developed by the Microsoft and the Sun Microsystems respectively, it is essential for any company to ensure proper integration of the two technologies so that the customer support is ensured in spite of the technological divide.

Not just ordinary ODBC tools and drivers, it has become almost essential for the companies to obtain the JDBC drivers as well. With JDBC drivers, it would become possible to connect the Java applications with any type of databases and can query as well as update data from any data source across Intranets or the Internet.

Q9. Explain the security tools.

ANS : Securing an intranet is not a simple task. Just as articles in a house are protected by use of various types of security systems such as lock and keys, admirals, burglar alarms, etc., so also the intranet should be protected using various types of security systems.

A number of security products covering a broad range of methods are available in the market. Most popular of all the security measures are the firewall, the VPN and the SSL. While the firewall is supposed to be easily manageable and configurable as compared to all other security measures, the VPN and SSL are considered the most inexpensive and easy security methods.

Firewalls : While getting one firewall for the company's intranet it should be well known that firewalls come in both hardware and software forms, and that even though, all firewalls are programmed, they require proper configuration at the time installation to suit the requirements of the company. While doing so a number of considerations have to be taken into consideration.

The firewall vendors may be giving tall claims about the success of the product in the world, but the purchaser must keep a number of issues ready before actually obtaining one for the company. The customer must be cautious that firewall security can be highly complex and that just simplicity can not be a good measure for the performance, and finally that the firewall after installation requires proper configuration.

While deciding whether to buy a hardware or software firewall, the user must consider important factors such as performance and flexibility. Hardware firewalls can be easy to set up and may also be customized to improve performance, the software firewalls offer the flexibility of use on any hardware platform is available, and the platform and can be upgraded much easily and thereafter moved to a different platform altogether.

The Unix-based firewalls are considered most secured as compared to the Windows NT based ones. The firewalls binds the holes of the operating system under which it has been installed by closing all the security holes and by eliminating all possible services that could be used by attackers.

There are proxy servers that act as good firewall protection for the entire intranet system. In some cases, firewall comes as a separate server altogether, whereas in certain cases, firewall themselves can act as a proxy server.

It must be ensured that the firewall is being updated from time to time and the personnel responsible are alert and loyal.

Virtual Private Network (VPN) : Even though, many firewalls also include the features of the virtual private network, the functionality and capabilities of VPN capability are different from that of the firewall.

It is important to understand that installing a firewall is only one part of a security strategy. In addition to it, other aspects such as user authentication through username/password combination, Vans, a public-key cryptographic code and resource management should also be added to the policy of the company's intranet security.

When determining requirements for a VPN, carefully estimate the number of systems to be put behind the VPN, the number of concurrent users, the type of Internet connection in use, etc. It is also essential to study the degree to which internal systems must be protected, the available resources to maintain the VPN, and what security functions are intended from the VPN to perform.

Encryption/decryption using by SSL : Once a session is established, the SSL generates a session key using public-key encryption to exchange information between the client and server. This key is used to encrypt the transaction for both request as well as the response. It would be extremely difficult for the attacker to get into the system since each transaction uses a different session key. Hence, even it the attacker succeeds to crack the code of a transaction, he can not use the same key every time for cracking and will have to spend enormous amount of time as he did for decrypting the first key.

Most of the server and browser software developed by various vendors carry out encryption using either a 40-bit or a 128-bit secret key. It is felt that using a 40-bit key could be insecure since any possible combination of 2^40 can be computed easily using modern day computers. Relatively, use of a 128-bit key eliminates this problem as there would be 2^128 possible combinations instead of just 2^40.

Software are coming up in which the user can select what kind of security measure can be taken for encryption. One such example is the Netscape, in which the user can select from available encryption methods and size of key.

Q10. What is a Firewall? How will you configure it?

ANS : Firewalls are becoming an increasingly popular way to control access to network systems: in fact, well over one-third of all Web sites on the Internet are protected by some form of firewall. According to a recent survey, 10,000 firewall units were shipped during the whole of 1995, and this figure is expected to grow to 1.5 million by the year 2000.

The firewall sites between your private local area network and the Internet, and all traffic from one to the other must flow through the firewall; nothing is allowed to go around the firewall. Although the firewall monitors all the traffic that flows between the two networks, it's able to block certain kinds of traffic completely. If the firewall does its job, and intruder will never reach your protected internal network. The firewall also performs several other important tasks, including authenticating users, logging traffic information and producing reports.

Configuring your Firewall : Where you locate your firewall depends on the design of your network and exactly what you want to protect. A simple configuration in which the firewall sits between your intranet and the Internet. The firewall blocks access from the Internet for everything except incoming e-mail.

A slightly more complex example of what's usually called a dual-homed firewall, a common configuration that's currently used by companies that have Web servers. This type of firewall has two network connections: the first to the secure internal network, and the second to the Internet. Network traffic originating in the secure network can pass out to the Internet, to the bastion host, or to the server that contains the firewall; incoming traffic from the Internet can only access the bastion host and the services it offers.

The bastion host (the name come from the highly fortified projection on the outside walls of medieval castles in Europe) is your public presence on the Internet and therefore is exposed to possibly hostile elements. But even if the bastion host is compromised (and you should plan on it), your internal network is isolated and remains secure.

Don't allow user accounts on the bastion host if you can avoid it; they make the host more susceptibility to attack while at the same time making it more difficult to detect those attacks when they do occur.

A variation on the dual-homed firewall configuration that brings the bastion host inside the secure area.

1. An external connection to the Internet

2. A connection to the secure internal network

3. A connection for the bastion host

IP routing must be turned off on the bastion host machine, which prevents IP packets from getting to the rest of the network.

Although this arrangement brings the bastion host inside the secure area, it's still isolated from the secure internal network.

Q11. What are different Intranet Server Software available in the market? How do you select one of them? **[JUN01;Q5(a)]**

ANS : Web server software is available for various operating System like Win NT Server, Win NT Workstation, Win 98, Machintosh, and even win 3.11.

The web server software runs on the hardware and operating system combination. Price of the software varies from free to few thousand rupees for high-end servers.

Windows based Web Servers :

- Commerce Builder: it runs on Win 95, or Win NT. It is properly integrated with Win NT so we don't have to create additional groups or users on Win NT. It has a built in Macro Language, which gives flexibility to connect to any ODBC data source.
- EMWAC https: European Microsoft Win NT Academic Center runs on Win NT Server and Win NT workstation. A major drawback is it is little secured. No user accounts, passwords or directory access permissions.
- Microsoft IIS: Internet Information Server is a powerful web server-side Java, and ISAPI applications.
- It supports SSL, CGI.Perl, server-side Java, and ISAPI.
- Java support, Database support like Access, SQL, Oracle, Sybase and Informix adds more functionality.
- Peer Web Server: PWS runs with Win NT Workstation and Windows 98. It offers less functionality than IIS.
- Netscape FastTrack Server and Netscape Enterprise Server: These were founded by Netscape Communications; are very powerful server software for the Internet.

The features includes :

- Enhanced monitoring and logging features
- Server-side digital certificate authentication
- Client side authentication
- Full text integrated search engine
- SNMP(Simple Network Management Protocol) Support

Many other web server software includes:

- Netscape SuitsSpot
- Open Market Secure Web Server
- Purveyor IntraServer
- Website
- Apache Web Server for Unix/Linux
- Samba Server

Selecting the right Software is a crucial issue. Following questions should be considered:

- Does the software have to run on specific Operating System?
- What level of performance is needed?
- Is price a major issue?
- Is there any planning for to connect to the Internet? Is yes, there is a need for proxy server.
- How to plan Intranet? What level of security is required?
- How much technical support is needed and what it will cost?

Q12 . "Hardware needs for the Intranet are to be accessed based on the current business requirements. It will be premature to think about future business needs." Do you agree with this statement? Justify with an example. [DEC02;Q2(a)]

ANS : No, I do not agree with the statement.

In the current scenario, technology changes rapidly. So as there will be much software available in the market, one should always consider future growth of the Intranet as well as future requirements of the advanced technology.

If hardware is selected that best suits the Intranet currently, it is possible that the same not be efficient enough for grown Intranet. At that moment, either Hardware has to be upgraded or in the worst case, it might have to be replaced.

For example, current Intranet requires simple data sharing and web browsing. For the same, a server running Pentium II processor with 64 MB of RAM is selected. This best suits the current requirement. But as time passes, now there are many applications being developed and running on our Intranet, it uses Database and e-mail services, this server would no longer work. Only database support recommends 128 MB of RAM and the total memory requirement reaches 512 MB. It is easy to upgrade memory rather than processor. Still when it is required to upgrade the processor, its better to replace the existing server with a new server.

So future growth of the Intranet should be always considered when choosing hardware for Intranet.

Q13. What is the process of customizing Internets Explorer? [Jun 2001;Q1(b)]

ANS : There are many different things you can do with the Internet Options Dialogue box. You get that dialogue box by first opening up Internet Explorer, going to Tools on the menu bar, and then selecting Internet Options.

Your Homepage : Your homepage is the web page that automatically opens up when you load the browser. You can change the homepage by clicking in the address bar in Internet Explorer, copying and pasting the address into the address bar under Internet Options. This way you can't mistype the address.

Temporary Internet Files : When you visit a web page, the files associated that web page goes to a folder on your computer called Temporary Internet Files, or the Cache. Why does it do this? Well, the next time you visit a web page, your computer does not have to re download the files associate with the page, because they are stored in that folder on your computer. Therefore, the page loads faster. It is good, however, to delete these files every so often, because it is said that in newer computers and operating systems, when the folder gets too full, it can cause your internet connection to be even slower. To delete these files, you can click on the button that says "Delete Files."

Sometimes, you may need to increase the size of that folder, if you feel that your internet connections is way too slow, or you may need to decrease the size of the folder to save space on your computer. However, if increasing the size of the folder doesn't help, you may want to decrease the size of the folder just in case. Try it both ways and see if it makes a difference. On dial-up, there is not much you can do to make your connection faster. To increase or decrease the size of your cache folder, you click on the Settings button, and then.

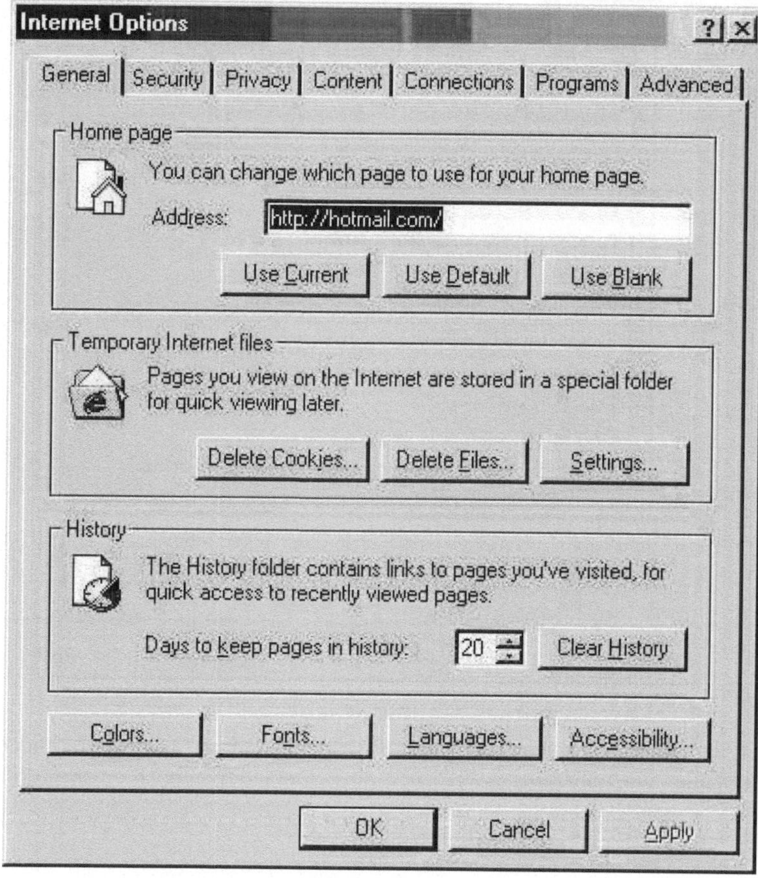

move the slider to the left or to the right. Also, when you click on Settings, it is probably a good idea that you have the Automatically box checked to make sure that your browser is always loading the newest version of the web page.

History : You can view what web pages you have visited and you can control how long the web pages stay in your history.
You control this by the Internet Options box, and you can tell it how many days to keep pages in your history, or you can clear your history.
Disable Image Loading : Sometimes you are doing research on the net, and you really don't care about viewing any images on web pages You can disable images from loading to speed up your connection.
In the Internet Options box, click on the Advanced tab.

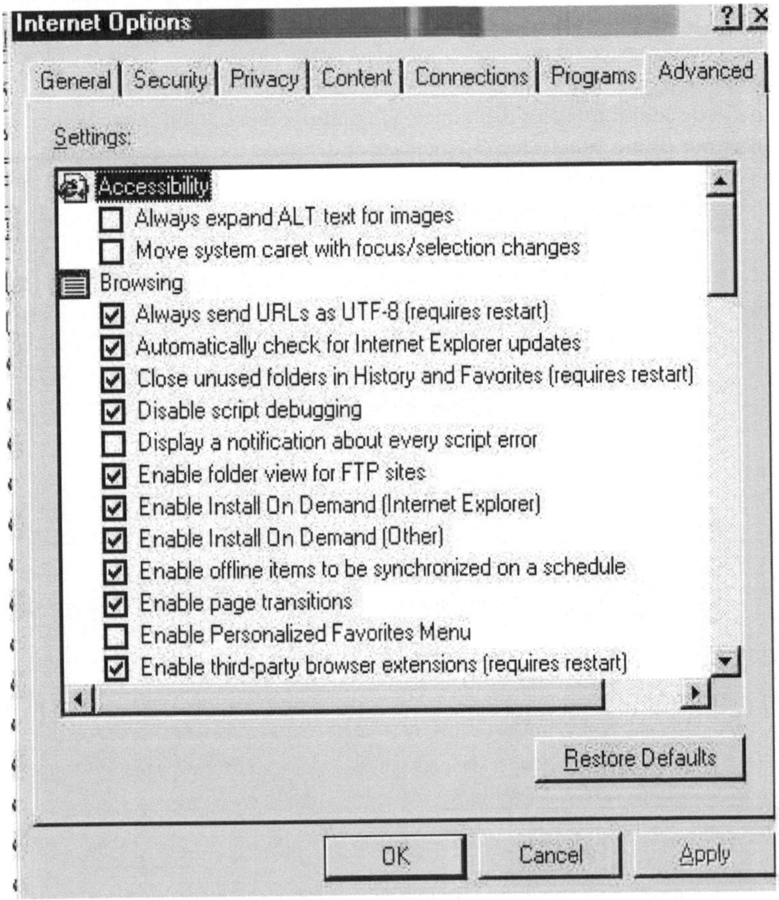

Then scroll down, until you find "Show Pictures." Uncheck that box. To notice the new change, you may have to close your browser, and then open up an entire new one.
0

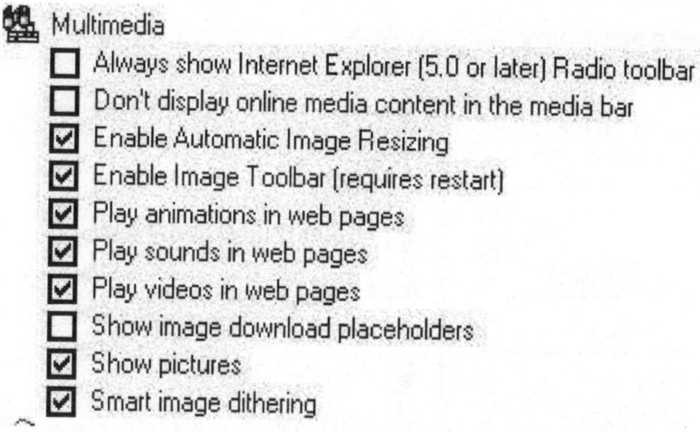

Viewing your History : The fastest way to view your history is by holding down Ctrl and H on your keyboard. You can choose from which day you want to view the history. **Add to Favorites :** To view your favorite web pages, click on the favorites icon at the top of Internet Explorer. To add a page to your favorites, simply click on the button "Add."

Organize your Favorites and Delete your Favorites : You can organize your favorites into folders, and rename your favorites by clicking the Organize button in the favorites pane. (Hint: if you do not see this, make sure you have your favorites open.) To create a new folder, click the Create Folder button, and to get your pages into the folder, just click and drag them into the folder. You can rename your favorites, by highlighting the name of the favorite, and clicking Rename. You can also move your favorites to a folder by highlighting the favorite, and then by clicking Move to Folder, and then choosing the appropriate folder. Then click OK. To delete your favorites, click on the delete button after you highlight the favorite. Hint: If you want to delete ALL of your favorites, you can go into the C drive, click on the Windows folder, and then click on the Favorites folder. You can then highlight all of them and delete.

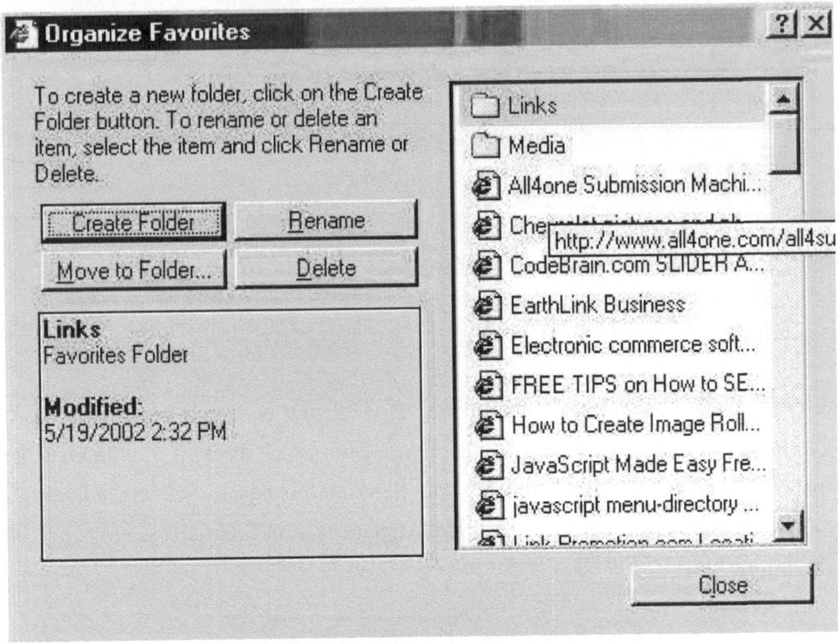

Text Size : You can change the size of your text in IE. Go to View, Text Size, and then choose from the menu. Note: doing so may display web pages in a way they were not meant to be viewed. The default is medium.

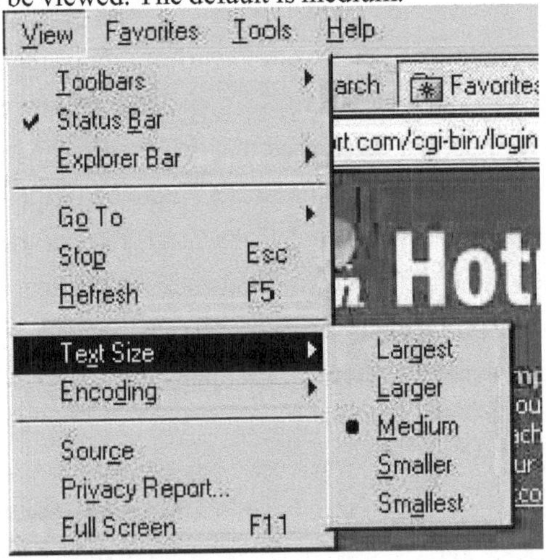

Q14. What are different pentium based Webserver systems available? Write a short note on each of them. **[DEC01;Q2(a)]**

ANS :

Microsoft .net Enterprise Servers

The Microsoft. NET Enterprise Servers are Microsoft's family of server applications for building; deploying and managing integrated Web solution and getting them to market fast.

The .NET Enterprise Servers integrate with other Microsoft products, such as the Microsoft 2000 operating system and the Microsoft Visual Studio development system, to give developers everything they need to create powerful Web solutions.

Windows NT Server 4.0 is the only true multipurpose server operating system. From rich application, communication, file, and print services to advanced media and Web features, customers choose Windows NT Server 4.0 for a complete end-to-end solution.

Microsoft Windows 2000 Advanced Server

In the simplest terms, server reliability means you can count on your systems to be available when you need them. "Five nines" is a measure of reliability for server operating systems that translates into just over five minutes of server downtime per year. Windows 2000 Server-based systems is designed to deliver up to 99.999% server uptime.

Red Hat Linux made its name as a server. As a workstation, Red Hat Linux is easier to install, use, and support than ever before. Because Red Hat Linux is flexible, it plays well with others - Windows, UNIX, Macintosh, other versions of Linux - all can run with Red Hat Linux on your network.

Microsoft SQL Server 7.0 makes giant strides in performance, reliability, and scalability, giving your organization many opportunities to create intelligent, real-world business solutions. SQL Server scales from laptop databases and small business servers all the way up to terabyte-size databases. It integrates well with existing applications, and it provides a cost-effective environment for customizing and building new applications that meet unique requirements.

Microsoft SQL Server 2000

With better performance, greater scalability and more concurrent users, SQL Server 2000 is helping e-business leaders bring robust applications online quickly, helping your business adapt to ever-changing competitive and operational environments.

Oracle8 is the world's most popular database for e-business. As more and more companies transform themselves into e-businesses, Oracle's internet-enabled solutions provide a cost-effective way to expand market opportunities, improve business process efficiencies, and attract and retain customers.

Microsoft Internet Information Server 4.0 Windows NT Server 4.0 with Internet Information Server 4.0 (IIS) is one of the easiest way to publish information and bring business applications to the Web.

Internet Information Services 5.0

Windows 2000 Server meets the needs of a broad spectrum of users, from corporate intranets to Internet Service Providers hosting Web sites receiving millions of hits per day. Because Internet Information Server 5.0 (IIS) is fully integrated at the operating system level, Windows 2000 Server lets organizations add Internet capabilities that weave directly into the rest of their computing infrastructure.

Apache 1.3.x is a general webserver, which is designed to be correct first, and fast second. Most sites have less than 10 Mbits of outgoing bandwidth, which Apache can fill using only a low end Pentium-based webserver. In practice, sites with more bandwidth require more than one machine to fill the bandwidth due to other constraints (such as CGI or database transaction overhead). For these reasons the development focus has been mostly on correctness and configurability.

Mediasurface 3.0 helps customers to rapidly publish and effectively manage content across their organisation for both internal use and to facilitate online business to business (B2B) and business to consumer (B2C) e-business. By separating design and navigation from content, Mediasurface software allows a wide range of users within an enterprise to monitor, update and administer prescribed areas of an enterprise's content over the Internet and other digital networks in an easy to use, secure and centrally controlled process.

Running as a multi-threaded process, **ColdFusion Server 4.5** provides a runtime environment for application logic and dynamic page generation. The server supports a broad range of services from database connectivity to full text searching to load balancing and failover. Developers and server administrators can use these services to deliver complex applications quickly and easily.

Microsoft® Exchange Server 5.5 Businesses today rely on their messaging and collaboration servers more than ever. This reliance means that you do not just need a way to send e-mail or create groupware. Businesses need a comprehensive messaging platform that includes the tools necessary to create rich collaboration applications. Microsoft® Exchange Server 5.5 is that platform. Microsoft Exchange Server 5.5 has: a solid messaging foundation; connectivity and co-existence; common, familiar tools for collaboration, management and administration.

Q15. There is a need for user training as browsers change. But, what should technical support staff do in the face of constantly changing browsers?

[JUN03;Q5(a)]

ANS : Training is an essential part of the intranet setup. Technical staff should always make out schedules and keep lectures, seminars to train the employees to use intranet and in short we can say to use Web Browsers.

But in this face of constantly changing Web Browsers it is a big question for the Technical staff to continuously upgrade employees.

One of the best way to overcome this problem is at first make the employees expert with the present Browsers.

Also on the web while planning contents place training materials, tutorials and informational links to the site to help users answer their own questions and train themselves.

All the new features which have come in the new browsers can be placed on the site only as a new page which will help the employee self train themselves.

A form that asks the users to ask questions and make suggestions can give feedback on what users want and need to know.

Then a seminar or lectures can be arranged on the new features especially giving those features more emphasize which users have written on the feedback form.

Thus with less effort it will help the employees and technical staff to overcome this difficulty.

Q16. What are the various tasks associated with maintaining an Intranet? Explain them. **[JUN03;Q5(b)]**

Ans : Once the Intranet site is running, it has to be properly maintained. The maintenance of the intranet site includes to keep the system free from the errors and bugs, adding new functionality, migrating from old software to new software, migrating from old technology to new technology.

There are many threat to the computer system like threats to Hardware, software and information. The maintenance section of an organization should be capable enough of handling all the threats and keeping intranet free from it.

Threats to Hardware : The first component of computer system is the hardware used. Some of the common threats to the hardware are:

- Theft of a computer, printer or other resource.
- Tampering by a disgruntled employee who interferes with dip switches or cuts a cable.
- Destruction of resources by fire, flood or electrical power surges. Don't forget those sprinklers in the ceiling can put out hundreds of gallons of water a minute; most of the damage to computer systems comes not from the fire but from the water used to put out the fire.

Threats to Software : The second component of your system is software. Threats to software include the following:

- Deletion of a program, either by accident or by malicious intent
- Theft of a program by one of your users
- Corruption of a program, caused either by a hardware failure or by a virus.
- Bugs in the software. Their effect sometime is immediate and catastrophic and sometimes they come in limelight years later.

Threat to Information : The third component of your system is the data and data files used by the corporation. Threats to information can include:

- Deletion of a file or files
- Corruption, caused either by hardware problems or by a bug in the software
- Theft of company data files.

Maintenance of the intranet means to deal all the above threats and keep the system free from it. For hardware solution system should be checked continuously, if any hazards occur like fire etc. cease fire should be kept in handy position, electrical power switches, cables and surges should be maintained.

For software solution system and information security should be kept high. For most confidential systems even password protection should be incorporated. For removing bugs continuous testing of the intranet system should be done. Backup should be taken regularly. Antivirus programs should be run continuously.

CHAPTER 4

CONFIGURING INTRANET

- *Introduction*
- *Objectives*
- *Configuring Intranet*
- *Installation*
- *User management*
- *Disk Quotas*
- *Security Configuration and Analysis*
- *Account Policies*
- *Permissions and restrictions*
- *Tuning server performance*
- *Configuring network settings*
- *Networks and Security*
- *Tuning applications over Intranet*

The next step in setting up an intranet is to configure intranet that is to how to create and host the web pages and step to secure the network. There are different types of web page authoring tools for content creation. Managing user and granting permission and restriction is also important part of Intranet administration. Decision like risk level and how much exposure one can stand. Once that is done it is now time to find out where the network is vulnerable.

Unfortunately, there are dozens and dozens of ways network can be compromised, and the first step in finding them is by looking around.

Q1. What are the four basic steps of your Intranet project? Explain them. [JUN03;Q6(b)]

ANS : The four basic steps of the Intranet project are Planning, Constructing (Content), Implementing and Maintaining. Each step is followed by the other.
Following parameters are to be considered when planning your own Intranet:

- **What is the purpose :** One need to make sure that why I want to have an Intranet?
- **Advantages :** What advantages I am going to get if I am replacing my LAN with the Intranet?

- **Save Money :** Does an Intranet save money for me?
- **Security :** What sort of security I need to implement for my Intranet?
- **Software required :** What software do I required to build Intranet I want.
- Hardware should not be forgotten.
- What is going to be on my Intranet? That is content. Content is again a crucial issue.

The purpose of the Internet is simple. It is to corporate all the advantages of the Internet protocols and technologies which are not possible with LAN.

One need to make sure the security level required and the budget which can be spend for implementing security. Both the things need to be balanced in order to get proper security model for Intranet.

The software required depends upon the field of the company. There is variety of software available which can be used or which is supported by the Intranet protocol stack (TCP/IP protocol Stack). To get start with the Intranet, following softwares are required:

- Web Server Software
- HTML authoring Tool
- Browser
- TCP/IP based network

Selection of Hardware is to be done again with the Software being used and Software requirement. For example, an Internet with 1000 clients requires 256 MB of memory and the same server uses Oracle as Back-End tool, which requires additional 256 MB of RAM. Memory requirements increases as number of hosts of the Intranet increases.

Content of the Intranet : The content that is going to be put on Intranet must serve purpose. One needs to make sure that whatever is going to be put on Intranet is worth or not.

Moreover, good design of the content includes structure as well as appearance. The design, which is created, should reflect the mission defined while planning the Intranet.

Creating each page : Once content is available, it is time to convert the material to a form suitable for display.

It is needed to decide what percentage of existing material can be used and who will be responsible for converting that information.

Testing : Once the content is formatted, test your pages and then test them again!!!!

It is a sort of feedback of content. That whatever is worked out really works nicely or not.

Part of content plan should include a test plan detailing :

- What should be tested?
- Who will perform the tests?
- What to do if there are problems?
- When to do retest?

Tracking results and taking feedback : Once Intranet is up and running, emails and comments will start coming. We have to get ready to deal with these comments in an effective manner.

A typical Intranet site may include following Heads as content :

- News
- Organizations under us
- References, Tools & Utilities
- Feedback
- About Us
- Contact Us
- Search
- Go to Home on each
- Go to specific page (when required)

Q2. How will you add interactiveness in a site?
#: How will you make a site attractive?

ANS : Once the construction of basics like text, hyper text links and graphics are over, interactive additions such as image maps, sound, video, search capability, database retrieval, forms and even encryption security is desirable depending on the type of requirement. These advanced functionalities require the help of technologies such as Java programming, common gateway interface (CGI) scripting or the addition of plug-ins. They usually require additions to and modifications of the server software. Such a discussion is beyond the scope of this topic.

Hosting Web Pages on the Internet : Organizations that will host the web pages, can be asked from the Internet service provider (ISP) or system administrator. Another option to serve the web pages is dedicating a computer to run Web server software. The advantage of a dedicated computer is personal control of Web server software. This option requires a dedicated Internet connection. Some ISPs also provide a option to keep web server computer at their site for a direct Internet connection. This usually requires remote control software or many trips to the ISP. Personal server software is becoming popular for small-scale Web sites on office computers with a dedicated Internet connection.

After finding an organization that will serve the web pages or choosing own Web server software, some question can be asked:

1. What kind of file name extensions are used? The Web is very particular bout file names, the file names must end with an extension that indicates the file type. For example, a Web page coded in HTML needs a .htm or .html extension. The specific extension and the length of the file names depend on the server that serves the files. The beginning Web page may need to be called homepage.html, default.html or index.html depending on the server software.

2.How to updates pages? This is usually accomplished by using file transfer protocol (ftp) to transport all the html documents and graphics files to a specific directory on the server. FTP access to the server along with a password is required for this.

HTML code is easily downloaded for review. It is also possible that if some web site technique that is of interest, can be simply saved as HTML from its code. This will provide special techniques that are used in developing own web pages. Web site graphics are also easily downloaded as HTML files but there is need to consider infringement of copyright laws, if any, before incorporating them into own Web site.

Q3. Explain the term network and security.

ANS : A network, whether it is a small home office network or a 5000 node LAN/ WAN, securing it should be a top priority. From the smallest to the largest network steps should be taken to make sure that it is secure from attack or theft. How to protect the integrity of network information can be handled aggressively or casually depending upon what one have and how much one need to protect. For doing a good job there are specific steps that one should take and in a specific order. Bear in mind that not all steps are necessary for all network situations. Like any major project to be undertaken, one should start with a plan, and a good plan starts with an outline. Below is a sample outline of the process of securing the network.

Risk Assessment
Vulnerability
Budget Analysis
Security Policy
Implementation
Auditing

SQLBase 7 offers five connectivity interfaces for linking client applications with SQLBase databases. One can choose the connectivity interface that best suits the needs based on the development tool/language users are using and application requirements:

SQL/API is a low level, high performance interface suited for use with C and languages that support external functions in DLLs. It provides complete access to the SQLBase feature set, including "administrative" operations.

SAL is the 4GL scripting language used in Gupta's development environments for coding business logic.

SQLBase++ is an object oriented "wrapper" around the SQL/API for use with C++ Applications.

The SQLBase JDBC driver provides a native interface for Java applications and applets.

The SQLBase ODBC driver provides a simple and portable interface via ODBC. SQLBase 7 fully supports multi-threaded ODBC applications. It is also fully compatible with the older ODBC 2.0 API.

Q4. What are the tuning application over intranet? Explain three of them.

ANS : ***SQL:*** The Structured Query Language/Application Programming Interface (SQL/API) is a function library designed for use with the C programming language, and development environments that support C-style external function calling conventions. SQL/API is a call level interface (CLI) analogous to SQL*Net in Oracle environments and CT-LIB in Sybase environments.

One can make calls to SQL/API functions throughout the application to interact with SQLBase. Typical function calls include connecting and disconnecting to a database, passing SQL statements to the server for compilation and execution, providing bind variable data, and retrieving result sets.

Additionally, the SQL/API provides functions to perform administrative tasks such as performing database backups and restorations.

ODBC : Not just an ODBC driver, Recital ODBC Developer provides a complete industry standard ODBC database solution for Unix, Linux, or OpenVMS. Consisting of an ODBC driver, and an Application Server, which has a complete SQL-92 database engine, Recital ODBC Developer can create, query and update Recital databases from Windows applications. If Recital applications are running on Unix, Linux, or OpenVMS, one can provide full read and update access to the databases from Microsoft Windows clients with Recital ODBC Developer. Using Recital ODBC Developer one can use industry standard management reporting tools such as Crystal Reports to generate high quality reports against live data in a Recital based application.

JDBC : Not just a JDBC driver, Recital JDBC Developer provides a complete industry standard JDBC database solution, consisting of an all-Java type 3 driver, and an Application Server that implements a complete SQL-92 database engine. With JDBC Developer, Java applications can query and update data from any data source across Intranets or the Internet.

Q5. What are the differences between a Proxy Server and a Firewall? How will you configure your Proxy Server? [DEC02;Q5(a)]

ANS : 1. A proxy server, sometimes referred to as an application gateway or forwarder, is an application that mediates between two networks segments. While a firewall is a network component that provides a security barrier between networks segments.

2. A proxy does not Route any traffic while Firewall route traffic.

3. Proxy provides logging and statistics on network usage while these types of information not provide by Firewall.

4. Proxy Server are application specific while Firewall type is spread across four areas:

- Embedded
- Software
- Hardware
- Application

Proxy receives the request, it identifies what type of service the internal host is trying to access and then forward request to related application but in Firewall, there are no such type of activities performed.

Configuring Your Proxy Server : Proxy servers can be configured with what are commonly referred to as bad addresses. A bad address is not really "bad"- it's one of the special IP addresses that aren't routable through the Internet. These addresses are commonly used to configure networks behind a proxy firewall server. One common set of bad addresses is the 10.0.0.0 class A network. InterNIC (the organization that licenses domain names and maintains unique addresses for all computers connected to the Internet) has set aside this entire block of addresses for testing purposes, which you could certainly use behind a proxy server. Here is an example of how to do this:

1. Set up your proxy server hardware with two network cards. One network card has a real, routable Internet address of something like 204.176.47.2, and the other uses a bad address of 10.0.0.1.

2. Plug the 204.176,47.2 network card into your Internet router connection, and plug the 10.0.0.1 network card into your local network. This is the first step in creating the isolated barrier between the Internet and your network.

3. Now, configure each workstation with a unique address on the 10.0.0.0 network, using a gateway address of 10.0.0.1 or the server's bad address.

4. Configure each application that understands and uses a proxy server with the proxy server address of the server, 1.0.0.0.1.

That's it! Now when the client software needs to access the Internet, the requests are sent to the network card in the server that has the address 10.0.0.1, at which point the proxy server actually forwards the request to the destination after including its own valid address of 204.176.47.2. When the request is returned to the server, the proxy server returns it to the originating workstation.

For workstation to use a proxy server, however, it must have software that knows how to talk to proxy server. The Netscape Navigator and Microsoft Internet Explorer Web browsers can both use a proxy server, as can many other e-mail, news, FTP, Web, and Telnet software packages.

Q6. On what basis does any organization decides to set up an Intranet? [DEC01;Q4(a)]

ANS : Any organization before deciding to setup an Intranet, generally look into the basic business needs that Intranet can fulfill such as finding information, getting current information, manipulating information and sharing information provide to each and every employee of company and outside the company. Intranet can eliminate printing, publishing binding documents and saves costs. A corporate intranet offers a single point of entry into information stored in diverse ways. People can locate information quickly and intuitively through a combination of hierarchical organization, search capabilities, unstructured links between sources. Another basis may be Intranet application can be designed to run largely from the server and to install any necessary client components automatically. This can significantly reduce the burden of distributing, configuring and upgrading application throughout an organization.

Q7. How are corporations using Intranets? Explain with examples. [JUN03;Q1(a)]

ANS : An Intranet is an internal company network that uses the Internet standards of HTML (Hyper Text Markup Language) and HTTP (Hyper Text Transfer Protocol) and the TCP/IP (Transmission Control Protocol/Internet Protocol) communications protocol along with a graphical web browser to support business applications and provide departmental, interdepartmental, and countrywide communications solutions.

The ways in which an intranet can be used by industries, corporations, or organizations are as numerous and as varied as the enterprises themselves.

Here are few examples of several companies using intranet.

1. At Genetech pharmaceutical company, employees can access the employee directory, find out how to get business cards, read company announcements, get information on research seminars, building facilities, commuting options, benefits and child care.

2. At Compaq Computers intranet is used by the employees to reallocate investments in their 401(k) plans.

3. Silicon Graphics uses their intranet to connect several departmental intranets, allowing them to share data with other groups in the organization and to network with departments who may not have an on-site office but can dial in conferencing, or other tasks.

4. At HBO, researchers, programmers, and high level executives use an intranet to access a database that contains information on every movie ever made, whether it's on videocassette, and when it's scheduled to air for the next two years.

Thus intranet is a source of information for the employees of an organization regarding the various activities of organizations. Employees of one department can have knowledge regarding the other departments with the help of intranet. Suppose an employee of the accounts department want to know recent details of the production now he won't be needing to go to the production department and get details from there instead he has to just get connected to the intranet and get details from there. Information regarding the company seminars, entertainment programmes, and announcements all are available on intranet.

Q8. What Exactly Is Content Syndication?

ANS : Content syndication on the web refers to a technology that facilitates the distribution of content from one computer to any number of other computers via the Internet. Content syndication does not entail the distribution of the complete articles, images or files. Rather, it offers information about the website where the content can be found, and headline information with links to the web pages where the complete content can be accessed. The basic element of content syndication is the syndication file, which is located on the web server of the distributor of the content. This file contains information about the site, the headlines and the links to web pages containing the content.

For example, the syndication file on the server of a newspaper could include:

i. the title of the newspaper;

ii. the headlines of articles published on its website; and

iii. links to the full texts of these articles. An example of such a syndication file can be viewed by opening the BBC's news syndication file in your browser.

Content syndication was first popularized by Netscape in 1999, for adding and updating news from selected web sources to its personalized *My.Netscape* pages. For this purpose, Netscape developed RSS ('Rich Site Summary' or renamed by some: 'Really Simple Syndication'), a format for syndication files based on XML, a computer language used for describing, storing and exchanging information.

With these RSS files, Netscape no longer required an army of editors to gather content to fill its ever-growing portal. Instead, webmasters or content distributors could create newsfeeds by placing RSS files on their servers and submitting information about their exact location. All that Netscape then needed to do was to collect these newsfeeds at regular intervals and display their contents on its portal, thus offering its visitors a continuously updated set of headlines and links to the latest information posted on many websites.

Netscape thus created a mutually beneficial relationship between the visitors to its portal and the content distributors. The visitors could view the latest news headlines published on a wide range of websites from which they could make their own selection, and the content distributors benefited from the increased numbers of visitors who followed the links attached to the headlines to their websites.

Syndication Servers : News can be syndicated directly among websites or intranets, or it can be gathered by so-called syndication servers, or content aggregators, that bring together many newsfeeds in a central location. Examples include Moreover, Syndic8 and News is Free.

These syndication servers offer many facilities for selecting newsfeeds (e.g. BBC World News, SciDev or Oneworld) and displaying their content in a variety of ways. For example, syndicated content from selected newsfeeds can be included on an organization's website simply by cutting and pasting a single line of code into the HTML code of the webpage where this content is to be displayed. Once this code has been inserted, any changes in the content (such as new articles added to or old ones deleted from the BBC World News section or Oneworld site) are reflected in the headline information and links displayed on your website.

Q9. How can content syndication benefit your organization?

ANS : The decision as to whether your organization actually needs to adopt content syndication, and how best to use this Internet technology, will depend on your organization's mission, and the purpose and functions of your website. For example:

1. Content distribution: Your organization wishes to promote the information services offered by your website. Applying syndication, you can offer a newsfeed via which headlines and links to the content on your site can be picked up by any number of organizations and displayed on their websites or intranets.

2. Content gathering: Your organization wishes to monitor developments in a particular field of interest. You can pick up other organizations' newsfeeds (one or more) and display the headlines and links on your intranet. In this way, your staff will be able to access – via your intranet – daily updated headline news from various selected websites. This feature of content syndication could also add value to your website by displaying the latest headline news and links of selected organizations on your website. This could be useful, for example, if your organization is preparing a conference, conducting an advocacy campaign, or monitoring a specific situation, such as a regional conflict.

3. Content brokering: Your organization functions as a knowledge centre, and wishes both to distribute and to gather content related to one or more topics. In this case, you could strengthen your organization's position by distributing your own content as well as providing web pages where visitors can find thematic headline information with links to the complete articles posted on a large number of other sites.

4. Content networking: Your organization is part of a knowledge sharing network that wishes to exchange content among the members on a regular basis. For this, each participating organization could install a newsfeed on its website and pick up the headlines and links provided by the other network members.

These are early days for content syndication, and new applications of this novel means of exchanging and sharing information are actively being explored. For example, content syndication can be used to compile automatically the content of email newsletters, as well as to update discussion forums, conference agendas, theatre programmes, or sales promotion campaigns for games, photos and software.

Q10. What is the process of forming a Project Team? What are different designations given to its team members and what are their functions?

[JUN01;Q2(b)]

ANS : Team is a group made to achieve a single goal, in which all works together to achieve this goal. Here the employee in the organization or new recruits are selected on the bases of goal. Right candidate for the right work is selected. And the goal is broken into smaller sub-tasks and assigned to all the team members. The team will cross traditional boundaries in your organization and may include members from several departments, including the following:

- Technical Services, sometimes called (Information Systems), DP (Data Processing), or MIS (Management Information Services)
- Marketing
- Sales
- Product Research and Development
- Customer Service
- Public Relations
- Publications or Creative Services]
- Training or Education Services

Technical Services people will focus on the technical aspects of setting up the Web site and be invaluable as security consultants; however, in most corporations, this is one of the least important aspects. Deciding what the intranet will actually do, defining the appropriate level of system security, and defining rules for maintaining the site will generate much more discussion and will turn out to be much more important issues than which hardware to use in your installation.

First, you'll want to give each member of the team a copy of your corporate Web browser-if you have one-and be sure they all spend some time surfing the Web and looking at all sorts of sites: the good, the bad, and the ugly. And this should be a part of their ongoing education. If you haven't decided on a browser yet, download at least two different browsers and use this part of your planning to evaluate them.

Companies that already have some sort of centrally focused computer system will find that it's relatively easy to adapt their approach to developing an intranet site.

The person or group in charge of an intranet will need all sorts of skills, some technical and some diplomatic. Here's list of some of the major jobs by category:

Webmaster The Webmaster is the point of contact with users and is responsible for replying to complaints and suggestions and for coordinating with other sites in your company or organization. This person receives all the e-mail sent to your intranet and usually has the overall view of how the site works and is responsible for each area of the intranet. Sometimes the Webmaster address is an e-mail alias set up to forward e-mail to an existing account or set of accounts if a team is responsible for the overall site. Many Webmasters also reform the duties of the Web administrator.

Web administrator : This person is responsible for the day-to-day running of the intranet, monitoring the usage logs, adjusting the configuration as needed, and making the backups and system upgrades as needed.

Content authors : These people create the content used on the intranet. They are not necessarily technical people, but they must know their subjects be able to prepare an HTML document, and be able to write well. They will also be responsible for submitting new material and updating old material as things change within the organization.

Intranet developer : This person develops the scripts and programs needed to do the things that you can't do using HTML. The intranet developer is essentially a programmer who can develop code to make your intranet do new things.

Some companies will find it easier to assign site maintenance responsibilities to the departments that originate the content for the site, rather than having one person or group manage all the Web sites within the company. This approach is useful for large intranets where someone closer to the material may be better off maintaining it. For small intranets, the Web master fulfills all of the duties described here.

As well as deciding who has access to what kinds of information, you must also keep tabs on network usage, check usage statistics, and continue efforts to fine-true the daily operation of your intranet.

Q11. Write short notes on the following:

(i) RAID

#: What is RAID? Explain it. Can you replace SLED with RAID? [JUN01;Q6(a)]

ANS : RAID Explained : Windows NT Server includes several levels of RAID (Redundant Array of Inexpensive Disks) support. RAID is a technology used instead of the old SLED (Single Large Expensive Disk) design, in which a hard-disk failure spelled disaster. Instead of using one enormous disk drive and writing all data to that disk, RAID uses an array of less expensive and one of several methods for writing data to ensure redundancy. Each level of RAID is designed for a specific purpose:

RAID 0 Data is written to one or more drives, but there is no redundant drive. RAID 0 provides no fault tolerance because the loss of a hard disk means a complete loss of data. For this reason, some classifications omit this level of RAID.

RAID 1 Two hard disks of equal capacity duplicate or mirror each other's contents. One disk continually and automatically backs up the other disk. This is also known as disk mirroring or disk duplexing, depending on whether one or two independent hard-disk controllers are used.

RAID 2 Same as RAID 2, except a single parity bit is written to a parity drive instead of checksums to checksum drives. A parity bit is just extra information that is written at the end of a file used for error checking. Checksum is an error-detection scheme where each transmitted message is accompanied by a numerical value based on the number so set bits in the file to make sure the message isn't garbled.

RAID 3

1. It requires only single redundant disk, which is used as parity bit.

2. It also employs parallel access as that of level 2, with small data strips.

3. Parity bit may be used for reconstruction of data in case a disk fails.

4. As the data strips are small, level 3 may achieve a very high data transfer rate. However, only one request can be processed at a time so there is low input/output request fulfillment rate.

RAID 4

1. It uses independent access technique, where each of the physical disks may be accessed independently, thus, enabling fulfillment of separate input/output requests in parallel.

2. Data strip is large and bit by bit parity strip is created for bits of strips of each disk.

3. In level 4, paity strip is stored on a separate disk.

4. Write operation requires updation of parity bits also. This causes user software to read old strips of data as well as old parity strips.

RAID 5 Data is written across drives in sector, just as if it were ordinary data. RAID 5 allows overlapping writes, and a disk is only accessed when necessary. This level of RAD is faster and may be more reliable than some of the other methods.

In terms of speed, there is not much to choose from among these RAID levels-the appropriate level of RAID protection depends on how you use your network, Levels 1,3, and 5 are available commercially, and levels 3 and 5 are used most often, Level 2 is generally considered too expensive for commercial use and Level 4 is comparable to Level 5 but isn't used because of the poor performance.

Schedule and make frequent backups and test them to ensure the contain what you think they do. Store your backups at a secure off-site location, preferably one that can provide temperature, humidity, and access controls, as well as fire protection. Install callback modems to prevent unauthorized logon attempts from remote locations. This type of modem takes note of the caller's logon information and then breaks the connection. If the telephone number that originated the call and the logon information are both appropriate, the modem dials a predefined number and allows the user access to the network. You can use callback modems with Windows NT Server.

(ii) Packet Filtering **[JUN01;Q6(b)]**

Packet filters either allow or block data packets (discrete units of information), often while routing them from one n network or network segment to another and most often between a private network and the Internet. Packet filtering can be done in a router (which is often called a screening router) or on an individual host computer using special software; both implementations are considered a form of firewall, a secure barrier behind which your local area network operates in safety. We'll look at firewalls in more detail later in this chapter.

Packets can be filtered on the basis of

Packet source address

Packet destination address
Source port number
Destination port number

Packets can also be screened based on whether they're trying to initiate a connection. For example, you might decide to block connections from sites of addresses that you consider untrustworthy, or you might decide to block access from all addresses external to your own network.

Before a packet can be screened, you must establish a set of rules that the router uses in blocking or allowing packets. These rules are usually stored in the router in a specific order and then applied in that same order once a packet is received-so be sure the order makes sense. Once you've set these rules, test them. In most packet-filtering routers, the packet is automatically blocked if a packet does not satisfy any of the rules you set up, this being the safest course of action for the router to take. When compared with a software-based firewall system running a host computer, most routers have very limited reporting functions, but they can maintain internal information about the state of connections passing through them and the contents of various data streams. Packet-filtering routers tend to be fast and invisible to users.

Router vendors such as Cisco Wellfleet, 3COM, Digital Equipment Corporation(DEC), and many others supply routers that you can program to perform packet-filtering functions.

Provide virus protection for all users, and scan all file servers and workstations daily. Use virus scanners that stay loaded and run all the time.

Ensure all operating-system patches are installed immediately when they're distributed. Don't expect the manufacturer to track you down and tell you about them.

Don't send confidential information in clear text across the network. Instead, encrypt all sensitive messages and files before transmitting them across any network, including an intranet.

Limit the services offered on your network to those that are necessary. If you're not using one aspect of the server package (for example, if you're using the Web server, but not the Gopher or the FTP servers in Microsoft's Internet Information Server), turn it off or uninstall it.

Limit the number of logon account on the host, and be sure to look for and then remove any inactive accounts that you find .

All these recommendations have their place in your security plan, but the best security plan in the world is worthless unless you carefully and precisely put it in place and then follow up by taking the appropriate steps to keep it working.

(iii) KSA **[JUN01,Q6(c)]**

(Kane Security Analyst)

KSA is a package, which runs on Windows NT Server.

KSA is an extensive and well-supported commercial package that runs on Windows NT server.

Future versions of KSA will be available for Unix systems, Novell NetWare versions 3.x and 4.x, and networks using Lotus Notes.

KSA examines your server system and then presents you with three-dimensional bar charts in the following six major categories:

Account Restrictions Assesses password controls, use of logon scripts, and password-expiration dates.

Password Strength Rates your password policies. A future version will include a password-cracking dictionary to show you how easily your passwords can be guessed.

Access Control Checks user rights and removable drive allocations.

System Monitoring Collects together a miscellaneous set of security-related concerns.

Data Integrity checks the UPS installation and configuration.

Data Confidentiality Tests to see if passwords are stored in clear text or in encrypted form.

KSA's Report Manager is easy to use and offers almost 30 reports; data can be exported in the usual database formats.

KSA creates no accounts or services, however. To use it, you must be logged in as the administrator; although once the analysis is complete, the results can be shared with all user who have access to the system. KSA takes an instant snapshot of the state of your system; as you follow its recommendations and make improvements in your security policies, return the program to see how you're doing.

Software packages such as KSA can do little to actually catch intruders; that's up to the appropriate law-enforcement agencies. What they can do is highlight the security weaknesses in your system in a way that is just about impossible to ignore.

Q12. Write short notes on the following : [JUN02;Q6][DEC01;Q6(c)]

*** Windows NT**

*** SATAN**

ANS : ***Windows NT*** workstation also has the Windows 95 interface and it includes a slightly restricted version of internet information server called peer web services. This package is also capable of running a small to medium sized Intranet without difficulties.

Windows NT is one of the various Windows operating systems platforms available is. Other operating systems available are Windows 3.1, Windows 95, , Macintosh and Unix. You can select according to satisfy yours business needs.

Windows NT adds the popular windows 95 interface, the internet information servers (IIS), capable of running web, FTP and Gopher services – search engine called index server, the front page HTML authoring package and Internet Explorer.

Microsoft Windows 95, Windows NT workstation and, Windows NT server all contain TCP/IP. Therefore upgrading one of these systems can help make TCP/IP easier to deploy. These operating systems are easy to handle, capable of handling protocols on the desktop and on the server. Windows NT ensures best security system.

Windows NT is a multi-user and multi-tasking operating system. It is a big setup from Windows 95 in terms of price capabilities. Windows NT server is capable of supporting a major Intranet.

SATAN : lets potential entruders take advantage of the information contains to learn how to infiltrate systems more effectively.

SATAN is system administration by system administrator tool for analyzing network. It is a set of programs used in UNIX for system administration by system administrator.

SATAN is available free on the Internet, and for this reason, many critics have argued that

SATAN collects data from each host in the specified network and create reports for each host by type, service, vulnerability and trust relationship. SATAN also offers several tutorials that explain the system security weakness and how a system administer can eliminate them. It also includes Faq.

SATAN (Security Administrator tool for analyzing network) is available free on the Internet.

SATAN lets potential intruders take advantage of the information it contains to learn how to infiltrate systems more effectively. You can use SATAN to your advantage. Run it against your own site to check for security holes. SATAN collects data from each host in the specified network and creates reports for each host by type, service, vulnerability and trust relationship. It offers several tutorials that explains the system security weaknesses and how a system administrator can eliminate them, it also includes FAQ.

SATAN lets potential intruders take advantage of the information it contains to learn how to infiltrate systems more effectively. You can use SATAN to your advantage. Run it against your own site to check for security holes. SATAN collects data from each host in the specified network and creates reports for each host by type, service, vulnerability and trust relationship. It offers several tutorials that explains the system security weaknesses and how a system administrator can eliminate them, it also includes FAQ.

SATAN (Security Administrator Tool for analyzing Network) is available free on the internet.

Q13. Write a brief note on the following:

(i) Domain Name System

ANS : The Internet Protocol address is a 32- bit integer. If somebody wants to send a message it is necessary to include the destination address, but people prefer to assign machines pronounceable, easily remembered names (host names). For this reason the Domain Name System is used. These logical names also allow independence from knowing the physical location of a host. A host may be moved to a different network, while the users continue to use the same logical name.

The Domain Name System (DNS) is a distributed database used by TCP/IP applications to map between hostnames and IP addresses, and to provide electronic mail routing information. Each site (university department, campus, company, or department within a company, for example) maintains its own database of information and runs a server program that other systems across the Internet can query. The

DNS provides the protocol which allows clients and servers to communicate with each other.

The system accesses the DNS through a resolver. The resolver gets the hostname and returns the IP address or gets an IP address and looks up a hostname. As we can see in the resolver returns the IP address before asking the TCP to open a connection or sending a datagram using UDP.

The domain name system uses a hierarchical naming scheme known as domain names, which is similar to the UNIX file system tree. The root of the DNS tree is a special node with a null label. The name of each node (except root) has to be up to 63 characters. The domain name of any node in the tree is the list of labels, starting at that node, working up to the root, using a period ("dot") to separate the labels (individual sections of a name might represent sites or a group, but the domain system simply calls each section a label). The difference between the UNIX file system and the tree of the DNS is that in the DNS we start on the ground and "go up" till the root. Writing them in this order makes it possible to compress messages that contain multiple domain names. Thus, the domain name "tau.ac.il" contains three labels: "tau", "ac", and "il". Any suffix of a label in a domain name is also called a domain. In the above example the lowest level domain is "tau.ac.il" (the domain name for the Tel-Aviv University Academic organization in Israel), the second level domain is "ac.il" (the domain name for Academic organizations of Israel), and the top level domain (for this name) is "il" (the domain name for Israel). The node il is the second level node (after root) (Fig.2)

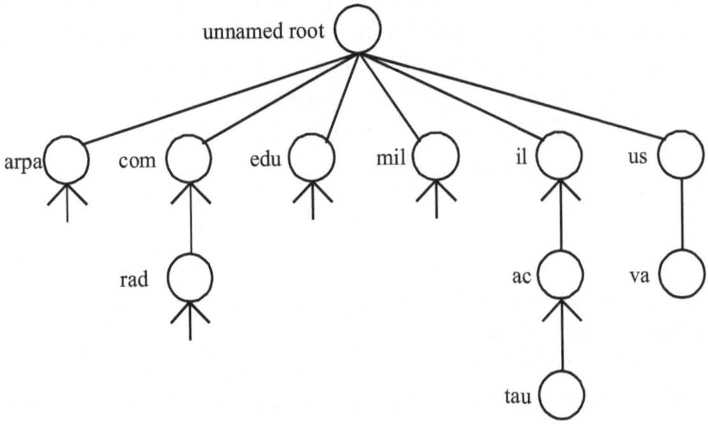

Fig. (2) Hierarchical organization of the DNS

Every node in the tree must have a unique domain name, but the same label can be used at different points in the tree. The top-level domains are divided into three areas:

1. area is a special domain used for address-to-name mapping.

2. The seven 3-character domain names (generic (organizational) domains).

3. The 2-character domains are based on the country codes. These are called the country (the geographical) domains.

The seven generic domains are depicted in the fig.3 :

Domain Name	**Meaning**
COM	Commercial organizations
EDU	Educational institutions
GOV	Government institutions
MIL	Military groups
NET	Major network support centers
ORG	Organizations other than those above
INT	International organizations

The Internet scheme can accommodate a wide variety of organizations, and allows each group to choose between geographical or organizational naming hierarchies. Most sites follow the Internet scheme so they can attach their TCP/IP installations to the connected Internet without changing names. The zone is a sub tree of the DNS that is administered separately. A common zone is a second-level domain, "ac.il" for example. Thus a lot of second-level domains divide their zone into smaller zones.

Whenever a new system is installed in a zone, the DNS administrator for the zone allocates a name and an IP address for the new system and enters these into the name server's database. A name server is said to have authority for one zone or multiple zones. Often, server software executes on a dedicated processor, and this computing machine is called the name Server.

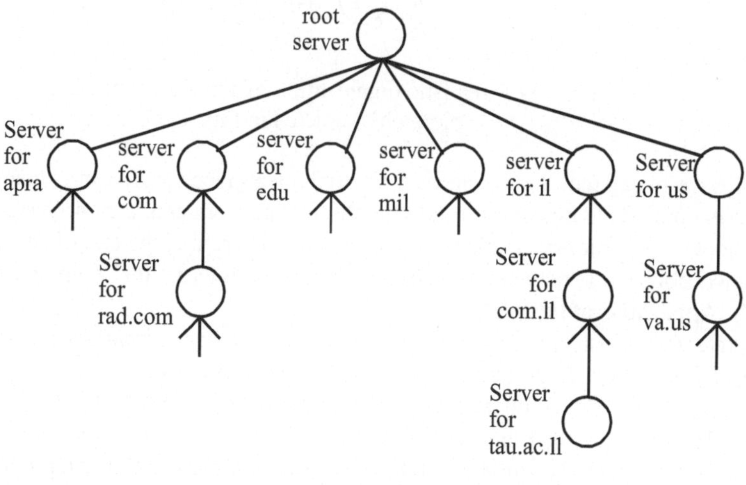

Fig. (4) The conceptual arrangement of domain name servers in the tree depicted in Fig. 2.

The person responsible for a zone must provide a primary name server for that zone and one or more secondary name servers. The main difference between a primary and a secondary is that the primary loads all the information for the zone from disk files, while the secondaries obtain all the information from the primary. When a secondary obtains the information from its primary it is called a zone transfer.

When a new host is added to the zone, the administrator adds the appropriate information (name and IP address) to a disk file on the system running the primary. The primary name server is then notified to reread its configuration files. The secondaries query the primary on regular basis (normally every 3 hours) and if the primary contains newer data, the secondary obtains the new data using a zone transfer.

If the name server doesn't contain the information requested, it must contact another name server. Not every server, however, knows how to contact every other server. Instead, every name server must know how to contact the root name servers. The root servers then know the name and location (i.e. IP address) of each authoritative name servers for all the second-level domains. There are six root servers in the world and every primary name server has to know the address of one of root server. The fig. 2 we can depict the tree of servers fig.4.

In practice, the organization often collects information from all of their sub-zones into a single server. Thus we can depict fig.5 which is more realistic than fig.4.

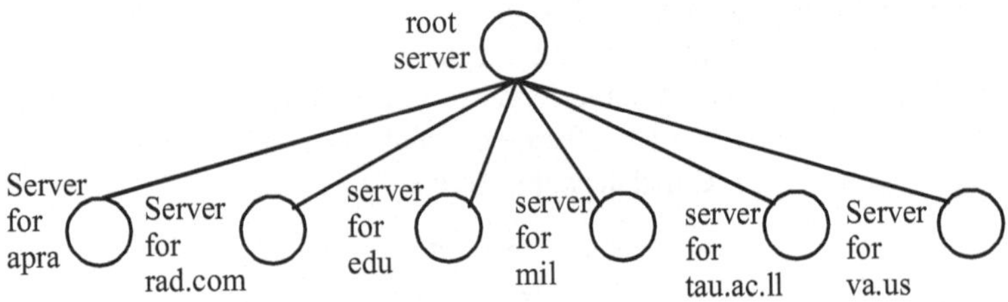

Fig. (5) A realistic organization of servers for naming hierarchy depicted in Fig. 2

We have to say that the tree in fig.5 shows how a given server can contact other servers only. This tree doesn't indicate physical network connection. Servers may be located at arbitrary locations on the network. Therefore, the tree of servers is a logical connection between servers, which uses the Internet for communication.

(ii) Application of Internet

@ Internet:-*Internet is a web which has very large numbers of computers connected to each other. Or it can be said that Internet is a network of networks.*

One can have many applications of the Internet such as the following:

(a) To exchange electronic mail with friends all over the globe for a small price.

(b) To participate in-group discussions on topics of interest, through public news groups.

(c) To find educational tools. Universities around the world, book stores, and libraries are sharing online information.

(d) To shop-commercial electronic store fronts are growing in number in the USA and Europe. One can order different products over the Internet.

(e) In the case of business one can get technical support for products one is using. One can publish information such as technical or marketing literature.

(f) Because the Internet is electronic, one can make changes to reflect late breaking news that would be impossible for printed publications. Change becomes easier, updates are simpler and information is instant.

(g) The Internet has become the first global venue for publishing information. This network has enough users now and it is benefiting from the positive feedback loop: the more users it gets, the more content it gets; and the more content it gets, the more users it gets.

(h) Internet's main asset is freedom. An alternative to controlling its freedom is to train and educate the user.

(i) You can refer to the pictures of an art gallery.

(j) One can get an electronic copy of classics such as Alice in Wonderland.

(k) One can get an electronic copy of journals and magazine from the Internet.

(l) One can create campus wide information systems.

However, the Internet is used for the four main applications, which are given in details in the following :

E-mail : E-mail is the most heavily used feature of the Internet. You can use it to send messages to any one who is connected to the Internet or connected to a computer network that has a connection to the Internet, such as an online service. E-mail messages are sent in the same way as most Internet data. The TCP protocol breaks your messages into packets, the IP protocol delivers the packets to the proper location, and then TCP reassembles the message on the receiving end so that it can be read.

You can also attach binary files, such as pictures, videos, sounds and executable files to your e-mail messages. Because the Internet is not able to directly handle binary files in schemes are MIME and unencode. The person who receives the attached binary file (called an attachment) must decode the file with the same scheme that was used to encode the file. Many e-mail software do this automatically. When you send e-mail to someone on the Internet, that message has to travel through a series of networks before it reaches the recipient. Different networks might use different e-mail formats. Gateways perform the job of translating e-mail formats from one network to another so that the messages can make their way through all the networks of the Internet.

News Groups : News groups are specialized forums in which users with a common interest can exchange messages. Thousands of newsgroups exist, on technical and nontechnical topics. Each newsgroup has its own style and customs.

Remote Login (Telnet) : Telnet is short for Telecommunication Network. It is a virtual terminal protocol allowing a user logged on to one TCP/IP host to access other hosts on the network.

One of the remarkable features of the Internet is the way it lets you use the resources of a distant computer somewhere else in the world. From your own home or office, you can log onto another computer, issue commands as if you were at that computers keyboard, and then gain access to all the computer resources. You do this with an Internet resource called Telnet. Telnet follows a client/server model, which means that you run a piece of software on you PC (the client) to use the resources of a distant server computer. This distant computer is called the host.

File transfer and file transfer Protocol (FTP) : We have just seen the use of Telnet to allow remote logins to computers over networks. Now we look at another very useful protocol. This one is concerned, not with letting us log into a remote computer, but with allowing us to *transfer files* between two different computers on the Internet. It is named "File Transfer Protocol", but is usually just called FTP. FTP can be used to fetch files from many different sources on the Internet.

Anonymous FTP : There are various implementations of the FTP protocol available. One is called WS_FTP Limited Edition (or WS_FTP LE), which is free for educators and non-commercial home use.

FTP runs on a client/server model. So, in order to use it you will need client software to run on your computer.

To begin an FTP session, you run the FTP client software and contact the FTP server that you want to download files from. You can use FTP client software available in Windows NT. The FTP client talks to an FTP server. FTP uses TCP to handle communications and creates a session between the two hosts. The FTP daemon runs on the FTP server. This daemon handles all FTP transactions. When an FTP client contacts a server, the daemon will ask for an account number (or user name) and password. Many FTP sites let anyone log on to them to download software. This is called anonymous FTP.

Some FTP clients will automatically log on to the FTP server for you when you connect so you won't be asked to log on. It is so because your client software does it automatically for you. When you log on to the FTP server, a connection called a command link is opened between your computer and the server. This link is used for sending commands to the server from your computer, and sending messages and information back from the sever to your computer.

When your want to change directories on the FTP server, your client software sends an instruction to the FTP daemon, using the command link. The daemon changes directors and then sends back a listing of files on that directory via the command link. On your client software, you will see a listing of files in the new server directory. When you want to download a file, the request is issued over the command link.

When you issue a command to download a file, a second connection is opened up, called the data connection (also called the data link). This connection can be opened up in one of two modes:

(a) The ASCII mode

(b) The binary mode

The ASCII mode **:** The ASCII mode is used for sending text files and alters things such as line feed and carriage return.

The binary mode **:** The binary mode is used for sending binary files and lets files through untouched.

The file is downloaded from the server to your computer via the data connection. After the file is downloaded, the data link closes automatically.

When the file is downloaded and the data link closes, the command link stays open. You can then change directories or download more files. After you have done, you log off and command link closes. You are no longer connected to the FTP server.

Q14. Compare different ways of connecting to Internet. Also, list the advantages of each mode separately.

ANS : ***Types of connectivity :*** There are several ways to connect to the Internet. The more expensive services provide more features, more flexibility, and greater data transfer capacity. Large companies choose dedicated Internet access or LAN dial-up. Smaller organizations are happy with PC dial-up access and terminal emulation, which provides E-mail and other services through a service provider's computer.

Dial-up and Terminal Emulation : Here you need is a computer with a modem (attached to a phone line) and any of the popular telecommunications packages. The individual user dials-in to an Internet service provider. When you use PC dial-up (also called a terminal account), your computer runs a terminal emulation program to communicate with the service provider's host computer, and you ask the host computer to go out onto the Internet to do what you want to be done. Most host providers will send and receive E-mail, transfer files from a remote Internet computer to the host which you can then download to your local computer, and provide access to USENET (the typical bulletin boards/newspaper/discussion groups on the Internet).

Many Internet access providers also allow dial-up users to interactively roam the Internet in real-time, logging on to remote hosts with TELNET, searching indexed databases with WAIS, and locating esoteric information with Gopher.

Advantages :-

1. This is the simplest and cheapest type of connection to Internet.

2. Some people use a UNIX computer to connect the LAN to the Internet. The advantage is that UNIX interfaces easily with Internet.

Dedicated Internet Access : The most popular Internet access for companies and institutions is a dedicated phone line connecting your LAN to the Internet 24 hours a day. However, a dedicated Internet access also requires substantial initial investment in equipment. The main continuing cost is a flat monthly fee for the use of the line. It varies with line capacity, and line capacity determines how many users can connect to Internet simultaneously.

Leased Line : Running a Web server, handling a large volume of mail, connecting an entire network of users or, offering other information services require a permanent connection to the net and higher bandwidth than a normal modem can deliver. The solution is a leased line connection to the Internet. These are fast and permanent. Depending on your bandwidth requirements. ISP's can provide leased line ranging from 24kbps to 2mbps.

Advantages : An inexpensive modem based connection, which is set up only when it is needed, is the ideal solution for occasional use on the Internet.

TCP/IP Account : For a TCP/IP account, in addition to the browser and e-mail applications, you may need software for other applications, like Telnet and FTP. Internet software such as "Chameleon" and "Internet in a Box", usually, have many of these applications bundled in. application software packages for networking employ a design called client/server architecture, where the software sitting on the

PC, can send request for the files to the server. Software packages are optimized for ease-of-use and may be referred to as the "Client".

Shell Account : Using dial-up access to GIAS HOST-the primary level of access for Internet users-one can dial-up access to GIAS HOST computer set up by VSNL, at each of the nodes. By connecting to the host computer, the users would be able to use all Internet services. In this mode, the users would be using a simple terminal emulation from their PCs and will not require any special software on their machines. The limitation of this access mode is that the access is primarily limited to text-based services.

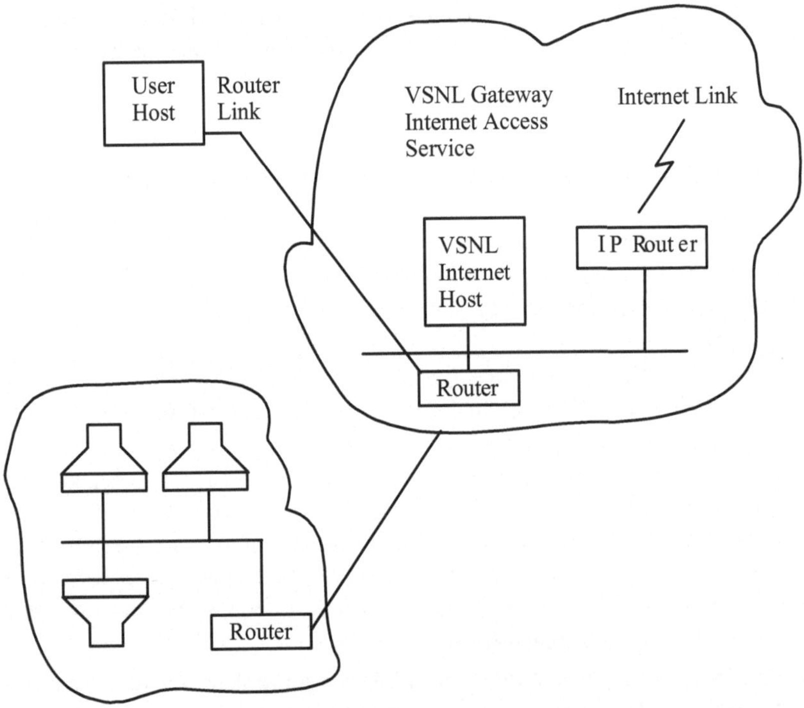

VSAT Links : VSAT stands for Very Small Aperture Terminal. It can be described technically as an intelligent earth station connected to the geo-synchronous satellite suitable for supporting a variety of two-way telecommunication and information services such as voice, data and video.

The main function of the hub equipment is to receive inbounds and formulate outbounds. The hub equipment can be sub divided into two groups, namely, unit (NCU) whose main function is to formulate TDM outbounds (1024 kbps), and a master control unit (MCU) , which keeps the clocks of the VSATs in synchronism with the clock at the hub. In addition, there are subchannel control units (SCUS) to take care of the various VSAT installations through link control processor (LCP) cards.

Q15. List the differences between E-mail, FTP and TELNET. Give an application, which can be done with more than one of the above.

ANS : E-mail is the one of the very useful thing about the Internet is that it allows you almost instantly exchange of electronic message (e-mail) across the world. E-mail is a popular way of communication on the electronic on the selected paper. E-mail is mainly used for sending electronic piece of text.

While e-mail does not provide running a program available on another computer, this facility is provided by telnet.

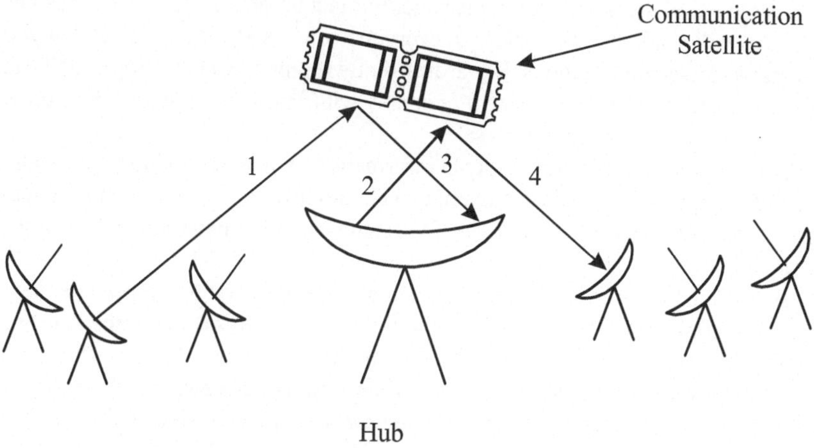

We have just seen the use of Telnet to allow remote logins to computers over networks. Now we look at another very useful protocol. This one is concerned, not with letting us log into a remote computer, but with allowing us to *transfer files* between two different computers on the Internet. It is named "File Transfer Protocol", but is usually just called FTP. We will see how FTP can be used to fetch files from many different sources on the Internet.

Telnet is a program that allows an Internet host computer to become a terminal of another host on the Internet.

Ftp opens a connection solely for transfer of files either way from terminal to host computer (uploading) or from host to terminal (downloading), however, Telnet allows you to become a user on a remote machine. You can run the Internet computer program available on that machine.

Downloading and Uploading of files can be performed through both ftp and Telnet.

Q16. How are companies using Intranet to distribute information in faster and less expensive ways to communicate with employees in a more timely manner? Give examples. **[JUN03;Q6(a)]**

ANS : One of the primary reasons for which Intranet was thought of was to use it as a means of faster communication within an organisation having presence at many locations.

Keeping everyone in a corporation up to date about the latest news in the corporation is a never-ending, often impossible task. It is particularly difficult in large corporations with many departments and divisions that are geographically separated.

There are many ways that Intranets cab be used to solve the problem and keep everybody in an organisation informed about corporate news. Companies can post their company newsletter on Intranet Web pages. Because Web pages can be updated so much more quickly than newsletters are less inexpensive too.

Intranets can also be used to deliver literally up-to the minute news flashes. The Java language can be used to create news tickers that can flash the breaking news across the top of the newsletter home page. Intranet broadcast technologies can be used that will send out a news flash to everyone connected to the Internet that will run on top of whatever actions they are currently running. And electronic mail can be broadcaster to everyone inside a company with important news, such as press releases, or news about quarterly sales.

Intranet can also deliver more in-depth information in more involving ways. Audio and video clips can be send via streaming technologies, so that people can listen to interviews with corporate executives, for examples, or see news reports about the company.

A new offline news readers technology can also be used. With it, corporate news and news from outside world can be delivered to everybody on an Intranet. Offline news readers work on a client/server model. An offline news server carries the latest corporate news. Only certain people are allowed to update news on this server. Since people on Intranet may want to read news about the outside world also, the server gets this news from Internet and distributes it on the Intranet.

This news flashes, Web page based newsletters, emails, Java tickers, news alerts, and offline news reader are some of the ways of distributing information to employees in a faster yet less expensive ways.

Here are some examples of how several companies are using an intranet to distribute information in faster and less expensive ways, to communicate with employees in a more timely manner and in general, to run their businesses more effectively:

1. Cargill International employs more than 70,000 people engaged in commodities trading around the world. Even with only 25 percent of company materials on its intranet, Cargill estimates it save tens of thousands of dollars annually by posting electronic updates rather than printing, binding and distributing them through traditional means.

2. Eli Lily, a pharmaceutical firm gives its 30,700 employees the ability to easily access timely information and thus a significant competitive advantage. By using internal web site, employees can find more information in one day than they could find out in several days in the library.

3. McDonnell Douglas distributes some 4 million pages of documentation every year and estimates that distributing this information in paper form costs twice a much as disseminating it via Web. Because manuals for an aircraft can run from 45,000 to 50,000 pages, McDonnell Douglas is experimenting with placing this information on its intranet so it can be accessed by maintenance crews and onboard by pilots using Pentium PCs.

CHAPTER 5

INTRANET AUTHORING AND MANAGEMENT TOOLS

- *Introduction*
- *Objectives*
- *Intranet Authoring Tools*
- *Intranet Management Tools*

The success behind the intranet or Internet is the authoring and management tools. On one side, they provide opportunity for higher productivity and on the other hand, the tools give tremendous manageability. It is needless to mention that good powerful tools improve the management of tasks as well as make the processes fast and organized. Another hidden aspect is that use of tools make the processes more and more computer processing intensive thereby leaving the users to put their else for other tasks.

An activity as simple as web page designing could be many times more complex and tedious than preparing similar output using a general word processor. Many software developers have extended the features of general application software used in day-to-day activities by adding up a number of features. Many have properly analyzed the requirements of the developers and tried to give a proper organized shape to them.

With the advancement in the object oriented technologies and the software engineering concepts, the software developers are seeing all application software as tools for achieving higher goals. Earlier this was not the concept and every piece of software developed was considered a masterpiece in themselves. But as the time passed, it was found that adoption of advanced concepts such as OO techniques and OO based software engineering, it had become possible to visualize and realize essential features required in different software (thereby making them complete).

There were days when designing and management of just 10 web pages for a corporate was viewed as a major project and a task such as changing the reference to a web page in all web pages could consume almost half a day. Whereas these days life of designers and developers has become very easy due to the sophisticated and elegant tools, more than 20000 pages can be handled with few mouse clicks and tasks such as changing web page reference can be as easy as a kids play.

The impact of the tools has been so strong on the computing line that a number of new employment opportunities evolved in no time. There has been great demand for graphic designers, animators, publishers, creative artists, information or content specialists, and many more. Needless to mention that due to the impact, an era of "dotcom" companies came for about a decade before the dotcom culture burst off. The use is still functioning due to certain major players in the industry such as companies running search engines, newspaper, massive portals, etc.

This unit contains information on various authoring as well as management tools available in the market for intranet. These are the tools that help in improving the look and feel of the information to be hosted on the Intranet and can be used for Internet also. Tools with lots of features are available which can improve the productivity of the professionals as well.

Q1. What are the Intranet Authoring Tools? Explain in detail.

ANS : With the active involvement of major developers such as Microsoft, Netscape, Macromedia, Adobe, Trellix, Sun, etc., there are a number of tools ranging from small applications such as image animation up to powerful email response handling applications available to everyone. Most of them are even free on the web and those available commercially can be obtained at reasonably low cost.

Editors : In the yesteryears, not very far but just about 5 years ago, the web page developers used a standard text editor or basic word Processor, such as notepad, to create HTML file. This involved very laborious activities such as coding everything by hand and then saving the HTML pages as text files. Then finally test the output offline using browsers like the Netscape or Internet Explorer. Not many tools were available for carrying out petty activities such as animation, placement or presentation of material, elegant user interface, etc.

It was essential to know almost all the HTML tags and take care of every tag and parameter of the HTML syntax. This need has led to invention or development of appropriate tools to take care of relevant activities. These tools are being updated very quickly to suit to the requirements of various newly added features, integration with other tools as well as to allow cross-platform functionality.

Today, there is no need to remember all the HTML tags and their parameters. Interestingly, there are a number of versions and variations of HTML available that makes it much more complicated to remember the features and variations.

All that is needed is to obtain the tool, install it, practice a little and then straightaway start working on it. Many better and convenient ways are now available with the availability of software tools for web authoring such as the following:

- Adobe PageMill
- Microsoft FrontPage
- Netscape Web Tools
- Macromedia Dreamweaver Ultradev
- Trellix Authoring Tool
- Chili! ASP (Active Server Pages from Sun for UNIX)
- Claris Homepage

- **GlobalX CORE System**
- Revize
- SmartTable (converts spreadsheets into Java applets)
- Web Wizards (create and edit MS Office documents through a web browser)

While the above tools are very popular, this is not the end. Though there a number of editors are available, it is felt worthful to make a little note on these tools that they offer flexibility and manageability that are very new and highly creative.
All efforts have been made to bring out most of the features that are both essential as well as desirable for all editor tools to offer.

Features of editor tools should provide for:

1. Autocoding : The tool should provide for automatic coding in the background when the developer assembles the objects on the web page, thereby relieving the developer of remembering the HTML code. When the editor itself inserts the basic framework of actual code on which the developer can add the required features, it becomes quite obvious that the time and efforts of developers reduce by many times. Moreover, the chances of committing errors also reduce substantially.

2. Modifying the code : The developer should be free to change or modify a portion of the code or change certain setting through HTML coding, but the corresponding output has to be properly affected by the editor.

3. Object library : There are many editors that are more than just editors as they perform the tasks of debugger as well as code generator by use of concepts like the object libraries. Such software tools are considered intelligent and are highly reliable. They also guide the developer on-line during any syntax mistakes.

4. WYSIWYG kind of output : The software tool should generate output exactly as designed and laid out by the developers. If the developer designs the page in a particular format, it is essential for the editor to prove coding in a manner to generate the same output.

5. Compatibility with other server architectures : The editor should support powerful web server such as Apache, iPlanet or Zeus web servers.

6. Compatibility with other platforms : The editors should produce output acceptable to all platforms such as Unix, Solaris, Windows, Linux, HP-UX, AIX, Sun Cobalt, etc.

7. Less memory usage : The tools should not consume all the memory space and swap area for want of enormous amount of memory for storing images, texts, links and other parameters.

8. Preview of the output : This feature proves to be of great use to the developers since the need to switch over to other browsers to the affect of every small change would consume memory space, time and efforts. Almost all editors are providing this feature.

9. ActiveX Data Object Support : New properties and methods to provide a tighter integration with the editor tools should be provided. Popular Web authoring tools (e.g., Macromedia's Dreamweaver UltraDev, Adobe GoLive!) give this support.

10. Java support : The editor tool should providc for support to use of Java technologies such as JavaScript, Java Beans, Applets, etc.

11. Acceptability of variants : Though this aspect purely depends on the changing market trends, it is desirable that the editor should be able to accept coding specific to variants of the HTML such as DHTML, XML, SGML, VRML, WML, etc. and be capable to generate output in these formats whenever felt necessary.

12. Site map : A proper view or estimate of how the web site is organized and how massive it is makes the web site more attractive. Editors should provide a broad view of the web in the form of an GIF or JPG image whereas some even provide this as a web page.

13. Simple and elegant user interface : The use of various objects such as colours, background, textures, buttons, banners, etc. make the web pages look more beautiful. The editors should support such things and the product would be readily accepted if it contains features related to handling of graphical representations nearer to photo-realistic nature.

14. Compatibility to popular word processing, spreadsheet and presentation software : It has become common now-a-days that most features of a web page editor are integrated directly into the word processors since the features of both are not much different. In addition to this, it should also be possible to publish the work done using spreadsheet or presentation software on to the web site as well as use the existing pages to load and accordingly process using these software.

15. Clipart support : Most editors come with a huge gallery of clipart and some even provide a collection of sounds, music and multimedia clips. Though, this is optional, it is desirable to provide one such library to enable the developers to use ready available objects.

16. Audio support : The editors should provide for playback of audio files of various formats.

17. Multimedia capabilities : The editors should also give the option of playing multimedia files so that the web site gives a much better look and feel.

18. Extension of support to various file formats : As it is known that there are hundreds of file formats available, the editors must give the support of a majority of the file formats. There are different sets of formats for images, audio, video, multimedia, text, support files, fonts, compressed files and many more.

19. Powerful search and replace facility : The editors should be smart enough to locate for a particular word or phrase in the entire web site on click of the mouse button.

20. Managing different peripheral devices : Devices such as web camera, scanner, light pen, etc. can be handled directly through the editor for better flexibility.

Q2. Explain the Supporting applications for services like FTP, Telnet, etc.

ANS : There are a number of tasks identified for hosting applications on the web. After the designing tasks are over, the next important activity would be to host on the server, and to carry out this task, it is essential that the developer is aware of the developments in this line. There is a huge range of software available for communication and file transfers between the developers' computers and the web servers.

This issue could be as simple as clicking the mouse to transfer thousands of files and it could be as difficult as using a set of programs to execute and test the developed software. It may also be possible that the developer may have to use character user interface (CUI) many times.

The developer must also know what are all the possible activities that can be performed and what objective would be achieved by use of particular service. In addition, it must also be known what additional features would be covered under that particular service and what software are available to carry out this task easily. Take for instance, a service like the file transfer. It is possible to carry out using software designed for Unix, DOS, Windows and other platforms. They are offered to work through different user interfaces such as CUI, GUI, etc. Those offered through the GUI technology are much popular and provide the easiest way to transfer files across the intranets and Internet connecting to an FTP site in seconds, even if the user is a beginner. Whether publishing a Web page, downloading the images, software and music or transferring high-capacity files between branch offices, such software provides the flexibility users need to make the tasks more enjoyable and productive.

It may be noted that there are a variety of tasks such as FTP, Telnet, Gopher, etc. that the users want to use without knowing much about the software tool they would be using and the underlying technologies. Users as well as the developers would like to look out for better user interface while hiding the supporting details and technologies.

The actual details of the protocol services would be dealt with in the next unit, but for now it is sufficient to remember that telnet clients are part of the larger category of terminal based applications such as FTP, Gopher, etc., and are programs designed to allow one computer to emulate another type of computer. It gives a feel as if the user is actually working as a part of a big network group situated geographically distant from his place and that too may be on a separate platform. Some of the popular software for telnet are as follows:

- NetTerm - One of the best telnet clients available — features remote host file editing
- HyperTerminal - A must-have free upgrade for the standard Windows Hyper Terminal client
- CRT - Combined Rlogin and Telnet — one of the best terminal applications on the 'net
- SecureCRT - CRT with SSH2 (Secure Shell) support and RSA authentication
- CommNet - One of the better telnet clients available — features Zmodem support
- QVT/Term - The standalone terminal client found in the QVT/Net Internet suite
- Anzio Lite - A solid terminal emulator with extensive connectivity options
- EWAN - A good Emulator Without A good Name
- Kermit - Kermit and a whole lot more for Windows 95/98/NT/2000 users

The features considered essential and relate to most of the services that the supporting software tools should provide are given as follows:

Features common to all :

1. Simple Drag'n'Drop based Instructions : The tools developed in recent times offer this feature and it will here to stay. One should look for this service if easy transfer of files, less command based interface, etc. are desired.

2. Extensive host type support : The software should offer full support for various host types that the user can choose from, which may include VMS, MVS, NT, OS2, AS400, Novell, Chameleon, and VM/ESA.

3. Quick connect URL : Some software have icons and simple text entry boxes for easy connectivity so that FTP URLs, usernames and passwords, etc. can be entered and directly connected into the server just like a browser.

4. Macro record/playback scripting : Automation has never been so easy with software offering recording of macro scripts. Clicking the record button, performing the tasks required and then storing the performed actions as a "macro" can record a group of activities or commands. These macros can be used time and again so that the entire group of actions need not be repeated again and again.

5. Dial-up networking support : The ISP should be automatically dialed as soon as attempt is made to connect to a remote site and still further the ISP should also be automatically reconnected after if the connection with ISP is lost due to certain reasons.

6. Right-click shell integration : Should allow performing a range of activities by just right-clicking anywhere and selecting from the choices given. The intention is that the users have to know little about the complexities of the program and gives the minimum input to the process. If required, it should also lead to the shell execution of the platform.

7. Record sessions log : The details of the logging should preferably be recorded at some place to a file so that the details can be updated daily, weekly or monthly.

8. Force upper/lower/preserve file case : Most software can be forced to transact with files in lower, upper or preserved case.

9. Auto-renaming of file extensions : Though most of the platforms do not support this, it is desirable that the users should be relieved of the job of knowing the file extensions and types. Renaming of a file extension should be done automatically during upload or download or any other process.

10. Change file attributes (such as chmod) : Bringing up a GUI for easy manipulation of file attributes would be highly useful for every user.

11. Wildcard macro support : Transacting activities through macro scripts that are masked with wildcards.

12. URL parsing/pasting : The laborious task of parsing URLs should be automatic whereas pasting/copying URLs from the clipboard to the software for automatic connection to a site could be boon to the users.

13. Support for relevant international standard : It is essential that the software should function based on the established international standard in order to provide proper compatibility to all other platforms, formats and architectures.

14. Book-marking of remote directories and sites : Ability to store the addresses of sites and location of directories of remote sites should be essential so that the user do not have to remember hundreds of sites for information. Once selected, the software should automatically lead the user to a specified directory when connected through FTP or telnet or otherwise.

Exclusive for FTP service

15. Simple Drag'n'Drop file transfers : The tools developed in recent times offer this feature and it will here to stay. One should look for this service if easy transfer of files is desired. Note that it is an essential feature for all the FTP software.

16. Transfer queue and file transfer scheduling : Selection of multiple files from various folders or directories as well as sites, and queuing them for transferring later sometime should be possible. Queued transactions should be open for being edited, saved, and scheduled for later recurring file transfers.

17. Caching of directories on remote servers : During a FTP session, one of the most time consuming task is updating the directory display after almost every process. This could be simplified by means of proper caching or storing and processing at the users' end.

18. Resume upload and download : If the files could not be downloaded due to any reason, the software should be smart enough to resume downloading or uploading immediately once the connectivity has been established. This could save tremendous efforts and precious time.

19. File finder feature : When it is required to search a massive site for simple information, the software should be capable to search the site for files using multiple search engines or similar strategy.

20. Site to site transfers : Sometimes it becomes essential to transfer files from remote server to another remote server very quickly. During such a situation, the software should be intelligent enough to keep minimal processing at its end and ensure success.

21. Directory Comparison : Local and remote directory contents can be compared based on case, name, date, or size. Files that are different from each other can be highlighted and selected for directory wide changes.

22. Directory upload and download : Some software allows the user to upload and download entire directory tree structures to and from the remote server.

Exclusive for security

23. Site security : The software should allow the developer or user to protect the entire site using combination of username and password pairs or any other security method. Whenever required, it should be able to generate reports about the type of user logged into and other details such as the users' address, platform used, date and time of logging, files or information requested, etc.

24. Extensive firewall support : It is the responsibility of the software to handle proper firewall security to keep the site secure. It is desirable that the depth of firewall implementation should be considerable. The software should be easily configurable and manageable.

Exclusive for Telnet

25. File filters : The file filters allows the users to specify the type of files in the local window. In short, the software should ensure that the commands are easily provided through single interface and provides excellent manageability. For example, if the user specifies that only .doc files are needed to be displayed, then other unwanted types are suppressed allowing easy operation on those files.

Q3. What are the Intranet Management Tools? Explain.

Tools other than web or intranet authoring tools fall under the category of web or intranet management tools. They include tools ranging from simple solutions to massive deployment tools.

Groupware can be considered as one good solution but not the only suitable solution or tool. Databases, application servers and other software tools for controlling the operations such as tools for discussion forum, emailing, chatting, etc. come under this category.

These tools are sophisticated and require higher expertise to tackle with.

Q4. What is Web Servers? Explain.

ANS : Web servers allow serving information about the organization, its services and products over the intranet or Internet. At the most fundamental level, it uses the Hyper Text Markup Language (HTML) for presentation of the content.

The job of web servers does not end there; they accept requests from browsers like Netscape and Internet Explorer generated by users at the client end and then returns the appropriate HTML documents. With the advancement of technologies, thousands of new features are being added day-in and day-out. A combination of many server-side computing techniques and technologies can be used to enhance the power of server beyond its ordinary capabilities; which may include implementation of CGI scripts, server-side includes, SSL security, and Active Server Pages (ASPs).

Note that the software are described separately as web servers and application servers. There is a little difference between the two. While the web servers perform functions encompassing those of application servers and other services like security, multithreading, communication, and many more. Some application servers available are as following:

- Allaire Cold Fusion
- Bluestone
- CreDO
- Cyberprise
- FastTrack
- Infoscape
- Intertop - I-Xpresso
- NetDynamics
- NetObject Fusion
- Netscape Application Server
- Netscape Enterprise
- NeXT WebObjects
- Persistence
- Perspecta (XML Based)
- Progress/Apptivity (Java Only)
- RadNet WebShare
- WebStar Pro

Primary Web Servers : The primary web servers apply all that have been discussed just now (as above) as the most fundamental services. Products such as AOLserver, Apache, WNServer, IIS, PWS, etc. are very well known and are easily configurable and manageable.

At the first instance, all the servers offer similar services; however, all of them differ in terms of certain additional value added features, better manageability, etc.

There is absolutely no shortage of free web servers on the market, especially those based on Unix. Apache is the most popular of all the available web servers and it is a freeware. Apache is a Unix-based software package that rules on about 60 percent of the web server market in the world as estimated by a survey.

The situation is different in the web server world other than Unix based. There are few freeware available and requires lot of searching for one such server. It is a well-known fact that most Windows-based servers are either costly or integrated into the operating system thereby making the process more complicated.

As a professional, the purchaser must ensure that the web servers provide support for two major standards, i.e. the HTTP 1.1 and CGI 1.1, both of which have become the most popular and widely used.

Most web servers are based on the content of a file and consequently are purely based upon the file extension. For instance, if a file of HTML format has been named "html.txt", then it would be served as a text file only.

AOLserver : AOLpress and AOLserver were formerly known as GNNPress and GNNServer (and much before they were popularly known as NaviPress and NaviServer) respectively. America Online combined or bundled the features of web authoring tools and web server into one.

The basis of AOL's complete web development service is known as PrimeHost, which combines the fineness of the HTML editor and web server. Joining the PrimeHost service, as a member will allow the user to have own domain name, a web site space of 20 MBs or more, counter programs, SSL support, and CGI capabilities. Using PrimeHost user accounts can be easily set up with appropriate and moderate inexpensive monthly rates. Also offered are membership categories such as an individual, commercial, or dedicated user. Using the AOLserver software, whenever any a page is saved through AOLpress, it gets automatically hosted on the site. This cuts out the time and efforts required for saving files locally, transferring them to the remote server using FTP, and then making additional changes for maintenance thereafter.

In addition to seamless integration with the AOLpress client, the AOLserver offers the following services:

- Secure Sockets Layer (SSL) support (40-bit encryption)
- Multithreading and multi-homing capabilities with the ability to configure hundreds of virtual servers in a single process
- An integrated search engine
- Hierarchical access control (for restricting access to parts of the web site)
- Built-in TCL scripting language capabilities (for quickly building custom Web applications)
- Internal image map support

- SQL database services
- A complete C API for writing custom functions, drivers, and applications
- Support for AOLserver Dynamic Pages (ADPs) which make it easier to create dynamic content
- An integrated nsftp module (a fully-functioning FTP server that uses the AOLserver's permission system)
- Support for server-parsed HTML
- HTML caching (allows pages to be served more efficiently)
- An nsvhost module for virtual hosting (non-SSL only)
- And many more…

AOLserver also offers native support for server-side includes, CGI, HTML-forms based configuration, remote site and page administration, custom error responses, page trailers, and more.

There are certain drawbacks of this server application as well. Most important being its support for the Windows NT platform only, the server also ignored the famous 128-bit SSL security technology support responding to the export regulations of US.

Overall, it stands as a good solution for serving anything from personal home pages to right up to corporate web sites. The presence of the AOLpress and the PrimeHost web-hosting service makes the duo-combination even much better.

Q5. What is iServer?

ANS : Server was developed by Servertec, written entirely in Java for any Java-enabled operating system, has the dual purpose of serving both web pages and Java servlets. In other words, it can be said that this is a special kind of product that offers the functionality of both a web server as well as an application server.

As a web server, iServer provides support as a simple multithreaded web engine generating threads for multiserver type environment and managing them. The iServer offers the following features:

- The server supports HTTP 1.1
- Uses minimal resources as the basic installation takes up to only 85K and the full package occupies space less than 125K
- Since it can manage Java servlets, it supports the more advanced protocols like IIOP and CORBA as well as fundamental protocols like ODBC, JDBC, SSI and CGI
- It is a unique combine of BASIC and Java, permitting users to create BASIC-like scripts for Java environment. Also supports TCL and Perl.
- The administration is done very easily through web while detailed log files help tracking usage levels and problems with the site.

As an application server, iServer has some attractive features, including:

- Load balancing (which allows management of incoming requests to a cluster in the most efficient manner and could include redirection to a less busy server)
- Fault tolerance
- Database-connection pooling
- Since it can run on a server with Java, it can be easily installed on the smallest PC based machine to the largest mainframe computer

These features are usually found in enterprise-level application servers but not in web servers and hence offer flexibility for a scalable web-server installation. However, there are some downsides in iServer:

- There is no provisioning for any other third-party authentication
- Users, access rights, resources, and access control lists must be set up manually i.e. it is not even possible to import any user lists even from a Windows database or from the outside
- Separate Perl support is not available (one could implement through CGI)
- No support provided for the Microsoft FrontPage extensions.

Q6. What is WN Web Server?

ANS : WN is a free web server that runs on a number of variants of UNIX platforms. It provides support for both the major standards, HTTP 1.1 and CGI 1.1.

In the WN server the method of operation is unique and easy. The server is not based on the file extensions but a separate database called "index" is maintained in which the filename, extension, type, security information, etc. are entered. All requests or references are checked with the entries in the index. A file is loaded only when there is a reference and permission for execution or service. The WN does not serve files unless specifically instructed by the index.

Obviously, the database called index makes the process of searching the website very easy. This is in line with the basic objective of WN to create an easy-to-search website. It becomes possible for the end users to search for desired data in many different ways and in different portions of the files.

Most important and notable point is that the security is implemented by the process of minimization rather than by authorization. The concept is as clear as that if the malicious users cannot see it, they would not know what to hack.

WN was one of the original web servers developed in this line. It is not just one of the nicest web servers available, but combine the features of stability with decent security features.

Q7. What is Sambar Server?

ANS : Sambar is excellent web server software and had taken a lead further by being functional, reliable, and free. Sambar 5.0 is the latest version and provides the following:

- It is functional that means Sambar not only works like the server but also works very well in a wide variety of applications. At any time, if it is found that the server does not work according to the desired pattern, the system administrator can program APIs using languages like C and C++.
- A web-based step-by-step guidelines for configuration of Sambar
- Supports ASP Web pages via the Sambar Server CScript language so that the system administrators can create dynamic and database-driven web pages
- Sambar uses the HTTPS protocol in both 40- and 128-bit versions. Also, the OpenSSL libraries are supported
- Sambar is reliable. When matched with a Windows-NT-based system, Sambar's reliability can come very close to that of a Unix/Apache-based system, so long as

the supporting, custom APIs are programmed properly.

- Sambar can run as a Windows NT System Service by executing a file named ntserver.exe binary in the "bin" directory
- Provides features similar to Unix daemons, i.e., the use of a system program without the need to log on to a machine and keep it connected.
- Provides a module called the Watcher Daemon that will try to restart the Web server and build up the system status automatically, and also arrange to send e-mail the administrator if server crashes.

It would be interesting to note that the basic Sambar Production Server is available free. The professional version of Sambar (that is priced at few thousand rupees) features such as DNS, mail, telnet, and proxy capabilities are offered.

Q8. What is the Internet Information Server?

ANS : Microsoft's IIS 5.0 is a great improvement over the existing versions of web servers and now bundled with the Windows 2000 Server operating system. This version contains many new features along with enhanced performance and reliability. Notable improvements include

- Better and clearly documented security policies
- Support for the new WebDAV publishing standards
- Faster restarts of both Web and FTP services.
- Support of clustering, Microsoft has significantly improved the configuration and setup to enable multiple machines to share the load and deliver more reliable web services

Microsoft has also added a few new wizards to perform common tasks much easily. Three important wizards are

- The Permissions Wizard (to synchronize and align Web and NTFS security settings)
- The Web Server Certificate Wizard (to obtain and install server certificates)
- The CTL Wizard (to create and modify certificate trust lists)

There is a strong support of a number of standards in IIS 5.0 including:

- Fortezza (a new U.S. government security standard)
- Transport Layer security using SSL 3.0
- Digest Authentication (a method of hashing authentication information introduced in IE 5.0)
- Replacing NT LAN Manager authentication with the stronger Kerberos 5.0 authentication protocols used in Windows 2000.

The greatest improvement in IIS 5.0 is supposed to be the web-based distributed authoring and versioning or in short WebDAV. It is a newly developed standard designed to make the construction of intranets simpler. It also helps many simultaneous users to publish and host documents on a common web server. A step ahead, this protocol allows the users to use the web directories through Office 2000 and IE 5 tools running on Windows 98, NT and Windows 2000 as if they were shared over Windows file system.

The minimum specification required for running IIS is a 200 MHz Pentium based computer with 128 MB of RAM. Another product from Microsoft that acts as complementary to the IIS i.e. the Advanced Server that is meant for clustering purpose. Companies planning for running the Advanced Server clustering should double the RAM and CPU speed. Similar step is required even if it has been planned to run MS-SQL or Transaction services on the same machine as the web server. It should be remembered that for setting up clusters through Windows 2000, it is essential to think of Advanced Server that works fine with IIS.

Q9. What is Personal Web Server?

ANS : Microsoft's Personal Web Server (PWS) also functions on the lines similar to the IIS or in other words, it can be that PWS is a lowered version of the IIS introduced and bundled along with the Server edition of Windows NT. Even though, it has been designed for Windows 95 and Windows NT Workstation users, the PWS has made greatest impact on the design, development and publishing of web documents by bring them to the personal computer range. It proved to be boon for small web sites and intranets.

While it is extremely easy to install and use PWS in terms of the clients, there are wizards that help the developers to quickly publish, share and administer the documents. The Explorer interface or the Personal Web Manager of the PWS can be used to share folders, start or stop the server services and do other similar tasks. The documents intended to be published on the web site can be tested before hand for dead or invalid links, scripting errors and many other possible loopholes.

Once the site is ready to go live you can either continue using PWS to serve your Web site or you can use Microsoft Front Page to copy the Web site developed on PWS over to IIS. PWS and IIS are packaged together as part of the freely downloadable Windows NT 4.0 Option Pack; Microsoft FrontPage is a commercial Web design client that must be purchased separately.

Certain advanced features such the Index Server, Certificate Server, and Site Server Express found in IIS are not present in PWS. Further, the server does support the famous Active Server Pages (ASP), script debugging, and many other important features. PWS offers the ability to develop web applications using the Microsoft Transaction Server.

In general, it can be said that though large organizations may prefer other high-end web servers such as the IIS, the PWS remains a best option for smaller companies and personal computer users.

Q10. What are the different buttons available in the Netscape Tool Bar? Explain each of them. **[DEC02;Q1(c)]**

ANS : ***The Toolbar*** **:** The row of buttons at the top of your web browser, known as the toolbar, helps you travel through the web of possibilities, keeping track of where you've been. Since the toolbars for Navigator and Explorer differ slightly, we'll first describe what the buttons in common do:

The **Back** button returns you the previous page you've visited.

Use the **Forward** button to return to the page you just came from.

Home takes you to whichever home page you've chosen. (If you haven't selected one, it will return you to the default home page, usually the Microsoft or Netscape website.)

Reload or **Refresh** does just that, loads the web page again. Why would you want to do this? Sometimes all of the elements of a web page haven't loaded the first time, because the file transfer was interrupted. Also when you download a web page, the data is **cached** (pronounced "cashed"), meaning it is stored temporarily in your computer's memory. The next time you want that page, instead of requesting the file from the web server, your web browser accesses it from the cache. But if a web page is updated frequently, as may be the case with news, sports scores or financial data, you won't get the most current information. By reloading the page, this timely data is updated from the web server.

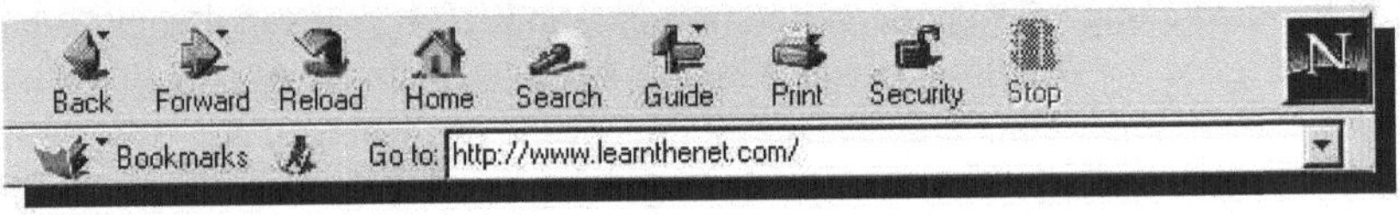

Print lets you make a hard copy of the current page loaded in your browser.

The **Stop** button stops the browser from loading the current page.

Search connects to directories and search tools on the Microsoft or Netscape websites.

Bookmarks or **Favorites** lets you to record the addresses of websites you want to revisit. Once you add a URL to your list, you can return to that web page simply by clicking on the link in your list, instead of retyping the entire address.

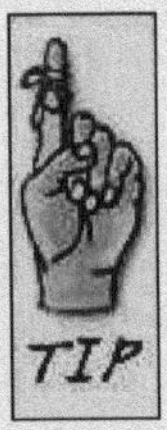

When to Use the STOP Button

There's a good reason why the Web is referred to as the World Wide Wait. If you can't connect to a site, use the STOP button and try again later, especially if you are trying to access a popular site.

The Location Bar : Just under the toolbar, you will see a box labeled "Location," "Go To," or "Address." This is where you enter the address of a website you want to visit. After you enter it, press the **Return** or **Enter** key to access the site. By clicking the small triangle to the right of the Location box, you will get a drop-down list of the most recent websites you have visited. To revisit a site, just click on the address.

The Menu Bar **:** Located along the top of the browser window, the menu bar offers a selection of things you can do with a web page, such as saving it to your hard drive or increasing the size of the text on a page. Click once on a word to access the drop-down menu, then click on the appropriate selection you want to make.

The Access Indicator **:**

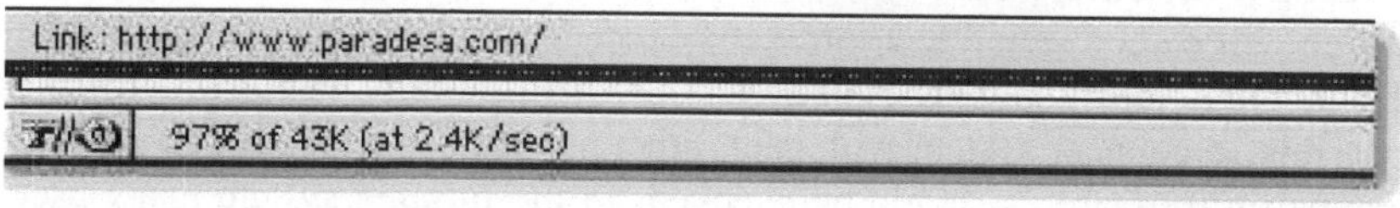

Navigator has a small picture in the upper right-hand corner of the browser. When this image is animated, it means that your browser software, known as a **client**, is accessing data from a remote computer, called a **server**. The server can be located across town or on another continent. Your browser downloads these remote files to your computer, then displays them on your screen. The speed of this process depends a number of factors: your modem speed, your Internet service provider's modem speed, the size of the files you are downloading, how busy the server is and the traffic on the Internet.

The Status Bar **:** At the bottom of the web browser you'll find a window known as a **status bar**. You can watch the progress of web page transactions, such as the address of the site you are contacting, whether the host computer has been contacted and the size and number of the files to be downloaded.

The Scroll Bar **:** The vertical bar to the right of the browser lets you scroll down and up a web page. You can do this by placing your arrow cursor on the up or down arrows and holding down your left mouse key. You can also place the arrow on the slider control, hold down the left mouse key and drag the slider.

If a web page is too wide to fit your screen, a horizontal scroll bar will appear at the bottom on your browser window. This scroll bar works the same way.

Some Browser Tricks : As with most software, there is more than one way to accomplish a task. Here are a few other features to help you navigate:

As you hop from page to page and website to website, your browser remembers where you've been. With Navigator, select **History** from the drop-down list under the **Communicator** menu. With Internet Explorer, click **History** button on the toolbar. There you'll find a list of all the web pages you've visited during a specified period of time. To revisit a page, just click on address.

Another way move between pages with Navigator is by clicking the right mouse button. A pop-up menu will appear and you can choose to move forward or back.

Q11. How will you test your Intranet? Will you initially test it with a small number of users or a large number of users? Justify your answer. Also, explain the testing process step-wise. [DEC02;Q3(a)]

ANS : Testing is a set of activities that can be planned in advance and conducted systematically. When we design a intranet system then we should test it before sending it for practical usage. Testing is a very essential part for any system and for Intranet it is also very important. In a Intranet system hundred or thousands of users are working together and all the work is related to one-another. If due to any problem, system fails then work become held. It will effect the efficiency of the system also. While testing a Intranet all the system which will be connected to a intranet system should be checked individually. Their compatibility should be checked. The hardware components which makes possible to connect system with each other should be checked. The browser compatibility features should be checked. In the Intranet system many users will work simultaneously so it should be checked that there should not be collision .

If data will lost, then it can be recovered or not, it should be checked.

Recovery testing checks whether recovering is automatic of manual.

Security testing should be done for better security.

It is advisable to test the Intranet in two steps:

lAs it is under development mode, test it with a small number of users.

lBut as one of the few module is up and ready to run, it should be tested with the load actually it is suppose to carry.

Q12. Write a short note on the following : [JUN03;Q2(b)]
(i) Intergraph Inter Serve Wed 30
(ii) Pacific Internet Web Cube

ANS : ***(i) Intergraph Inter Serve Wed 30* :** The system can be configured in way a customer may want and can be upgraded as his Internet needs grow.

Intergraph Internet web 30 is a Web server system offered by the Intergraph corporation. It has been declared as the Best Web server system for 2003 by the computer experts.

The Web 30 is one in the series of web servers offered by Intergraph corpn. Although the system is in a desktop case these machines ran the entire Oscar site and still supported several million hits per day with video downloads, audio clips, and graphics.

The bare specifications of the system are 256 MB RAM and 20 GB of disk. It has three PCI and two ISA slots and Ethernet controllers on the networking side, the units built in interface is 10 MB. Intergraph recommends that 10 MB Fast Ethernet is fine for any Internet connection up through a T 1.

Full multimedia authoring system: The web 30 goes beyond server functionality. It can be a full multimedia authoring system thanks to its workstation style audio and graphics capabilities.

The web 30 server has audio features like 16-bit CD quality stereo sound and come with a multimedia keyboard with built in amplifies-microphone. It offers excellent 2D/3D rendering applications. It can thus be used from content authoring to serve pages.

The web 30 has been found to be a solid performance as a web server and as a workstation.

(ii) Pacific Internet web cub **:**

The pacific Internet web Cub is a tool for managers of large size Websites. The cube provides a three dimensional model for classification of the issues and tasks of managing a distributed website. It focuses on the issues relating to large site management rather than those of content development

It is also a Pentium based Internet web server. It has 180MHz Pentium processor with 32MB of RAM. Backup of server data is taken every evening with different type of backup mechanism. It means, server will come operational in some hours after failure. This server runs on caldera Linux and uses Apache web server Window NT ans. Microsoft's Internet Information Server is also available as an alternative.

CHAPTER 6

INTRANET PROTOCOLS-TCP/IP

- *Introduction*
- *Objectives*
- *Basic Intranet Protocols*
- *Web Server Specific Protocols*
- *Latest Protocols*

Protocols are the rules guiding the communication over networks. In the context of intranet and Internet, protocols has greater significance since there are a number of networks trying to communicate to one another, trying to talk in different languages, formats, etc.

This is just similar to the situation where there are different people trying to talk to one another but there are a number of barriers separating them including language, culture, nationality, etc. Protocol helps in translation from one format to another and one network to another.

Some protocols are used for communication, some for conversion from one form to another, some for specific tasks, and some even for carrying out cash transactions (also called e-commerce). New protocols are being created for making mobile computing a reality.

Take it for granted that without ensuring proper customer protection, the commerce and trade over the Internet can not function at all. Hence, methods should be evolved to protect the consumer/customer interest first and business next.

The list of protocols is very long, however, attempt has been made to cover details of most of the protocols in this unit.

Q1. What are Communication cum Mail Protocols?

ANS : Address Resolution Protocol (ARP) : One of the basic communication protocols is the ARP that resolves the IP addresses used by various networking equipment into network usable format that used by LANs. ARP addresses two basic services to the clients viz., it obtains the media access control address for the requesting device and recording of the media access control address in a table called the ARP cache for future use.

The Address Resolution Protocol (ARP) is situated at the bottom half of the Network layer. It can be considered as a mechanism for mapping or translation of addresses between the Network logical addresses and MAC (Media Access Control) layer physical addresses. For instance, the MAC layer uses a 48-bit address whereas the Ethernet uses a 32-bit address. ARP provides the mechanism to translate the MAC addresses to IP addresses and vice versa using a lookup table like data structure called the ARP cache.

The greatest advantage of using an ARP is its simplicity since it does not have to perform any kind of computations or otherwise, except than to use the look up table and assign each machine an IP address and decide about subnet masks.ARP does the rest.

Simple Mail Transfer Protocol (SMTP) : The SMTP protocol is used in the TCP/IP based networks for transferring mail messages between user computers. Most popular freeware for Unix based SMTP mail programs are Elm and Pine. The other Windows based software also such as Netscape or Eudora that have become very popular. The Microsoft Outlook that comes with the Windows operating system also uses SMTP to transfer messages and is very popular.

The most notable aspect is that the SMTP works only when both the mail sender and receiver are ready to transact at the same time. Suppose that the receiver computer is not connected or available at that moment, then the messages are stored in a temporary server (may be the nearest gateway or hub). A post office protocol (such as IMAP or POP) must then be used to retrieve the mail.

Since the mail messages cannot have control characters in them, the binary files must first be converted into ASCII. A program called Unicode usually does the process of this conversion. Once the mail is sent to the other end, it is converted back to binary or ASCII or whatever format required using another utility program called the Unicode.

It should be clear that two separate protocols are used for sending and receiving email (or mail messages). For sending messages, the SMTP is used whereas for receiving at the other end either POP or IMAP is used at their local server. While configuring the email accounts, certain addresses are exclusively declared, viz., the addresses of an SMTP server, a POP server, address where returned messages are to be sent, and the basic server where the user has his email account.

There are two main difficulties using the SMTP protocol, i.e., the message of size more than 64 KB cannot be handled and the second is the timeout. Whereas the first problem could be overcome with newer implementations of the operating systems as well as attaching files as attachments to the main messages, the second problem continued as both the client and server can have different timeouts, and quite naturally, one of them may timeout very quickly keeping the other busy or unexpectedly terminate the connection.

Post Office Protocol (POP) : As the name indicates, the POP delivers all the messages stored on the server to the user's email account. It can be configured in such a manner that the user can obtain emails from his multiple email accounts into his only email software installed on the computer such as the Microsoft Outlook or Outlook Express. This facility is also available on almost all the Internet based email web sites such as Hotmail, Yahoo, etc.

Like the SMTP, the POP is also a very simple protocol and can be easily written for a command-line-based application. With the advent of a number of Windows based applications, the difficulty of writing such command-line based applications has totally vanished and the work of user has become much easier. Similar applications have evolved over the Unix based implementations as well.

Note that it is easy to write code for simulating a client by use of telnet to connect to the server, and then enable the client to do email-related tasks such as logging into the account, logging off, downloading the emails, deleting them, etc.

The transactions begins with the initiation of a session when newly logged in and it is possible to do only three things viz., get the username, password or quit the session. Once logged into the mail server, the transactions allow doing the following tasks:

STAT	Gives the number of messages in the box as well as total size of those messages in bytes
LIST	Gives the list of messages in the mailbox
RETR **msg**	RETR retrieves a message. It uses the message number as generated using the LIST command
DELE **msg**	Deletes a message. Message would be permanently deleted with the sessions ended using the quit command. Message can be undeleted using RSET command
TOP **msg n**	Returns the headers of desired message and also **n** lines of its body

Internet Message Access Protocol (IMAP) : Internet Message Access Protocol (IMAP) is a standard protocol for accessing e-mail from the local server. The method of functioning of IMAP is very much similar to POP but there is a little difference between the two.

While both POP and IMAP deal with the receiving of e-mail from the local server, POP just stores and then sends the messages whereas IMAP acts totally as a remote file server.

IMAP is more popular for the Internet based email services but the POP is gradually taking up the lead. IMAP acts more or less like a client/server type protocol wherein the messages are kept on a server and the user connects to it for viewing. In order to download the mail message, the user has to decide it by viewing only the header part and name of the sender. The only interesting part of the IMAP services is the creation and use of folders (also called mailboxes), delete messages, or search for certain parts. The downside is that the IMAP requires continuous access to the mail server while the user is session in order to keep the content and connection alive.

IMAP has the ability to view the mail messages not only by arrival number but by using attributes as well. In this kind of output the folder or the mailbox looks like a relational database table rather than just a collection of messages.

Q2. What is Service Protocols?

ANS : Many Internet users are familiar with the protocols such as TCP/IP to connect to the Internet. These include those protocols that permits the users to logon to remote computers, such as the following:

- ✓ World Wide Web's Hypertext Transfer Protocol (HTTP)
- ✓ File Transfer Protocol (FTP)
- ✓ Telnet (Telnet)
- ✓ User Datagram Protocol (UDP)
- ✓ Simple Mail Transfer Protocol (SMTP)

These and other protocols are often packaged together with TCP/IP as a "suite." Protocols related to TCP/IP include the User Datagram Protocol (UDP), which is used instead of TCP for special purposes. In combination with the IP, it is known as the UDP/IP suite.

Though not very well known otherwise, other protocols are used by network host computers for exchanging router information such as

- ✓ Internet Control Message Protocol (ICMP)
- ✓ Interior Gateway Protocol (IGP)
- ✓ Exterior Gateway Protocol (EGP)
- ✓ Border Gateway Protocol (BGP)

Personal computer users connect to the Internet through the Serial Line Internet Protocol (SLIP) or the Point-to-Point Protocol (PPP). These protocols use the Internet Protocol (IP) at the base so that the data can be sent over a dial-up phone connection to an access provider's modem.

Transmission Control Protocol (TCP) : As it is well known that the Internet uses different types of topologies, data transfer rates, packet sizes, and other related technologies. Keeping these issues in view, the TCP has been specifically designed to provide a reliable end-to-end service over an unreliable connection. The TCP was initially designed for either proprietary or Unix based operating systems so that they communicate with one another avoiding unreliable and slow physical transport of data. It attained such great popularity that it has become the standard protocol for every software and hardware to communicate with one another.

The entire message or data to be sent over Internet is divided into various units or packets for efficient routing through the Internet. The TCP is a protocol that is used in conjunction with the Internet Protocol (IP) to send the data in the form of message units between computers over the Internet. While IP takes care of handling the actual routing or delivery of the data, TCP keeps track of each individual units of data.

Even though every packet has the same destination IP address, they arrive at the destination through different routes over the Internet and finally reassembled at the at destination to make it a complete message or data as was sent. This breaking of message or data into packets before transmission and then rearranging at the destination in proper order after receipt of all packets is called disassembling and assembling respectively and done by a specific portion of TCP called the packet assembler and disassembler (PAD).

TCP falls under the category of connection-oriented protocols, which means that a connection or session is established and maintained until the message or messages has been exchanged totally.

Internet Protocol (IP) : The Internet Protocol (IP) is responsible for sending data from one point to another (may be through different routes) on the Internet and is also used for intranets. Every point or computer must have a unique IP address that gives an identity to that particular computer on the Internet. This unique address of the sender as well as the destination machine is put on the data packet before sending and the Internet gateway decides where to send this packet based on this IP address. The packets keep traveling through gateways to smaller networks till it reaches the nearest machine or the immediate neighborhood or server and then finally delivered to the destination computer. When all the packets have arrived at the destination, the TCP (which is a connection-oriented protocol) keeps track of the sequence and puts all of them into a proper order so that the message or data is built up as was sent originally.

IP falls under the category of connectionless protocols, which means that there is no permanent established connection between the sender and receiver of the message or data. In other words, each packet is permitted to pass through the Internet as an independent unit of data. In the Open Systems Interconnection (OSI) communication model, IP sits in the third layer called the networking layer. It is the responsibility of the Internet authorities to assign appropriate range of IP numbers to different organizations. There after, it becomes the job of the organizations to assign IP numbers to its departments and uses.

For an organization, there are two sets of IP addresses. This is where the difference between the Internet and intranet comes into picture very clearly. One is used to communicate with the outside world, also known as the static IP. This is, in other words, used for Internet connectivity, whereas the other is the one used for internal use. The internal IP is not communicated outside the network limits and is usually called the internal IP address or subnet address. The internal IP identifies a network component for use over the intranet or sometimes on the LAN. The server handles the task of network address translation (NAT) using which the IP address for external use is translated or mapped onto the one for internal use and vice versa.

The purpose and benefit of a second set of IP addresses for internal use is that the second set makes it possible to address a large number of computers and other network devices or a group of LANs that further have a number of devices installed within an organization by the method of pooling the IP addresses. With a broad view, it looks as if a number of devices and subnets might be using one single (static) IP address to communicate with the outside world. Compare this with the concept of an EPABX of an organization. The organization instead of leasing 300 direct telephone lines for internal use, prefers to have an EPABX installed so that the 30 direct lines from the telephone exchange are properly utilized or pooled among a large number of users as well as all the internal communication costs are reduced to zero.

When it comes to computers trying to connect to an Internet Service Provider or ISP such as VSNL, MTNL, etc., it becomes difficult to manage thousands of users at a time. Hence, a mechanism has been developed wherein an IP address is allocated to the user when he logs on to the ISP's network dynamically. This IP address is also called dynamic IP address and it changes every time the user logs on to the ISP's server.

The IP address are divided into four classes since networks vary in size, which the organizations decide when applying for a static IP address:

✓ Class A addresses are for extremely large networks or gateways, usually given at the level of one per country

✓ Class B addresses are for large networks, or extremely large organizations

✓ Class C addresses are for small networks (fewer than 256 devices) or may be for those at the level of organization

✓ Class D addresses are also called multicast addresses, normally for representing devices and computers on the networks

The class of addresses used by a device or network is identified by the first few bits of each IP address. The address structures look like this:

Class A	0	Network (7 bits)	Local address (24 bits)
Class B	10	Networks(14 bits)	Local address (16 bits)
Class C	110	Networks(21 bits)	Local address (8 bits)
Class D	1110	Multicast address (28 bits)	

The IP address is usually expressed as a combination of four octal numbers with each number representing eight bits, all of them separated by periods, such as 202.64.15.30. The number 202 represents the class A network (usually for India), the second number would represent a large organization or a service provider (in this case it is VSNL), third number represents a server (here it indicates a server of the VSNL at New Delhi) and finally the fourth number would indicate a particular user connected to that server.

The present version of IP is IPv4 that supports 32 bits. Very clearly, it is possible to address only 256 x 256 x 256 x 256 computers or devices or networks on the Internet, in short this amounts to 2^{32}. But the actual number of all devices or networks is many times more than this. The Internet's explosive growth made it possible to address (or pool or multiplex) many subnets for each IP address. However, it is proposed in the new version of IP called as IPv6 to use 128 bits thereby enabling addressing many more networks and computers to communicate simultaneously over the Internet without any difficulty.

Q3. What is Telnet? Explain.

ANS : TELNET : When it is required to develop and test software for another operating system such as Sun Solaris or SCO Unix when working on a Windows NT based computer, it is preferable to connect to a computer that actually runs on Sun Solaris or SCO Unix and run all the commands on that while viewing the output at this Windows based computer. This situation resembles something like a terminal emulation kind of working and is possible through the telnet protocol. It is possible to work on the ISP's server by connecting to it as a regular user (from a remote computer) and run all the Unix based commands on it even though the user might not be having Unix installed at his location.

The Telnet protocol is used to establish an on-line connection (or connection oriented service) to a remote machine. It gives an impression that the user can access someone else's computer (also called a host computer) and that all the required permission have been given.

A Telnet command for requesting connectivity to the Roorkee University (now IIT Roorkee) might look like the following:

telnet rurkiu.rurkiu.ernet.in

Once the connection is granted by the host computer, the user will get an invitation message to log on with a proper username and password pair. If the pair is acceptable to the host, the user would be logged on like any other regular user. Telnet is mostly used by program developers and anyone who needs to use specific applications or data located at the required host computer.

Q4. Explain any one application level protocol that has now become the standard web service protocol.

ANS : Hypertext Transfer Protocol (HTTP) : The Hypertext Transfer Protocol (HTTP) is an application level protocol and has become the standard Web service protocol. It enables transfer of files that may include text, graphic images, sound, video, and other multimedia files on the World Wide Web.

Essential concepts that are part of HTTP include (as its name implies) the idea that files can contain references to other files whose selection will elicit additional transfer requests.

A web server is a computer that has certain amount of space allocated separately and contains a lot of information in the form of HTML files along with other files such as images, voice, etc. An HTTP daemon or HTTPd is a program that is designed to wait for a number of incoming HTTP requests and respond them when they arrive. The standard web browser installed at the clients' computers generate requests that are handled at the server by this HTTPd. Users demand to see the web pages by typing in the Uniform Resource Locator or URL of the organization or web server such as http://www.hotmail.com or clicking on a hypertext link, the browser generates an HTTP request and sends it to the IP address indicated by the URL. This URL is translated to IP address by ARP or NAT at different stages to and from the client. The HTTPd at the server receives the request and after any necessary processing, the requested file is transmitted. It should be remembered that the HTTPd has the capability to handle multiple requests at a time.

In short, it can be said that the concept of HTTP is based purely on Request-Response combination, with the client "requesting" and the server "responding" to the requests. The server straightaway processes the request, generates a response, and closes the connection. Thereafter, the server keeps waiting for other requests.

The HTTP protocol consists of two distinct items viz., the set of requests from browsers to server and the set of responses going back to them. All the newer version of HTTP support two kinds of requests: simple requests and full requests. A simple request consists of just a single GET line pointing to the page desired, without the protocol version. The response is just the raw page (with no headers, no MIME, and no encoding) whereas in full requests protocol version on the GET request line is present.

Although HTTP was designed for use on the Web, most widely known methods are GET, PUT and POST. There are other methods also that offer greater flexibility of usage and have been put keeping in view the future applications. The details of usage of HTTP methods are not being dealt here as they are beyond the scope of this context and relevant HTML programming reference should be referred for further information. The built-in methods of HTTP are given below:

Method	Description
GET	Request to read a Web page
HEAD	Request to read a Web page's header
PUT	Request to store a Web page
POST	Append to a named resourse (e.g., a Web page)
DELETE	Remove the Web page
LINK	Connects two existing resourses
UNLIKE	Breaks an existing conection between two resources

Q5. What is file transfer protocol? Explain.

ANS : File Transfer Protocol (FTP) : File Transfer Protocol (FTP), is a standard Internet protocol that offers the simplest way to exchange files between computers on the Internet. Just as the HTTP transfers web pages and related files and the SMTP transfers e-mail, the FTP is an application protocol that uses the TCP/IP protocol suite. FTP is used to transfer files files from one computer to another on the Internet. It is a very popular and commonly used protocol to download and upload applications and other files from the clients computers to servers.

The FTP service is widely popular amidst the web site developers as well as the students' community for downloading or uploading documents or information to and from desired servers.

Initially, it was available through Unix based computers only when the users had to remember a number of commands and their combinations to use the FTP services, but with the advent of Windows based computers and tools, it has become to do the activities in a much easier manner; even the commands need not be remembered at all. Many browsers support FTP based URL such as ftp://www.abc.com (a fictitious address); the idea being that the protocol reference like http can be replace by ftp if file transfer or file based operations are desired by the user.

Q6. What is user datagram protocol? Explain.

ANS :

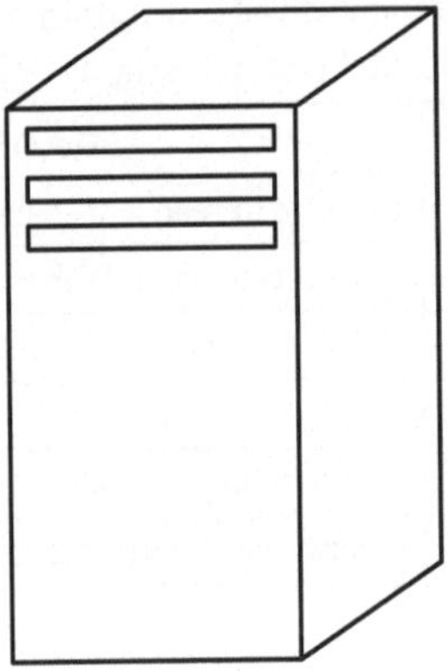

User Datagram Protocol (UDP) : The User Datagram Protocol, or UDP as it is known, is a connectionless transport level protocol supported by the IP. It offers a limited service as compared to the conventional TCP and can be used for transferring messages between computers in a IP based network.. In short, it can be said that UDP is more or less an alternative to the TCP and, it functions in a suite like TCP/IP called the UDP/IP. Unlike the TCP where the basic unit of data is called packet, under UDP a data unit is called a datagram.

```
          0   7 8      15 16    23 24      31
        +--------+--------+--------+--------+
        | Source | Destination
     |  Port   |  Port  |
     +--------+--------+--------+--------+
     |        |        |
     | Length |Checksum|
     +--------+--------+--------+--------+
     |
     |    data octets ...
     +----------------- ...
```

Figure: User Datagram Header Format

UDP does not divide a message into small packets (or datagram's) and then reassemble them after receipt as it is done with TCP/IP. The basic philosophy behind use of UDP is that the entire message is sent and ensured that the receiver has received the message properly without any errors. UDP is highly useful in those network based applications that aim at saving lot of processing time spent on breaking and reassembling them.

It may be remembered that a specific protocol called the Trivial File Transfer Protocol (TFTP) is based on UDP support rather than the conventional TCP. UDP can also be employed for Internet name server applications and usage. UDP offers two services not provided by the IP layer. First, it provides the port numbers where the request has actually received so that different user requests can be distinguished, and secondly, it provides a checksum that can be used to check whether the data has been received properly or not.

Q7. What is Common Gateway Interface (CGI).

ANS : It is a well established fact that an HTTP server is used as a gateway to a large repository of information related to an organization or a product or a concept. The repository could be further included with massive database based applications. The Common Gateway Interface or CGI provides mutual agreement between various HTTP servers on integrating information exchange through gateway scripts and programs. The CGI scripts are used in conjunction with HTML forms to build database applications and query processing.

Following are two most noticeable disadvantage of a CGI based applications:

1. That each time the application is executed, it runs as a separate process with its own address space resulting in execution of unnecessary extra instructions. This could be troublesome especially when many instances of the same application are running.

2. That the execution speed is extremely slow. It could be due to the references made by the applications, communication speed, the extremely slow compile/execute time and other factors.

A number of good text references are available on the CGI scripting that can be referred for in-depth information.

Q8. What is Internet Server Application Program Interface (ISAPI).

ANS : The Internet Server Application Program Interface or ISAPI is purely based on Windows technology of the Microsoft. It consists of a set of program calls that can be used to include while writing a Web server application. The advantage of ISAPI is that the applications run faster than its counterpart – a CGI based application. It is possible to create a dynamic link library (DLL) application file using ISAPI that can support the process and address space of the HTTP application. The DLL files are loaded into the computer memory when HTTP request is received and the application is started. They continue to remain loaded as long as they are needed; hence eliminating the chance of locating, reading into storage and executing as frequently as a CGI application thereby increasing the processing speed many times more.

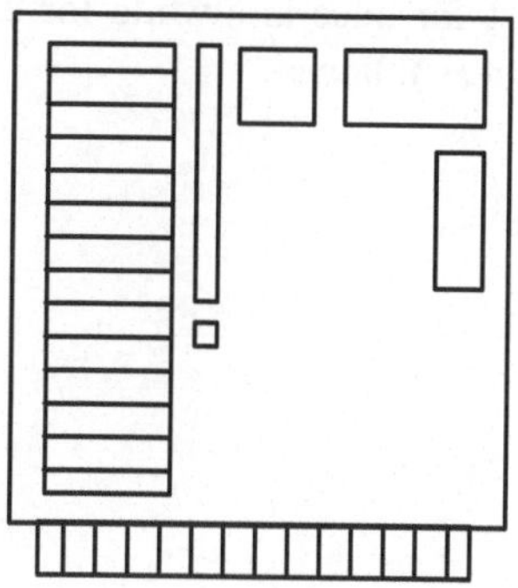

The existing CGI applications can be easily converted and configured into ISAPI application DLLs without having to rewrite the entire logic. But it is essential to make chances to accommodate the thread management part so that a single instance of the DLL application can support multiple users. In other words, the ISAPI supports the Component Object Module (COM) and Distributed COM (DCOM) concepts. An ISAPI filter is a special kind of ISAPI DLL application file that can be used to receive control of every HTTP request and thereafter they can be used for many purposes such as encryption or decryption, for logging, for request screening, etc.

Since the ISAPI supports COM/DCOM technology, it naturally provides a vendor-independent way of providing many features of the web server and quite naturally, it offers far more flexibility than the general CGI interface avoiding all performance limitations. Some of them have been given below:

✓ An ISAPI code or filter is compiled to a binary-shared library, which is loaded into the web server itself. For this reason ISAPIs must be compiled separately so that it becomes a position-independent shared library.

✓ An ISAPI extension or code can provides dynamic content on a web site. The functionality of an extension is defined by two required interface functions, GetExtensionVersion and HttpExtensionProc.

The first interface function, GetExtensionVersion, is called to check the version numbers and get information about the module. The file is then compiled as a shared library, and placed into relevant directory. If the file was installed then the server will load in the module, and then run the HttpExtensionProc, which will automatically send output to the browser.

✓ Filter is another type of ISAPI module that makes it possible to implement customized logging, encryption, and authentication or path-mapping support. Filters allow users to alter the behavior of the server whereas extensions can be used for generating content.

The process of serving a request is broken into a number of stages: a filter can ask to be 'notified' as a request reaches each of these stages, intervening at that point to modify the request and the web server's response. Some notifications come up a number of times for specific requests; some come up for a group of requests and some other take place just for once-in-a-while for each request. The ISAPI notifications are broadly put as follows:

- Read Raw Data
- Send Raw Data
- Preprocessed Headers
- Authentication
- Access Denied
- On URL Map
- Logging
- End of network session

Q9. What is Netscape Server Application Programming Interface (NSAPI).

ANS : Just as ISAPI is specific to the Microsoft technology, another arch-rival in the market i.e. Netscape developed the Netscape Server Application Programming Interface or in short, NSAPI. It was created as a more efficient and robust replacement for the CGI. It can also be used to develop applications involving customized authorization, encryption, or to change certain behavioral or functional aspects of the server operations.

It is an API provided with Netscape Web server to help developers build faster and more complex web-based applications by extending the server capabilities. NSAPI, CGI and the Java (along with JavaScript-based server API) are the three major components of the so-called Netscape's Internet Application Framework.

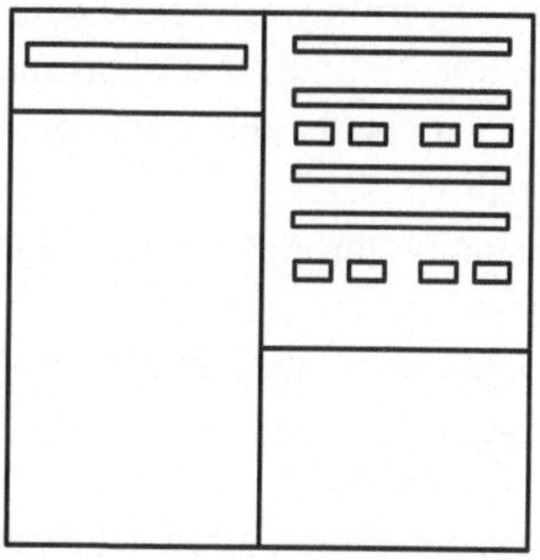

While the underlying technologies used for ISAPI and NSAPI are similar, the method of handling and addresses the request-response varies slightly. The HTTP transactions in the form of request-response process is handled on the Netscape Enterprise Server through the SAPI's functions called the built-in server application functions (SAF). Once initialized, the server waits for a HTTP requests from the clients for a file such as a HTML file, a CGI program, or an image file, etc. The following sequence of six steps constitute the request-response process which the SAF executes step-by-step and each step may involve more than one operations.:

✓ AuthTrans (authorization translation) verifies request information (i.e. username and password)

✓ NameTrans (name translation) translates request into a local file system path

✓ PathCheck (path checking) checks validity of the path and authorization of the user for path access

✓ ObjectType (object typing) determines the type of MIME (Multipurpose Internet Mail Encoding) resource requested by the client

✓ Service (service) in the form of response to the client

✓ Add Log (adding log entries) adds related entries to the log file

NSAPI was basically designed by the designers at the NCSA and CERN web servers. Thereafter, it has been under continuous observation and development of software developers so that the users may take advantage of its speed, tight integration with the server, and flexibility. The only downside of the NSAPI is that it requires an in-depth understanding of the server processes and their execution.

Unlike the ISAPI, for converting a CGI code or extension, the developers do not need NSAPI, rather the Web Application Interface (WAI) should be used. This WAI is a concept similar to COM/DCOM of Microsoft, but has not got wide popularity even though Netscape products are doing well on the Internet and intranet grounds. Just as COM components can be put in a distributed environment under the concept DCOM, the NSAPI can run in a distributed environment as well since it is based on Internet Inter-ORB Protocol (IIOP).

Q10. What is Code Division Multiple Access (CDMA).

ANS : The CDMA technology spreads the information contained in a particular signal of interest over a much greater bandwidth than the original signal. This technology offers a number of benefits to the cellular operators as well as to the subscribers. To name a few, the following are the benefits of CDMA:

✓ Capacity increases of 8 to 10 times that of an analog system

✓ Improved call quality, with better and more consistent sound as compared to system or near-wire line quality voice service

✓ Simplified system planning through the use of the same frequency in every sector of every cell

✓ Reduced installation time, error rates, inventory of components, maintenance, and many other related benefits

✓ Enhanced privacy

✓ Improved coverage characteristics, allowing for possibility of fewer cell sites or minimum number of fixed radio sites

✓ Increased connectivity time for portables

✓ Bandwidth available on demand

✓ Near-universal geographical coverage

✓ Low equipment cost, both subscriber stations and fixed plant

CDMA falls under the category of spread-spectrum technology, a family of digital communication techniques, used in military applications for many years. The basic principle of behind the technology is the use of noise-like carrier waves and bandwidths much wider than those used for point-to-point communication.

There are two philosophies behind the evolution of CDMA that has been derived from military applications viz.,

✓ That the enemy efforts to jam communications system should be prevented by use of anti-jam or AJ techniques

✓ That the enemy should not even know that communication was even taking place, by use of concept sometimes called low probability of intercept (LPI).

The history of CDMA traces back to the days of World War II when the application of this communication method was theoretically evolved. Somehow, the method did not get greater acceptability for civilian use but was put to use for military or defence purposes. In spite of the fact that the technology is so strong that it is poised to take over even the conventional mobile communication system, it found limited market in countries like the US and Germany, and interestingly, it is yet to get wide acceptance world wide.

The following factors of CDMA technology are altering the face of cellular and ordinary communication:

- ✓ Greatly enhanced the telephone traffic capacity also called the Erlang capacity
- ✓ Greatly enhanced the voice quality and eliminating the audible effects of multipart fading
- ✓ Minimized incidence of dropped calls due to handoff failures
- ✓ Providing reliable transport mechanism for data communications, such as facsimile and internet traffic
- ✓ Reduced the number of sites needed to support any given amount of traffic
- ✓ Simplifying site selection
- ✓ Minimized deployment and operating costs because fewer cell sites are needed
- ✓ Greatly reduced average transmission power
- ✓ Reducing interference to other electronic devices
- ✓ Reducing potential health risks

Availability of low cost, powerful digital integrated circuits, that reduced the size, weight, and cost of the exchanges or subscriber stations to minimal level. The two major break-through of this technology that made commercial applications possible are that the CDMA technology drives all operators, and it enables the users to use lowest transmission powers.

Since CDMA supports the digital technology, it changes the method the subscriber station operate. Programming the features has become extremely easy. Core technology has changed from extreme analog system to extreme digital system. CDMA receivers do not eliminate analog processing totally, but communication channels are separated by means of certain kind of modulation techniques that is applied and removed in digital form and not on the basis of frequency while all users occupy the same frequency band.

The original system evolved was called the Advanced Mobile Phone System, or AMPS. It is the system everyone use throughout the North American continent even today. Similar systems with slight variations are used in European and Asian countries.

Technically speaking, the spectral allocations for the channels are in the range of 800-900 MHz in which can be used for several hundred channels. One channel of one base station is used for each conversation. Upon handoff or change of cell area, the subscriber station is informed via switching message to discontinue the old channel and switch to a new one. Reuse of frequency is the core concept and central to the cellular telephony. The channel vacated at a particular cell area can then be dynamically allocated to another user. Contention could arise when all the millions of users try to use the services from one particular cell at a time, which otherwise is a rare or almost impossible situation.

Q11. What are the Wireless Application Protocol (WAP).

ANS : The Wireless Application Protocol (WAP) is client/server architecture based technology and has been one of the landmark developments in the communications industry because of the attempt to develop an open standard for wireless protocols, independent of vendor and air link.

The WAP is developed for micro-browser of the mobile or cell phone. These phones can be considered as hand-held terminals. The WAP servers are programmed to provide simple services to the users since it is not possible to provide complete flexibility of an ordinary browser. Limited services such as providing result of examination, amount balance in the bank account, temperature and humidity of the day, simple message service, etc. can be easily provided on the phones. Day-by-day, new services are being added to the features.

The WAP is the talk of the town due to the wide hype in the telecom industry as well as outside it. WAP is a standardized method wherein a mobile phone user talks to a server installed in the mobile phone network or exchange. The features of the phone are controlled by software and the phones themselves control switching. The growth in this industry has been so rapid that it forced all telecom and IT companies to open up departments for producing WAP based technologies in less than a year's time. WAP is in the news for the reason that it provides a standardized way of linking the Internet and mobile phones, thereby linking two of the largest and dynamic industries anywhere. The forum that founded the protocol includes major wireless corporate such as Nokia, Ericsson and Motorola, and Phone.com. While some companies support non-voice based services only, some provide voice mailing, some provide cell broadcast service. Some major players in this line are CMG, Siemens, Ericsson, Hutchison, Materna, Motorola, Nokia, NTT DoCoMo, AT&T, Spice and many more.

Initially, it was expected that mobile information services supposed to be the most important application for wireless based applications would be a grand success as many network operators envisaged but it did not happen.

It was with the advent of WAP that the entire scenario changed, however, it has its limitations such as the following:

✓ WAP phones are very difficult to configure for new WAP services, with about 18-20 different parameters must be entered to get access to simple WAP service.

✓ WAP is a protocol that functions in conjunction with an underlying bearer service protocol. The WAP has been actually developed to provide services in conjunction with wireless service protocols such as the Short Message Service (SMS), Circuit Switched Data (CSD), Unstructured Supplementary Services Data (USSD) and General Packet Radio Service (GPRS). It is notable that almost all these existing bearers have not been properly configured for WAP.

✓ The greatest difficulty is that the WAP standard is not yet complete, even with the latest WAP version (i.e. ver 1.2) that came in 1999.

✓ New protocols such as SIM Application Toolkit and Mobile Station Application Execution Environment (MexE) have already evolved before the proper standardization of WAP and this could be disastrous for WAP as they are widely supported and aimed to go ahead of WAP.

From the above discussion, it should be clear that the WAP could not attain great success due to the launch of technology much before actually being properly standardized globally, and the blame obviously goes to the wide publicity of the protocol while in its development or infancy stage.

WAP Technology : The basic philosophy behind the WAP approach is to utilize fewest resources possible on the handheld terminals and to utilize all the functionality of the network. Micro browser-based services and applications reside temporarily on servers as well as on phones. In the design of the WAP standard, application part has been kept separate from the bearer being used. This separation helps greatly in the switching over from ordinary applications like SMS or CSD to GPRS. In addition, the most important feature of WAP lies as under:

✓ Compatibility with any mobile network standard such as Code Division Multiple Access (CDMA), Global System for Mobiles (GSM), or Universal Mobile Telephone System (3GSM). WAP has been designed to work with all cellular standards and is supported by almost all major wireless leaders such as Siemens, AT&T and NTT DoCoMo.

✓ Support for multiple input terminals such as keypads, keyboards, touch-screens and styluses is provided.

WAP has a layered architecture as shown in the diagram below:

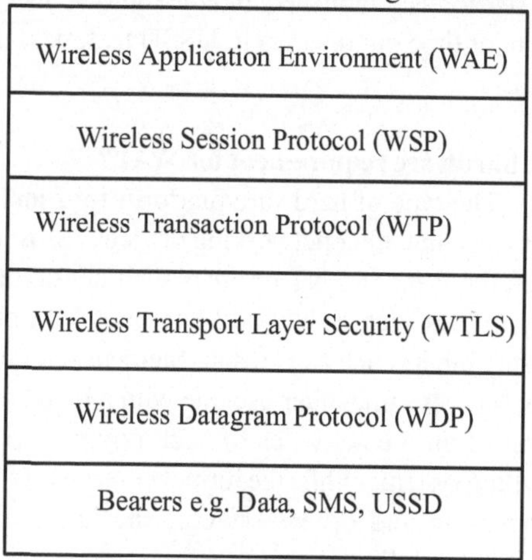

Figure: WAP Protocol Stack

Wireless Application Environment (WAE) : The WAE defines the user interface on the phone through the use of the Wireless Markup Language (WML), WMLScript – a scripting language similar to JavaScript and the Wireless Telephony Application (WTA).

Wireless Session Protocol (WSP) : A layer that links the WAE and the Wireless Transaction Protocol

Wireless Transaction Protocol (WTP) : Responsible for ensuring proper wireless enabled transaction using protocols such as Wireless Datagram Protocol or standard suite of TCP/IP protocols. WTP offers three types of services: unreliable one way request, reliable one way request and reliable two way request respond.

Wireless Transport Layer Security (WTLS) : Just as the transport layer of the OSI model, the WTLS also provides security features that are based upon the established Transport Layer Security (TLS) protocol standard. It also extends services such as data integrity checks, privacy on the WAP Gateway to client, and authentication.

Wireless Datagram Protocol (WDP) : This is a protocol very much similar to the UDP except that the WDP uses the wireless communication techniques.
The SMS, CSD and the USSD are three most important of the WAP's underlying bearers:

- ✓ Short Message Service: Supports a maximum length of 160 characters per short message.
- ✓ Circuit Switched Data: Since CSD has very few users as of today, the WAP could not have a good start with the CSD as well.
- ✓ Unstructured Supplementary Services Data: USSD is a means of transmitting information or instructions over a GSM network. USSD has some similarities with SMS since both use the GSM network's signaling path. Unlike SMS, USSD is not a store and forward service and is session-oriented such that when a user accesses a USSD service, a session is established and the radio connection stays open until the user, application, or time out releases it. USSD text messages can be up to 182 characters in length.

Q12. What are the hardware requirement for WAP?

ANS : Hardware : The type of hardware platform for running the WAP usually consists of a Unix server and other networking devices. Most operators use a Unix platform rather than the Windows NT or other such operating systems.
Even though many majors such as Nokia, Materna, CMG, etc. function on Unix based platforms many others such as Ericson, Siemens, etc. function on platforms based on Windows NT, yet some other use one with a blend or option of the other. The most important of all the activities of such powerful platforms are account management and billing system. While the former controls all the details of incoming and outgoing processing and other services, the latter manages to generate subscriber wise reports for billing.

Q13. List the applications of WAP.

ANS : Applications of WAP : Corporate applications that are being enhanced and enabled with a WAP interface include:

- ✓ Remote Point of Sale
- ✓ Customer Service
- ✓ Remote Monitoring such as Meter Reading
- ✓ Vehicle Positioning
- ✓ Corporate Email
- ✓ Remote LAN Access
- ✓ File Transfer
- ✓ Web Browsing
- ✓ Document Sharing/ Collaborative Working
- ✓ Audio
- ✓ Still Images

- ✓ Moving Images
- ✓ Home Automation

Consumer Applications that are being enhanced and enabled with a WAP interface include:

- ✓ Simple Person to Person Messaging
- ✓ Voice and Fax Mail Notifications
- ✓ Unified Messaging
- ✓ Internet Email
- ✓ Prepayment
- ✓ Ringtones
- ✓ Mobile Commerce
- ✓ Mobile Banking
- ✓ Chat
- ✓ Information Services

Days are not far when the WAP would be used to control the air conditioners and refrigerators installed at home directly from anywhere in the world. Users would be able to switch-on and regulate air conditioners much before coming back to home. Similarly, it would be possible to program the washing machines remotely.

Q14. What are the General Packet Radio Service (GPRS)?

ANS : The General Packet Radio Service (GPRS) is a new packet-based service that has been introduced on many GSM and TDMA mobile networks from the year 2000 onwards. It is immediate as there is no dial up connection, relatively fast (up to 177.2 kbps in the very best theoretical high side) and supports virtual connectivity, allowing relevant information to be sent from the network as and when it is generated. It is expected that the WAP based networks shall also support the GPRS services very soon. It is also possible that if the initial pull from the WAP side were strong through SMS and Circuit Switched Data services then SMS would take over GPRS. It is also possible that both the WAP and GPRS services can be provided on the same network and it is left to the user to select the one he intends to use.

By any means, it should be remembered that WAP will play an important role for the development of GPRS-based applications since due to the specific nature of WAP stack. The separation of bearer level from the application layer in the WAP protocol stack provides for the ideal, organized and standardized way to use the same application on different bearers.

Q15.What are the protocols for E-Commerce? Explain.

 # Explain the properties of Agora. [JUNE04;Q3(b)]

ANS : The technological development has been so rapid in the field of IT that the development did not stop after the design of wireless communication and related services. The standardization looked ahead towards performing commerce and trade in the virtual world with the use of various technologies available.

The world is fast moving towards Information Age wherein almost all the activities would be performed in the cyber space. This cyber era is poised to change the life style of every individual including day-to-day activities, the way people think and live. The age-old definitions of various entities as well as sentiments related to numerous issues are likely to get effected.

Electronic commerce is one of the foremost field that would be straightaway be redefined to suit the needs of the world. This field is relatively very new and good amount of development has already taken place with the deployment of certain e-commerce based protocols such as Agora, Millicent, etc.

Agora : Agora is a simple and inexpensive web protocol for electronic commerce. The feature that makes the protocol most attractive is that it supports high-volume of transactions with low incurred cost. It has the following properties:

Minimal: The incurred cost of Agora transactions is close to free Web browsing, where cost is determined by the number of messages.

Distributed: Since Agora is fully distributed, traders and merchants can permit customers without access to a central authority. It becomes possible for the customers to purchase from any merchant provided that they have valid accounts.

On-line arbitration: It is obvious that there arise a number of disputes in trade and commerce. With this property, an on-line arbitrator can settle certain customer/ merchant disputes.

The Millicent Protocol : Just as Agora, the Millicent is also a secure protocol for carrying out inexpensive electronic commerce and trading over the Internet. As the name indicates, this protocol was designed to handle purchases and other transactions costing less than a cent.

This protocol is based on decentralized validation of electronic cash at the vendor's server, and that too without incurring any additional processing for encryption, or communication delays or costs, etc. The greatest application has been from the brokers for taking care of operations during scrip fluctuations. This helps the brokers to check frauds including forgery and double spending. Most notable point is that this protocol is vendor specific.

There are a number of other existing and proposed protocols for electronic commerce that support e-commerce for higher denominations (i.e. of values more than $1 to over and above, such as those from DigiCash, Open Market, CyberCash, First Virtual, and NetBill.

The concept of accounts for carrying out transactions is not new in India as Internet users, credit cards as well as telephone users have account with the concerned offices that maintain proper account of usage, authenticity of user as well as transactions, provision of additional value added features, and many more. The customers are billed according the usage monthly or any other method that suits them well. But the concept of a protocol in lines with the Millicent is yet to make opening in India.

MilliCent reduces the overhead of managing accounts by the following ways:

✓ Communication costs are greatly reduced by verifying the scrip locally at the vendor's site since there are almost no MilliCent-specific communication costs for a normal transaction. Moreover, no centralized server for account management or authentication is required.

✓ Brokers handling all accounts and billing related activities further reduce the accounting costs. After the customer opens an account with a specific broker; it becomes the responsibility of the broker to maintain and manage the accounts.

✓ In normal practice especially in the account-based schemes, the vendor maintains the account whereas in MilliCent, the customer himself maintains the account.

MilliCent assumes a triangular trust relationships among the three entities of the system consisting of customers, brokers and vendors. In trustworthiness, brokers are assumed to be on the top followed by vendors and finally the customers. The only time customers need to be trusted is when they lodge complaint about services related problems.

Even though certain security measures are provided, it would be interesting to note that this protocol offers almost no security. Anyone can intercept the scrip with little effort use the change of scrip value. From the vendors' side there is absolutely no risk since a digital signature prevents the customer from changing and manipulating with the scrip value.

The following three activities make fraud from brokers' side unprofitable:

✓ It is possible for the customer and vendor software to independently check the scrip and maintain account balances, so any fraud by the broker can be detected instantaneously.

✓ Usually customers do not keep large scripts at any one time thereby the broker may have to perform a number of fraudulent transactions in order to make even a little profit.

✓ With fraudulent transactions, the reputation of a broker would quite obviously be at stake.

A good broker would attracting more customers and would work for increasing the customer base. It is very clear that a broker would quickly lose the entire business and reputation if any customer has trouble with the broker.

Most of the vendor fraud consists of not providing desired goods for valid scrip. The customers will lodge complaint to their broker, and in turn the brokers may drop vendors against whom a number of complaints has been lodged. This kind of third party evaluation also helps in policing on one hand and good vendor rating on the other hand.

There are three types of MilliCent Protocols with the "Scrip" as the basis of a all other protocols:

✓ "scrip in the clear" is considered the simplest and most efficient protocol. It is the basis for the other two protocols, but it may not be practicable as it is highly insecure

✓ "private and secure", offers good enhancement of security and privacy over the earlier, but it is expensive

✓ "secure without encryption", is a mix of the above two wherein security restrictions are available, but it also looks for privacy versus efficiency.

This protocol can be straightaway be implemented for simple transactions involving articles like those in print and information services that will be available in an online format – journals, articles, magazines, newspapers, encyclopedias, newsletters, and databases. It can be also be used to take care of purchase-selling of general items and essential commodities of use in day-to-day life.

Q16. What is secure electronic transaction protocol?

ANS : Secure Electronic Transactions (SET) Protocol : The SET based purely on the science of cryptography that speaks of encoding and decoding messages for communication. This science is not new to us rather it has been in use since the evolution of human. Preserving the secrecy of transactions through strong encryption algorithms, especially for applications like the military, trade and banking has been described infinite number of times in the history books. There has been tremendous advance in the field of encryption with the advancement in computing and mathematics.

Secure Electronic Transactions (SET) is a protocol developed jointly by Visa and MasterCard, involving other computing majors like IBM. SET is an open standard for protecting the privacy, and ensuring the authenticity, of electronic transactions, especially applicable to the banking sector where the transactions could be in terms of few cents to multi-million dollars.

Since the customer/consumer as well as the traders interest has to be protected, methods such as privacy, authentication, encryption, etc. evolved to provide back to back support for carrying out electronic commerce over the Internet.

The SET protocol is based on two different encryption and one authentication mechanisms. SET uses symmetric encryption using the well known Data Encryption Standard (DES) and asymmetric or public-key encryption to transmit keys for DES transactions. The DES algorithm has been used since the 1970's with advancements that took place later reduced the key size from the original 128-bits to 56 bits. The SET protocol also uses another popular encryption algorithm RSA known after the three scientists who developed it.

The difficulty with 56 bit key is that it can be easily cracked in few hours and with an investment of less than a million dollars, which is in reach of big companies. And this is possible for almost all security and military organizations as well. However, the algorithms and mechanism is proving to be highly useful for banking and commerce applications.

The customer can keep surfing through web sites and get every information about the products or services of the company, but when it comes to the money transactions, SET comes into play. The customer who intends to place order for certain products on a company makes payment through credit card number that is authenticated by a third party usually called as authenticator or intermediately. The third party do not carryout any financial dealing but their responsibility is only to authenticate the transactions. They in-turn communicate with the banks or vendors and also enable debiting of the amount from the customers' bank account and immediately crediting into the vendors' account. Any failures to do so is also suitably handled during the process and it is ensured that the transaction takes place smoothly and without any fraud.

Q17. List and explain at least five Intranet Browsers. **[DEC02;Q6(a)]**

ANS : Netscape Navigator : For many people, Netscape Navigator from Netscape Communications is still the browser to beat. Version 3 increases the capabilities of this market leader in almost every direction and effectively defines the industry de facto standards for many important features, including HTML, graphics, plug-ins, and JavaScript support, JavaScript gives HTML content developers a mechanism they can use to embed small but useful programs into their Web pages; they can also use JavaScript to manipulate programmable elements of the Netscape browser and the document that it displays.

In theory, the World Wide Web is based on open standards accessible to all; the facts, as you might reasonably expect, are somewhat different. It turns out that much of the material you see on the Web is actually quite craftily tailored to take advantage of little known and often poorly documented features of the Netscape Navigator.

One area in which Navigator can easily hold its own against Microsoft's Internet Explorer is in terms of speed. Navigator 3 is faster at rendering HTML pages in almost all cases than is Internet Explorer, and the difference is not only apparent over dial-up connections but also over local area networks and intranets. Navigator is also faster a reloading a page from its cache.

Because of Netscape's platform-independent philosophy, you can find a version for almost all the popular operating systems, including Unix and the Macintosh. If your company is interested in linking several of these systems together using an intranet, Netscape Navigator is still the best choice; Microsoft cannot match this range, at least not yet.

Microsoft Internet Explorer : With Internet Explorer, Microsoft finds itself in the somewhat unusual position of challenger rather than champion. Netscape Navigator has huge lead in terms of market share, and Microsoft is pulling out all the stops in an attempt to catch up.

Internet Explorer version 3, included with any new Microsoft operating system, goes a long way toward catching up with Netscape Navigator. Microsoft has done a good job of cloning all the important features found in Navigator, including support for Netscape plug-ins, support for JavaScript (which Microsoft insists on calling Jscript), and support for Navigator objects.

But Internet Explorer is much more than a simpleminded clone, and some people will say that the IE-the first truly competitive version of Microsoft's browser-has passed Navigator in one or two crucial areas, including operating system integration and support for both ActiveX as well as Java.

Some of the ground-breaking new features from Microsoft include ActiveX, a direct descendant of Microsoft's OCX control standard that is based on Microsoft's Component Object Model (COM). ActiveX began life as a 32-bit Windows-only project, but Recent developments to reach out to the Unix and Macintosh communities reflect Microsoft's attempts to broaden its appeal. Currently, between 1000 and 1500 ActiveX controls are available, and many third-party programming tools support the ActiveX standard.

Mosaic in a Box : Mosaic in a Box for Windows 95 from CompuServe Internet Division (previously known as Spry) has unfortunately not kept up with up with the changes made in the other popular browsers and lacks support for elements such as tables and frames. Currently Spry offers a replacement based on Microsoft's Internet Explorer called SpryNet Starter Kit. For more information, see http : / / www . spry . com / soft center / nettools / internet / browsers / index . html

NCSA Mosaic : Mosaic from the National Center for Supercomputing Applications (NCSA) tends to lag slightly behind the leading browsers. The NCSA likes to wait until a proposed new feature becomes well established before implementing it. The original Mosaic browser is now at version 3, and you can find out more at

http : // www. ncsa. uiuc.edu / SDG / SDGIntro . html

Netcom : Formerly called Net Cruiser, NET Complete, a customized software system containing Navigator or IE, is only available to owners of a Netcom Internet account. For details, see

http : / / www. netcom.com / Software / index . html

Spyglass Mosaic : Known previously as Spyglass Enhanced Mosaic, this capable browser is only sold directly to other companies for use in their products; you can't buy it directly. Companies such as O'Reilly & Associates, Open Text, AB Software, and Data storm all bundle this browser with their products. For Information, see

http : / / www . spyglass . com / products / mosaic /

Q18. What are the differences between Microsoft's Internet Explorer and Netscape Navigator?

Refer to Chap-1, Q30, Page-34.

Q19. What is the process of customizing Netscape Navigator?

[JUN02Q1(b)]

ANS : The process of customizing Netscape Navigator is done through Preferences menu bar of Edit menu. This is using for make the change in default settings of Netscape navigator. When we click on preferences menu bar we get a dialog box. This dialog box divided in to two parts:

1. Category Pane

2. Details Pane:- Shows the details of selected category.

1. There is seven categories in which it can be customized according to requirements.

(a)Appearance : This category uses to change the appearance of Navigator. We can specify that on startup which service will launch and also how toolbars icon will display. There are also two submenus in this option.

Namely :

(i)Fonts **:** Used for specifying the name of font, size and also whether document specified font override or not.

(ii)Colors **:** For specify the color of fonts, background, color, visited links and unvisited links and also override document color or not.

(b) Navigator : Use for specify the home page location, default site name, history size, language and applications which is supported by browser.

(c) Mail and Newsgroups : Settings for Mail and Newsgroups. Setting related with identity, Mail servers, Newsgroup Servers, Addressing, Messages, and Configuration about window layout, Disc space etc.

(d) Roaming Access.

(e) Composer : General setting for authoring web pages.

(f) Offline : Choose the startup mode of navigator either in online or in offline modes and also make setting which kind of messages will download in which order.

Q20. How to Select the Best Browser for Your Organization? [JUN02;Q5(a)]

#: What are different browsers available in the market? How do you select one of them for your organization. [DEC01;Q2(a)]

ANS : Selecting the best browser for Internet depends on how we use the Internet within the organisation and the technical level of the people involved.

If we are using all the latest technology, we will need the browser that supports all of those technologies.

Following are the ways for selecting the best browser for intranet.

❖ Evaluate the technical needs of Intrenet: For example, if will need to download PDF (Acrobat) files and need to read these files extensively, w need a browser with PDF support. In this case the browser itself will open PDF files for read!!!

❖ Evaluate technical knowledge of users: If the users don't know how to use the facilities of the browser, which can be learned. But what if the users' level isn't enough to learn those things?

❖ Evaluate browser those meet the needs: Selected browses should be compared and final decisions should be taken.

❖ Publish policy on Intranet so that your users will understand the reasons for the choice.

❖ Go back to the top and repeat the process as often as necessary.

If all user use same browser, network bandwidth, and viewing capabilities, we can develop content to take advantage of this environment much more easily.

Q21. Write a short note on the basics of a Web Browser. [JUN02;Q2]

ANS : A web browser-usually just called a browser-is the application you use to access any HTML-based information . That information-usually called pages-can be on the Internet or on an intranet. A browser is able to interpret HTML coding, called styles or tags, and use those codes to format and lay out the information in a window for you to see. In addition to HTML, browsers can interpret and display information stored in other formats, including sounds, graphics, Adobe Acrobat files, and Shockwave files. Some file types are readable byte the browser itself. Others rely on a helper application. Some helper applications run alongside the browser and some inside the main browser window. Those that run inside the browser are called *plug-ins.*

Plug-ins extended the capabilities of your browser and are usually available for free. Most plug-ins only allow you to read files-to modify them or create your own, you'll probably need to buy the plug-in vendor's authoring software.

If you're familiar with a word processor, page layout program, or graphics program, you'll quickly be able to understand how most browser functions work. One important difference between browser software and most other software is how you obtain and pay for it. Both Netscape and IE are primarily obtained by downloading the software from the Net. Currently IE is available free of charge from the Microsoft Web site. Netscape is also available in a trial version that you may download and use for free for up to 90 days, after which you pay a nominal charge.

Besides viewing Web pages, you can use your browser to access FTP, Telnet, Gopher, and e-mail and to read Usenet newsgroups. See Mastering Intranets from Sybex or your Browser's documentation for the exact procedures.

Besides viewing web pages, browsers are used to access FTP (File Transfer Protocol), Gopher, Usenet, and E-Mail.

FTP is used to transfer Files from one host to another. Gopher is obsolete now and was used before WWW arrived.

Usenet is a newsgroup on the Internet and E-Mail service is used to send and receive messages by means of SMTP (Simple Mail Transport Protocol) or POP(Post Office Protocol).

Here are few Browser Elements:

Toolbars

Icons

Menus and Dialog Boxes

Toolbars are used to make using the software easier. User can add or remove the toolbars as and when requires.

Buttons (Icons) are as a part of the Toolbar, click on the work is done!!!

Like other programs, IE and Netscape provide Menus to access some uncommon functions of the browser. If any of the options of the Menu are selected, we might get Dialog Boxs, on which we can configure specific parameters for the browser. For example, go to Tools Menu > Internet Options > Connections, Click on LAN Settings. Here we can specify IP address of the Proxy Server and the port number for the application. Number 80 is used for HTTP.

Browsers are available in various versions, currently, when this book is under construction, Microsoft has its IE version 8, known as MSN 8, default version of IE with Windows 98 is IE 4.

Browser selection is a very crucial issue and number of parameters should be considered when selecting a best browser for Intranet.

Q22. How will you use TCP/IP in an enterprise? [JUN01;Q2(a)]

ANS : One of the thorniest problems in crafting your intranet plan has to do with networking protocols and how any new additions fit into the overall corporate picture. The TCP/IP set of protocols is at the center of the intranet and must be at the center of yours. In some corporations, several protocols will be in use at the same time, and staff and machine resources will be needed to support each protocol. Many corporations will use Novell NetWare products with IPX/SPX protocols: others will use older, mainframe-based systems.

The recent releases of Microsoft's Window 95, Window NT Workstation, and Windows NT Server all contain TCP/IP, so upgrading to one of these systems can help make TCP/IP easier to deploy. These operating systems can also easily handle multiple protocols on the desktop and on the server.

Unfortunately, the cost of buying a TCP/IP package for every computer in an organization that has a large number of DOS/Windows 3.1 client computers can be quite significant, not to mention the costs of implementing the package on a slow computer that may already be at its memory and hard-disk capacity limits.

Q23. Write a brief note on the following:

ANS : (a) Host/Terminal Connections

Through Host/Terminal Connections is the simplest and cheapest type of connection to the Internet. Here, the connectivity to the Internet is in the mode where computer behaves as if it is terminal to an Internet host or server. When you use PC dial-up(also called a terminal account), your computer runs a terminal emulation program to communication with the service provider's host computer, and you ask the host computer to go out onto the Internet to do what you want to be done. In general, terminal will be remote to the host, therefore, requiring a dial-up modem to transfer information from your computer to the host and back. VSNL does provide this kind of connection.

Such connections may be well suited when you:

❖do not want to manage server by yourself

❖Want to connect from different locations using remote login facility, e.g. telnet etc.

❖Have a limited budget like home usage, or small office usage

❖Do not require constant connectivity, means you need it some times.

In this connection only the utilities offered by host are available to the user. Most of these connections do not provide any graphical interface. This machine can not exploit the multitasking features of the computer as this type of connections can perform only one type of communication at a time. Normally these shell accounts are on UNIX operation system.

(b) Individual Computer TCP/IP link

TCP and IP were developed by a Department of Defense (DOD) research project to connect a number different networks designed by different vendors into a network of networks (the "Internet"). It was initially successful because it delivered a few basic services that everyone needs (file transfer, electronic mail, remote login) across a very large number of client and server systems. Several computers in a small department can use TCP/IP (along with other protocols) on a single LAN. The IP component provides routing from the department to the enterprise network, then to regional networks, and finally to the global Internet. On the battlefield a communications network will sustain damage, so the DOD designed TCP/IP to be robust and automatically recover from any node or phone line failure. This design allows the construction of very large networks with less central management. However, because of the automatic recovery, network problems can go undiagnosed and uncorrected for long periods of time.

As with all other communications protocol, TCP/IP is composed of layers:

❖**IP** - is responsible for moving packet of data from node to node. IP forwards each packet based on a four byte destination address (the IP number). The Internet authorities assign ranges of numbers to different organizations. The organizations assign groups of their numbers to departments. IP operates on gateway machines that move data from department to organization to region and then around the world.

❖**TCP** - is responsible for verifying the correct delivery of data from client to server. Data can be lost in the intermediate network. TCP adds support to detect errors or lost data and to trigger retransmission until the data is correctly and completely received.

(c) Dial up Connection

Dial-up pertains to a telephone connection in a system of many lines shared by many users. A dial-up connection is established and maintained for limited time duration. The alternative is a dedicated connection, which is continuously in place. Dial-up lines are sometimes called switched lines and dedicated lines are called *no switched* lines. A dedicated line is often a leased line that is rented from a telephone company.

A dial-up connection can be initiated manually or automatically by your computer's modem or other device.

When you use PC dial-up (also called a terminal account), your computer runs a terminal emulation program to communicate with the service provider's host computer, and you ask the host computer to go out onto the Internet to do what you want to be done. Most providers will send and receive E-mail, transfer files from a re mote Internet computer to the host which you can then download to your local computer, and provide access to USENET (the typical bulletin boards/ newspaper/discussion groups on the Internet).

(d) Dedicated Link Connections

The most popular Internet access for companies and institutions is a dedicated phone line connecting your LAN to the Internet 24 hours a day. However, a dedicated Internet access also requires substantial initial investment in equipment. The main continuing cost is a flat monthly fee for the use of the line. It varies with line capacity, and line capacity determines how many users can connect to Internet simultaneously.

Q24. Explain the following:

ANS : (a) Web Portal : According to Doug Benzine, CUNA Service Group's director of e-commerce, "There's no one set definition of a Web portal." He states that "The field is so new that all companies involved in e-commerce still are struggling with the definition and attempting to determine what kinds of business plans even would work in an Internet environment. They're basically playing it by ear, forming the rules as they go along."

Nevertheless, portals are defined by a few key characteristics. They seem to be hot sites on the Internet that serve as "search engines or robotic Web crawlers" that categorize information into directors making sense of the vast information confusion. It assists a user searching for a particular item sifts through the endless sources of information. According to Leigh Gregg, "Today's most popular portals started as search engines, but they've extended their offerings to include e-mail, chat functions, instant messaging, and even personalized service."

An example of a web portal is famous Yahoo!. Yahoo! is a search engine that has more than 35 million registered users and hosts over 2,200 advertisers. According to MSNBC's Web site, "These companies operate from a strategy that they will continue to capture the Internet's biggest audience-the so-called "traffic." Nevertheless, as is explained in the site, since the audience isn't predictable, a web site's traffic cannot be guaranteed. The main reason for the problem is that web surfers aren't loyal to any one search engine. Web users utilize different search engines for different tasks. The majority of the major web portals service the same audience. There is no clear distinction between web portals users, says MSNBC.

@ **Portal :** A Web page that serves as a point of entry for surfers of the World Wide Web. *Note:* Most of the popular portals are designed to optimize their compatibility with one or more Web search engines. Many portals also offer value-added services such as e-mail accounts, Web page hosting, or filtered information flow, with the costs of these services being underwritten by advertising. *Loosely synonymous with* **Web-page** search engine.

(b) Mail Reflector

1. *Synonyms* e-mail exploder, **mail exploder.**

2. A program that forwards e-mail to individuals at a (usually) unchanging e-mail address, even when the individuals change Internet service providers.

@ **Mail exploder:** Part of an e-mail delivery system that allows a message to be automatically and efficiently delivered to a list of addresses, thus implementing mailing lists.

SOLVED PAPERS
CS-75

CS-75 : INTRANET ADMINISTRATION
JUNE-2001

Note : There are ***six*** *questions in this paper. Question number 1 is* ***compulsory*** *and carries 30 marks. Answer any three from the rest.*

Q1(a). What are the Hardware and Software requirements for setting up an Intranet? **[5]**

Repeated in Dec2002, Q1(a), Page no.-177.

(b) What is the process of customizing Internets Explorer? **[10]**

Refer to Chap-3, Q13, Page no.-66.

(c) What are the differences between Intranet, Internet and Local Area network.

Refer to Chap-1, Q5, Page no.-4. **[10]**

(d) How do you establish your Intranet Security Policy? **[5]**

Refer to Chap-2, Q13 , Page no.-52.

Q2(a). How will you use TCP/IP in an enterprise? **[7]**

Refer to Chap-6, Q22, Page no.-140.

(b) What is the process of forming a Project Team? What are different designations given to its team members and what are their functions? **[8]**

Refer to Ch-4, Q10, Page no.-84.

Q3. Write a short note on planning and content of an Intranet. **[15]**

Repeated in JUN 2003, Q6(b), Page no.-175.

Q4(a). What are various security threats to Intranet? How do you resolve them?

Repeated in JUN2003, Q3(b), Page no.-170. **[8]**

(b) What are the different ways of controlling access to Intranet? Explain them.

Refer to Chap-2, Q11, Page no.-51. **[7]**

Q5(a). What are different Intranet Server Softwares available in the market? How do you select one of them? **[8]**

ANS : Web server software is available for various operating System like Win NT Server, Win NT Workstation, Win 98, Machintosh, and even Win3.1.

The web server software runs on the hardware and operating system combination. Price of the software varies from free to few thousand rupees for high-end servers.

Windows based Web Servers:

❖Commerce Builder: it runs on Win 95, or Win NT. It is properly integrated with Win NT , so we don't have to create additional groups or users on Win NT. It has a built in Macro Language, which gives flexibility to connect to any ODBC data source.

❖EMWAC https: European Microsoft Win NT Academic Center runs on Win NT Server and Win NT workstation. A major drawback is it is little secured. No user accounts, passwords or directory access permissions.

❖Microsoft IIS: IIS is a powerful web server-side Java, and ISAPI applications.

❖It supports SSL, CGI.Perl, server-side Java, and ISAPI.

❖Java support, Database support like Access, SQL, Oracle, Sybase and Informix adds more functionality.

❖Peer Web Server: PWS runs with Win NT Workstation and Windows 98.It offers less functionality that IIS.

❖Netscape FastTrack Server and Netscape Enterprise Server: These were founded by Netscape Communications; are very powerful server software for the Internet.

The features includes:

❖Enhanced monitoring and logging features

❖Server-side digital certificate authentication

❖Client side authentication

❖Full text integrated search engine

❖SNMP(Simple Network Management Protocol) Support

Many other web server software includes:

❖Netscape SuitsSpot

❖Open Market Secure Web Server

❖Purveyor IntraServer

❖Website

❖Apache Web Server for Unix/Linux

❖Samba Server

Selecting the right Software is a crucial issue. Following questions should be considered:

❖Does the software have to run on specific Operating System?

What level of performance is needed?

Is price a major issue?

Is there any planning for to connect to the Internet? Is yes, there is a need for proxy server.

How to plan Intrenet? What level of security is required?

❖How much technical support is needed and what it will cost?

(b)What is the process of choosing Intranet Server Hardware? **[7]**

Refer to Chap-3, Q.2, Page no.-55.

Q6. Write short notes on the following: **[15]**

(a) RAID

Refer to Chap-4, Q. 11(i), Page no.-85.

(b) Packet Filtering

Refer to Chap-4, Q. 11(ii), Page no.-86.

(c) KSA

Refer to Chap-4, Q. 11, Page no.-87.

CS-75 : INTRANET ADMINISTRATION
DEC-2001

---

*Note : There are **six** questions in this paper. Question number **1** is **compulsory** and carries 30 marks. Answer any three from the rest.*

Q1(a). How can an Intranet save money for an organization? **[5]**
Refer to Chap-1, Q19, Page no.-22.

(b) Write a short note on the creation of a realistic Intranet plan. **[15]**
Refer to Chap-1, Q20, Page no.-23.

(c) How will you protect your Intranet from being accessed by unauthorised external people?
Repeated in JUN2002,Q4(a).
Refer to Chap-2, Q10, Page no.-50.

Q2(a). What are different browsers available in the market? How do you select one of them for your organization. **[8]**
Repeated in JUN 2002, Q5(a).
Refer to Chap-1, Q18, Page no.-22.

(b) What are different pentium based Webserver systems available? Write a short note on each of them. **[7]**
Refer to Chap-3, Q14, Page no.-70.

Q3(a). What is the process of Designing Intranet? **[5]**
Repeated in JUN 2003, Q6(b), Page no.-175.

(b) How will you calculate the cost of setting up an Intranet? Explain with example.
Repeated in DEC2002, Q1(b), Page no.-178. **[10]**

Q4(a) On what basis does any organization decides to set up an Intranet? **[10]**
Refer to Chap-4, Q6, Page no.-81.

(b) What are the most frequently asked questions about Intranet? **[5]**
Refer to Chap-1, Q22, Page no.-24.

Q5. What are various internal issues that have to be addressed while creating an Intranet business plan. Explain them. **[15]**
Refer to Chap-1, Q20, Page no.-23.

Q6. Write a short note on the following: **[15]**

(1) Servers and Security

Refer to Chap-2, Q12, Page no. 52.

(2) IP Addressing : Every computer that communicates over the Internet is assigned an IP address that uniquely identifies the device and distinguishes it from other computers on the Internet. An IP address consists of 32 bit , often shown as 4 octets of numbers from 0-255 represented in decimal form instead of binary form. For example, the IP address 168.212.226.204 in binary form is 10101000.11010100.11100010.11001100. But it is easier for us to remember decimals than it is to remember binary numbers, so we use decimals to represent the IP addresses when describing them. However, the binary number is important because that will determine which class of network the IP address belongs to. An IP address consists of two parts, one identifying the network and one identifying the node, or host. The Class of the address determines which part belongs to the network address and which part belongs to the node address. All nodes on a given network share the same network prefix but must have a unique host number. **Class A Network** — binary address start with 0, therefore the decimal number can be anywhere from 1 to 126. The first 8 bits (the first octet) identify the network and the remaining 24 bits indicate the host within the network. An example of a Class A IP address is 102.168.212.226, where "102" identifies the network and "168.212.226" identifies the host on that network. **Class B Network** — binary addresses start with 10, therefore the decimal number can be anywhere from 128 to 191. (The number 127 is reserved for loopback address and is used for internal testing on the local machine.) The first 16 bits (the first two octets) identify the network and the remaining 16 bits indicate the host within the network. An example of a Class B IP address is 168.212.226.204 where "168.212" identifies the network and "226.204" identifies the host on that network. **Class C Network**—binary addresses start with 110, therefore the decimal number can be anywhere from 192 to 223. The first 24 bits (the first three octets) identify the network and the remaining 8 bits indicate the host within the network. An example of a Class C IP address is 200.168.212.226 where "200.168.212" identifies the network and "226" identifies the host on that network. **Class D Network**—binary addresses start with 1110, therefore the decimal number can be anywhere from 224 to 239. Class D networks are used to support multicasting. **Class E Network**—binary addresses start with 1111, therefore the decimal number can be anywhere from 240 to 255. Class E networks are used for experimentation. They have never been documented or utilized in a standard way.

(3) SATAN

Refer to Chap-4, Q 12, Page-88.

CS-75 : INTRANET ADMINISTRATION
JUNE-2002

*Note : There are **six** questions in this paper. Question number **1** is **compulsory** and carries 30 marks. Answer any three from the rest.*

Q1(a). How will you ensure security of your Intranet? **[10]**

Refer to JUN 2003, Q3(b), Page no.-170.

(b). What is the process of customizing Netscape Navigator? **[10]**

ANS : The process of customizing Netscape Navigator is done through Preferences menu bar of Edit menu. This is using for make the change in default settings of Netscape navigator. When we click on preferences menu bar we get a dialog box. This dialog box divided in to two parts:

1. Category Pane
2. Details Pane:- Shows the details of selected category.

1. There is seven categories in which can be customized according to requirements.

(a) Appearance : This category uses for change the appearance of Navigator. We can specify that on startup which service (or s)will launch and also how toolbars icon will display. There are also two submenus in this option.

Namely :

(i)Fonts:- Use for specify the name of font, size and also whether document specified font override or not.

(ii)Colors:- For specify the color of fonts, background, color, visited links and unvisited links and also override document color or not.

(b) Navigator : Use for specify the home page location, default site name, history size, language and applications which is support by browser.

(c) Mail and Newsgroups : Settings for Mail and Newsgroups. Setting related with identity, Mail servers, Newsgroup Servers, Addressing, Messages, and Configuration about window layout, Disc space etc.

(d) Roaming Access.

(e) Composer : General setting for authoring web pages.

(f) Offline : Choose the startup mode of navigator either in online or in offline modes and also make setting which kind of messages will down
and in which order.

(c). What are the advantages of using Intranet? **[10]**

Refer to Chap-1, Q7, Page-6.

Q2. Write a short note on the basics of a Web Browser. **[15]**

Refer to Chap-6, Q21, Page-139.

Q3. Write a short note on planning and content of an Intranet. **[15]**

Refer to Jun-2003, Q6 (b), Page no.-175

Q4(a). How will you ensure security from external threats to an Intranet. [5]

Please refer Chapter-2, Q10, Page-50.

(b) Explain the role of an Intranet Server. [10]

Refer to Chapter-2,Q-10, Page no-51.

Q5(a). How will you select best browser for the Intranet of your organization?

[8]

Refer to Chapter-1, Q.18, Page no.-22.

(b) Distinguish between Microsoft Internet Explorer and Netscape Navigator [7]

Repeated in DEC 2002,Q6(a).

Refer to Chap-1, Q30, Page no.-34.

Q6. Write short notes on the following: [15]

(a) Windows NT

(b)SATAN

Refer to Chap-4, Q12, Page no.-88.

CS-75 : INTRANET ADMINISTRATION
DEC- 2002

*Note : There are **six** questions in this paper. Question number **1** is **compulsory** and carries 30 marks. Answer any three from the rest.*

Q1(a). What are the hardware and software requirements for setting up an Intranet? How do these requirements differ for each organization?

ANS : Hardware : An Intranet is simply a standard Wide Area Network (WAN). The use of the term Intranet recently to describe using software developed for the Internet on the company's WAN. Web servers are an example.

To setup a WAN, one will need to have some type of communications between the different sites. National ISDN, Very Small Aperture Terminal (VSAT) connectivity or a long distance Frame Relay could be the best choice. It will be essential to install a router at each site. Each router would connect back to a central site over dedicated phone lines. Note that the hardware should be configured for the following protocols/ services.

Protocol/Service	To be installed on
IP	Network
HTTP	Server
SMTP/POP3/IMAP4	Server
LDAP	Server
X509 Certificate	Server
Java	ORB
Document Server	Server

Scientists also describe how optimal performance of intranets is associated with a number of key hardware factors. In order to optimise performance, servers with fast processors and large amounts of memory are essential. They also noted how good multi-tasking and multi-threading ability is which is also crucial for most of the Web applications. In addition, sufficient memory and disk capacity at the user workstation would improve performance through increased caching. The limitation of large image files can also be considered important to improve performance, but images may be equally important to expand and illustrate data, and pages of text can be discouraging, especially in an educational context. Finally, the database itself, which forms the foundations of almost every intranet, can have a significant effect on performance.

Operating System for Server and Clients

On the Server : Since 1994, when the original pair of web servers — **NCSA HTTPd** and **CERN HTTPd**, dozens of commercial and shareware programs have been developed. While the Netscape Enterprise Server defines the commercial high end, the other is Microsoft's Internet Information Server (IIS) Netscape Enterprise Server and lightweight Fast Track Server.

On the Clients : All of the clients running popular operating systems such as Microsoft Windows, MacOS, UNIX, etc. could be used to function as backbone software for the Intranets.

Only one software is sufficient for working with the Intranet viz., the browser software that should be loaded on all the clients. This software serves as a single interface to both the Intranet as well as the Internet. At present, Microsoft Internet Explorer and Netscape Navigator both remain the top web browsers available. Apart for these, various other web browsers are also available to access the information such as NCSA Mosaic.

Language support : Intranet works on the basis of scripts written in any of the following languages, viz., SGML, HTML, DHTML, XML, ASP, CGI, Perl, UML, VRML, etc. Though almost all are variants of the basic markup language or development over it, all provide flexibility to program the needs of the organizations. It is essential to test minutely how the output looks when published on the central server, by using different browsers on different operating systems.

Some organisations need to connect various offices through their Intranet. Those organisations need to have additional hardware device like router to connect to different locations. If oganisation has great security issue, they also need to implement powerful firewall. This firewall can be software based or hardware based, depends on level of security, cost and efficiency.

The Intranet Software and Hardware requirements are a variable. As an organisation goes, we might want to add a search engine to help user find out informations quickly.

Some advanced features like Database support, logging, controlling access, Security etc. requires additional software to manage large Intranets.

If an organisation wants to provide several hundred to thousands of users getting connected to the Intrenet server and running applications, use remote login to connect, e-mail distribution software, or serve multimedia - video and audio, then hardware will need to be sophisticated and powerful enough to meet the peak-time demands that will put on the system.

(b) Write a short note on the cost factor involved in setting up an Intranet.

ANS : The cost of the Intranet depends on many parameters, as well as there are many variables.

If network is large, better hardware configuration is required, which results in high cost of Server itself.

For example, with 100 clients running a small Intranet requires one server with 100 MHz, 16 MB of RAM and 2 GB of IDE Hard Disk.

But if Intranet is having 1000 clients, with Database Support, it requires 3 Servers of 200 MHz, 32 MB of RAM and 4.3 GB Hard Disk with Disk Mirroring implemented (it means 6 Hard Disks are required). 2 servers will be used to share the overall load of the Intranet and hence the cost of the Intranet increases in this regard.

Similarly, if your Intranet requires software for Database, for Server side Scripting (ASP, ISAPI or any other), all this counts in terms of high cost as well as high resources in terms of Hardware.

Following are some approximate prices for Intranet Tools:
Server (133 MHz Pentium, 32 MB RAM, two 2 GB Hard Drives – Rs.2 Lacs to 3 Lacs.
Network Server – Rs. 1 Lac
Communications Server – Rs. 50000
Editors – Rs.10000
Search Engine – Rs. 0
Database – Rs. 1 to 2 Lacs
Proxy Server – Rs. 50000
Other Software – Rs. 100000
Client Hardware – Rs. 25000 per terminal
So, if we calculate for an Enterprise Network, it requires approximately Rs. 7 lacs just for setting up Intranet.

(c) What are the different buttons available in the Netscape Tool Bar? Explain each of them.
Refer to Chap-5, Q10, Page-111.

Q2(a). "Hardware needs for the Intranet are to be accessed based on the current business requirements. It will be premature to think about future business needs." Do you agree with this statement? Justify with an example.
Refer to Chap-3, Q12, Page-66.

(b) "When planning for an Intranet, there is no need to plan an Intranet Security Policy in advance." Do you agree with this statement? Explain.

ANS : "When planning for an Intranet, there is no need to plan an Intranet Security policy in advance." I am not agree with this statement.

As we know that anything done without planning is dangerous. No matter what we are doing. So, of you believe in above sentence, you are leaving yourself and your business on the luck! And nobody is going to leave his or her business on luck specially when it comes on security.

Security is one of the most critical issues that must be addressed before implementation. When you have implemented your Intranet without thinking of security, you will face strange problems. You will find that outsiders are trying and also gaining access to resources of your Intranet. It depends on you and your business that what contents are you publishing on your Intranet. If those contents are valuable for you, you can imagine the event when you will come to know that you valuable data has been stolen.

It is really foolishness to not to think about security. Even when organizations are planning and implementing maximum security that they can implement, they are not secure. They are always on the prying eyes of hackers, crackers and viruses. Then how will you ensure that your Intranet will be protected from these hackers, crackers and viruses? You will also face the problems from your employees as they might accidentally delete some documents, or maliciously destroy some or all your contents. And you have no way to identify the cause damage!

So, you must always think of security before implementing your Intranet.

Q3(a). How will you test your Intranet? Will you initially test it with a small number of users or a large number of users? Justify your answer. Also, explain the testing process step-wise.

ANS : Testing is a set of activities that can be planned in advance and conducted systematically. When we design a intranet system then we should test it before sending it for practical usage. Testing is a very essential part for any system and for Intranet it is also very important. In a Intranet system hundred or thousands of users are working together and all the work is related to one-another. If due to any problem, system fails then work become held. It will effect the efficiency of the system also. While testing a Intranet all the system which will be connected to a intranet system should be checked individually. Their compatibility should be checked. The hardware components which makes possible to connect system with each other should be checked. The browser compatibility features should be checked. In the Intranet system many users will work simultaneously so it should be checked that there should not be collision .

If data will lost, then it can be recovered or not, it should be checked.

Recovery testing checks whether recovering is automatic of manual.

Security testing should be done for better security.

<u>It is advisable to test the Intranet in two steps:</u>

- As it is under development mode, test it with a small number of users.
- But as one of the few module is up and ready to run, it should be tested with the load actually it is suppose to carry.

(b) "Intranet Planning is more than money." Do you agree with this statement? Explain your answer.

ANS : Yes, when you start planning your intranet, the first question you'll probably hear is "How much will this cost?" While costs are a major factor in deciding both the scope of your intranet and even whether or not to have one, the bottom-line setup costs aren't as important as deciding your overall return from your intranet. Your overall return factors in several cost elements including:

Cost of setup, including hardware and software

Cost of converting existing information for use on your intranet

Cost of creating new information

Cost of designing and programming for intranet applications

Cost of training

And while that quickly add up to a significant sum, you'll see that costs are reduced in other areas including:

Printing : Materials will still need to be printed, but users will only have to print the relevant information as needed.

Communication : Communication is improved. The way an organization communicated its message is vital to the success of the organization. Communicating with both the public and staff can change the way people see your company and your product. Employees often complain about poor communication; they feel left out of the loop or like they're working on a project that has no focus or purpose. Using an intranet, people can share information in an easy-to-use format that removes many organization constraints.

Technology : Skills are enhanced. Your staff and organization benefit by keeping employee's skills current. Intranets are an easy way to teach new skills or upgrade existing skills. The Web and the Internet are hot topics in the newspaper and on television and your employees have a natural curiosity to see what the type is about. You can use this natural curiosity to encourage your users do some simple self-training.

As you plan your intranet, keep in mind the costs are only one aspect of the plan and that costs will change as you assess your audience, intranet goals, content requirements resources (hardware, software, and human), and security issues.

Q4(a). What are the differences between a Home Page and a Web Page? List atleast 10 features of a Home Page.

ANS : Many browsers have a Home button on their toolbars and this yet another meaning to a web browser, "Home is that place to which you return when you get lost or tired of browsing – your browser Home page. It is a place to get your bearing before venturing out again.

A good Home page for your browser is one that loads quickly, contains information that you want to check regularly (such as headlines in your area of interest or a local weather forecast) and links to a wide variety of other pages. (So that you can quickly go where you want). Portals make good browser Home page and most let you customise the feature to display. By default, Internet Explorers Home button points to Microsoft portal site.

Web Page : Your browser's start page is the web page that the browser loads when you open the browser without requesting a specific page. Internet explorer automatically starts with the browser home page, but navigator allows the start page to be different from the browser Home page. You ISP's installation program may change your start page to the IPS's Home page on the web.

You can create a simple web page by using front page express, composer or any other web page editor Internet explorer provides many print options–

- Printing all documents linked to current page.
- Printing a list of links contained on current page.

Ten Features of Home Page

The ten features of Home Page are following:

1. Home page is the page you return to when you click home button on toolbar.

2. It is the page opens when you open Internet explorer.

3. "Home" is that place to which you return when you get lost or tired of browsing.

4. Home Page loads quickly and contains information that is of daily use.

5. The main (or starting) page of web site.

6. It is used to refer to a browser's start page.

7. It links to a wide variety of other pages.

8. Home Page is like magazine cover or the front page of newspaper.

9. It act as an introduction to the site, explaining its purpose and describing the information found on other pages throughout the site.

10. Home page act as the table of contents for the rest of the site.

(b) What are the various steps involved in the design of Intranet's structure? Explain each step with example.

Refer to Chap- 1, Q-9, Page-10.

5(a). What is a Firewall? How will you configure it?

ANS : For intranet developers, restricting access of unauthorized users to the web site has been the greatest challenge. In addition to preventing external users, a watchful eye on the users within the company may also have to be maintained. There are various tools to provide protection against unwanted intruders into the corporate wide networks, but the most popular amidst all security measures is the firewall.

The simplest way to restrict the users to peek inside the internals of the web site is to use firewalls, where the information cannot be seen or accessed from the Internet at large. Simple firewalls consist of software that prevents access to internal networks from the Internet. While general traffic such as email is allowed in to the mail server, programs such as FTP clients, telnet users or search engine queries cannot access machines beyond the safety premises of the firewall.

Firewalls also offer additional protection to local users who like to browse or surf out from the intranet to the Internet, by acting as proxy to obtain web pages so that the name and IP number of machines on the network are not revealed to other web sites that the users visit. Not revealing the IP address would help preventing hackers from knowing about the details of the structure of the intranet.

While firewall remains the basic foundation of Internet and intranet security, for many users getting into the corporate intranet would require increasing levels of technology. The intranet technology would need to be expanded beyond those physically present on the same intranet from time to time.

Though there exist a number of definitions of firewall, in simplest terms it can be defined as "a mechanism used to protect a trusted network from an entrusted network". It can also be defined as "A firewall is a system, or group of systems that enforce an access control policy between two networks, and thus should be viewed as an implementation of policy". From the above two definitions, it can be understood that a firewall is only as good as the security policy it supports.

It should be very clear right from the beginning that a firewall is not simply for protecting a corporate network from unauthorized external access via the Internet, but it can also be used internally to prevent unauthorized access to a particular subnet, workgroup or LAN within a corporate network.

Three broad categories of firewall configuration are:

Packet-filtering : Such low-level filters pass or drop packets based on their source or destination addresses or ports. Routers already provide this level of filtering. Such a firewall is easy and inexpensive to set up, but its capabilities are quite limited. A packet-filtering firewall can fail if its table of valid and invalid addresses is incorrect. Such a firewall is also susceptible to address spoofing (making a filter believe that a packet is coming from a different address).

Application-filtering : These higher level filters screen traffic involving specific applications or services (for example ftp or e-mail). The advantage of such a filter is that it allows for more sophisticated evaluation and authentication measures. For example, such a firewall could be designed to protect against a gopher server moving a file onto a machine or to check for an attack entering with an application. The large number of possibilities-for example, an application calling another application-makes it very difficult to build in safeguards against every possible attack.

Circuit-level : Such filter looks not only at source and destination addresses but also at the circuits (temporary paths) that have been established for a connection. Such circuits are established-for example, when using TCP (Transport Control Protocol)-during an initial handshaking session. Such a filter can detect address-spoofing, for example, because such a misleading packet would have no way of getting the circuit information that is set up during the handshaking. While very effective for certain protocols, circuit filters are of limited use with connectionless protocols (such as UDP), which may send packets over various paths.

(b) What are the differences between Firewall and Proxy Server? How will you configure your Proxy Server?

ANS :

1. A proxy server, sometimes referred to as an application gateway or forwarder, is an application that mediates between two networks segments. While a firewall is a network component that provides a security barrier between networks segments.

2. A proxy does not Route any traffic while Firewall route traffic.

3. Proxy provides logging and statistics on network usage while these types of information not provide by Firewall.

4. Proxy Server are application specific while Firewall type is spread across four areas:

Embedded

Software

Hardware

Application

Proxy receives the request, it identifies what type of service the internal host is trying to access and then forward request to related application but in Firewall, there are no such type of activities performed.

Configuring Your Proxy Server : Proxy servers can be configured with what are commonly referred to as bad addresses. A bad address is not really "bad"- it's one of the special IP addresses that aren't routable through the Internet. These addresses are commonly used to configure networks behind a proxy firewall server. One common set of bad addresses is the 10.0.0.0 class A network. InterNIC (the organization that licenses domain names and maintains unique addresses for all computers connected to the Internet) has set aside this entire block of addresses for testing purposes, which you could certainly use behind a proxy server. Here is an example of how to do this:

1. Set up your proxy server hardware with two network cards. One network card has a real, routable Internet address of something like 204.176.47.2, and the other uses a bad address of 10.0.0.1.

2. Plug the 204.176,47.2 network card into your Internet router connection, and plug the 10.0.0.1 network card into your local network. This is the first step in creating the isolated barrier between the Internet and your network.

3. Now, configure each workstation with a unique address on the 10.0.0.0 network, using a gateway address of 10.0.0.1 or the server's bad address.

4. Configure each application that understands and uses a proxy server with the proxy server address of the server, 1.0.0.0.1.

That's it! Now when the client software needs to access the Internet, the requests are sent to the network card in the server that has the address 10.0.0.1, at which point the proxy server actually forwards the request to the destination after including its own valid address of 204.176.47.2. When the request is returned to the server, the proxy server returns it to the originating workstation.

For workstation to use a proxy server, however, it must have software that knows how to talk to proxy server. The Netscape Navigator and Microsoft Internet Explorer Web browsers can both use a proxy server, as can many other e-mail, news, FTP, Web, and Telnet software packages. We'll look at how to set up both of these browsers with a proxy server in Chapter 8, "installing Intranet Software."

Q6(a). What are the differences between Microsoft's Internet Explorer and Netscape Navigator?

Refer to Chap-1, Q30, Page-34.

(b) List and explain atleast five Intranet Browsers.

ANS : Netscape Navigator : For many people, Netscape Navigator from Netscape Communications effectively defines the industry de facto standards for many important features, including HTML, graphics, plug-ins, and JavaScript support, JavaScript gives HTML content developers a mechanism they can use to embed small but useful programs into their Web pages; they can also use JavaScript to manipulate programmable elements of the Netscape browser and the document that it displays.

In theory, the World Wide Web is based on open standards accessible to all; the facts, as you might reasonably expect, are somewhat different. It turns out that much of the material you see on the Web is actually quite craftily tailored to take advantage of little known and often poorly documented features of the Netscape Navigator.

One area in which Navigator can easily hold its own against Microsoft's Internet Explorer is in terms of speed. Navigator 3 is faster at rendering HTML pages in almost all cases than is Internet Explorer, and the difference is not only apparent over dial-up connections but also over local area networks and intranets. Navigator is also faster a reloading a page from its cache.

Because of Netscape's platform-independent philosophy, you can find a version for almost all the popular operating systems, including Unix and the Macintosh. If your company is interested in linking several of these systems together using an intranet, Netscape Navigator is still the best choice.

Microsoft Internet Explorer : Internet Explorer version 3, included with any new Microsoft operating system, goes a long way toward catching up with Netscape Navigator. Microsoft has done a good job of cloning all the important features found in Navigator, including support for Netscape plug-ins, support for JavaScript (which Microsoft insists on calling Jscript), and support for Navigator objects.

But Internet Explorer is much more than a simple minded clone, and some people will say that the IE-the first truly competitive version of Microsoft's browser-has passed Navigator in one or two crucial areas, including operating system integration and support for both ActiveX as well as Java.

Some of the ground-breaking new features from Microsoft include ActiveX, a direct descendant of Microsoft's OCX control standard that is based on Microsoft's Component Object Model (COM). ActiveX began life as a 32-bit Windows-only project, but Recent developments to reach out to the Unix and Macintosh communities reflect Microsoft's attempts to broaden its appeal. Currently, thousands of ActiveX controls are available, and many third-party programming tools support the ActiveX standard.

Mosaic in a Box : Mosaic in a Box for Windows 95 from CompuServe Internet Division (previously known as Spry) has unfortunately not kept up with up with the changes made in the other popular browsers and lacks support for elements such as tables and frames. Currently Spry offers a replacement based on Microsoft's Internet Explorer called SpryNet Starter Kit. For more information, see

http : / / www . spry . com / soft center / nettools / internet / browsers / index . html

NCSA Mosaic : Mosaic from the National Center for Supercomputing Applications (NCSA) tends to lag slightly behind the leading browsers. The NCSA likes to wait until a proposed new feature becomes well established before implementing it. The original Mosaic browser is now at version 3, and you can find out more at

http : // www. ncsa. uiuc.edu / SDG / SDGIntro . html

Netcom : Formerly called Net Cruiser, NET Complete, a customized software system containing Navigator or IE, is only available to owners of a Netcom Internet account. For details, see

http : / / www. netcom.com / Software / index . html

Spyglass Mosaic : Known previously as Spyglass Enhanced Mosaic, this capable browser is only sold directly to other companies for use in their products; you can't buy it directly. Companies such as O'Reilly & Associates, Open Text, AB Software, and Data storm all bundle this browser with their products. For Information, see

http : / / www . spyglass . com / products / mosaic /

CS-75 : INTRANET ADMINISTRATION
JUNE -2003

*Note : There are **six** questions in this paper. Question number 1 is **compulsory** and carries 30 marks. Answer any three from the rest.*

Q1(a). How are corporations using Intranets? Explain with examples. [15]

ANS : An Intranet is an internal company network that uses the Internet standards of HTML (Hyper Text Markup Language) and HTTP (Hyper Text Transfer Protocol) and the TCP/IP (Transmission Control Protocol/Internet Protocol) communications protocol along with a graphical web browser to support business applications and provide departmental, interdepartmental, and countrywide communications solutions.

The ways in which an intranet can be used by industries, corporations, or organizations are as numerous and as varied as the enterprises themselves.

Here are few examples of several companies using intranet.

1. At Genetech pharmaceutical company, employees can access the employee directory, find out how to get business cards, read company announcements, get information on research seminars, building facilities, commuting options, benefits and child care.

2. At Compaq Computers intranet is used by the employees to reallocate investments in their 401(k) plans.

3. Silicon Graphics uses their intranet to connect several departmental intranets, allowing them to share data with other groups in the organization and to network with departments who may not have an on-site office but can dial in conferencing, or other tasks.

4. At HBO, researchers, programmers, and high level executives use an intranet to access a database that contains information on every movie ever made, whether it's on videocassette, and when it's scheduled to air for the next two years.

Thus intranet is a source of information for the employees of an organization regarding the various activities of organizations. Employees of one department can have knowledge regarding the other departments with the help of intranet. Suppose an employee of the accounts department want to know recent details of the production now he won't be needing to go to the production department and get details from there instead he has to just get connected to the intranet and get details from there. Information regarding the company seminars, entertainment programmes, and announcements all are available on intranet.

(b) Is it Intranet or Internet that is right for your business? How will you decide it? [15]

ANS : Generally an Intranet is different from an Internet in the following ways:

i. Intranet is a network within the organization whereas Internet is a worldwide network.

ii. Intranet has access to Internet but not vice- versa.

Once the difference has been defined, the immediate possible question in everyone's mind would be: Is an intranet faster than getting data over the internet? The answer to this would be mix of features of local area network (LAN) as well as that of Internet. Clear answer depends on the possible ways of connecting the client to the network that could be as follows:

If the network is totally contained within a LAN, then it will get LAN speeds. I.e. the web server is connected via LAN to the client computer. Following are some factors that must be considered whenever the organization needs to decide on internet or intranet.

(a) When you are trying to create a system that will be used for internal communication within the organization, intranet is best for that situation. This will allows only internal peoples to access and share information with each other. External peoples cannot access anything from your intranet. But, it requires security settings on your intranet server so that outsider cannot enter your network.

(b) If you are planning to provide up-to-date product information to all of you business branches only, then also intranet is good for your organization. Since only your authorized branches can access your intranet, they are safe too.

(c) If your business required more interactions with your customers, then internet is good option here. Doing so will enable customers to access your web site from internet and can show whatever you offer to them anytime, anywhere .

(d) If you want to improve interaction and communication between departments of your organization, you need to set up an intranet. But, if you want to get customer advice and feedback, you need internet to serve better for your purpose.

(e) If you are developing or creating some products and want to advertise about them, then internet is certainly the solution. Because public can only access your public web site not the private intranet.

(f) If you need a paperless office, so that every work of your office flow in electronic form, you need and intranet for the private intranet.

At last, we can conclude that anything that an organization wants to make accessible to public must be put on the internet. While anything that is going to be used by the persons of organization must be kept on the intranet.

Q2(a). How will you estimate your Intranet work requirements? **[7]**

ANS : An Intranet requirement estimate on the basis of its functions, load of traffic, tpe services provides b it to internal as well as external uses. Intranet reflects the working structure of its oganisation. To run an Intranet smoothly and perfectly the requirement estimate on the following three points:

(1) Hardware Requirements.

(2) Software Requirements.

(3) Use Training Requirements.

After all formality we first decide which kind of hardware components are required for Server as well as Client. In this we identify the configuration of server and client PCs. This is very critical. Because any oganisation is not making frequently change in the hardware of PCs. It also depends upon which OS you are going to use within Intranet on Client side and on Server side. Some about each components of PCs like

(a) Speed of CPU.

(b) Capacity of RAM.

(c) Capacity of HDD.

(d) Other Secondary storage device or Backup Device Etc.

In the software requirements we decide about OS for Serve as well as for Client PCs. To run an Intranet than we have must use Win NT or Win 2000 family OS. If use Linux, then this site not work properly because Linux does not support this. It also depend on hardware configuration so when selecting OS its obvious that you must aware with its minimum hardware requirements.

The User(s) training is plays major role in success of any Intranet. Because inefficiently user(s) never avail the feature of Intranet. So it's must that you provide proper training to user(s).

(b) What a short note on the following: [8]

(i) Intergraph Inter Serve Wed 30

(ii) Pacific Internet Web Cubes

ANS : ***(i) Intergraph Inter Serve Wed 30*** **:** The system can be configured in way a customer may want and can be upgraded as his Internet needs grow.

Intergraph Internet web 30 is a Web server system offered by the Intergraph corporation. It has been declared as the Best Web server system for 2003 by the computer experts.

The Web 30 is one in the series of web servers offered by Intergraph corpn. Although the system is in a desktop case these machines ran the entire Oscar site and still supported several million hits per day with video downloads, audio clips, and graphics.

The bare specifications of the system are 256 MB RAM and 20 GB of disk. It has three PCI and two ISA slots and Ethernet controllers on the networking side, the units built in interface is 10 MB. Intergraph recommends that 10 MB Fast Ethernet is fine for any Internet connection up through a T 1.

Full multimedia authoring system: The web 30 goes beyond server functionality. It can be a full multimedia authoring system thanks to its workstation style audio and graphics capabilities.

The web 30 server has audio features like 16-bit CD quality stereo sound and come with a multimedia keyboard with built in amplifies-microphone. It offers excellent 2D/3D rendering applications. It can thus be used from content authoring to serve pages.

The web 30 has been found to be a solid performance as a web server and as a workstation.

(ii) Pacific Internet web cub **:**

The pacific Internet web Cub is a tool for managers of large size Websites. The cube provides a three dimensional model for classification of the issues and tasks of managing a distributed website. It focuses on the issues relating to large site management rather than those of content development

It is also a Pentium based Internet web server. It has 180MHz Pentium processor with 32MB of RAM. Backup of server data is taken every evening with different type of backup mechanism. It means, server will come operational in some hours after failure. This server runs on caldera Linux and uses Apache web server Window NT and Microsoft's Internet Information Server is also available as an alternative.

Q3(a). What is RAID? Explain it. Can you replace SLED with RAID? [7]

Refer to Chap-4, Q11, Page-85.

(b) What are the different security techniques available for establishing effective security measures? Explain them. [8]

ANS : The Intranet requires security because of :

- Hardware causes
- Software causes
- Information

Hardware can be stolen, tampered by frustrated employee, destruction of the resources.

Whereas software causes include deletion or theft of a program, corruption of a program, change in program code and thus making it malfunctioning, bugs in the software or virus attack.

Third component of the system liable to be attacked in data which is so important and crucial for an organization/company.

Security should be provided in order to make an Intranet functioning successfully and reliably. There are many ways through which Intranet can be made secured and reliable. Those are :

(1) Certificates

(2) Firewalls

(3) Encryption/Decryption methods

(4) Multiple Level Security

(5) SOCKS

Certificates :

Digital Certificates or Digital Signatures are used for securing e-mails, money transactions. Certificates includes a Public Key which is assigned to the users and is required to be sent when user wants to make any transaction. The certificate acts as an evidence of the user's digital identity.

Digital certificates provide excellent means of controlling and monitoring access to the Intranets. The certificate itself acts as a token for access control. The certificate could contain a series of digits and alphabets combined together.

Firewalls :

Firewalls provide security by following:

(1) Packet Filtering

(2) Application Gateways for restricting applications

(3) Proxy Servers

Proxy servers are used to isolate IP address range from the Internet. One interface of the Proxy Server is connected to the Internet, whose IP address is known to the

Internet (Outside World). This IP address is also called Live IP address.

Whereas other interface is connected to the Intranet where all hosts are assigned unique IP addresses which are independent of the Internet (hidden to the Internet).

Firewalls can also be implemented on the proxy server either to give access or deny access based upon Applications or IP addresses.

NAT performs mapping between IP range of the Internet and IP addresses (resources such as web sites) of the Internet.

Encryption :

Public Key Solutions : The Public Key Solutions involves a third party provider which provides key and checks for the authentication based upon the key.

The Architecture is shown in the figure below:

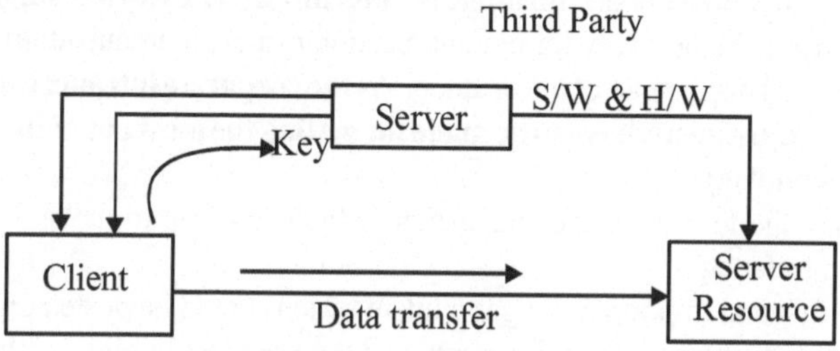

(-Public Key Authentication)

As soon as the third party server authenticates the key, data transmission takes place between the stations on the physical path.

Secured Sockets Layer (SSL) : It is used to secure the web server for authentication of the Users who want to access the resource. Resource requested may be HTTP or FTP or any other protocol supported by the Web Server.

Today, almost all commercial web sites are using SSL to ensure the authenticity of the server and integrity of the data delivered to web site users.

Virtual private Network (VPN) : If an Intranet is extended between two geographically separated locations, VPN is used to secure Intranet data.

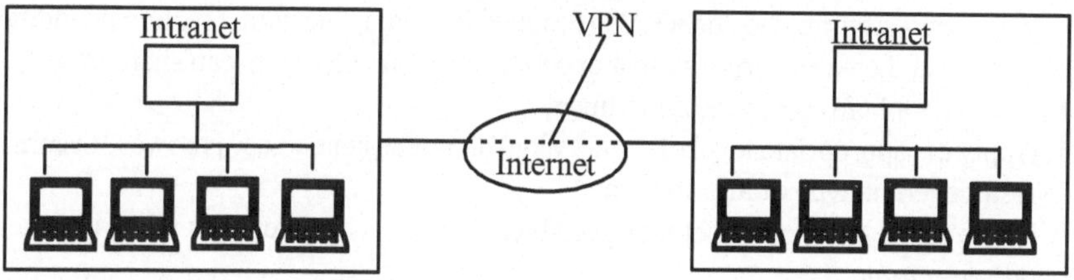

As shown in the diagram, when two geographically separated Intranets are connected using the Internet, VPN is established between the two to secure data of the Intranets. VPN uses IP addresses to differentiate between Internet and Intranet users.

Multiple Level Security : Multiple level security involves more than one type of security mechanisms implemented to secure data. It can be combination of any two described above.

Interaction : Where there are means of communication between the members of the company interaction becomes very easy. Hence the flow of information and responses are the loveliest thing present on the intranet. There can be a section on intranet where different employees will place their poems, stories, jokes and funny things which can be read by all just bringing the talent of the employees to the notice of others and making everybody gain something from it.

Discussion, scheduling, bulletin boards, desktop conferencing, doc management are few of the other benefits which are provided by the intranet.

Q4(a). List and explain various functions of an Intranet.

Refer to Chap-1, Q6, Page-5.

(b) How can you make maximum usage of your Intranet? List your suggestions. [8]

ANS : Intranet is the best way for communication inside an organization. It helps to give an individual many types of information. **As the corporate intranet evolves, many changes and adjustments have to be made for getting the most out of this young and emerging technology.**

Following are the few steps and suggestions which can help to make the maximum usage of the Intranet:

1. The very first and important thing is content which should be posted on the intranet site. Let us make the people in the company who are most familiar with the content recommend it and help the management in giving the final judgement. Those who are dealing with the contents are the best to know the value of the information they control.

2. Second step is the planning of the material which will be posted along with the justification of posting it. Whatever information is posted on the intranet should be for the benefit of the organization so there should be some solid reason for posting it.

3. It should be make sure that all material is easily identifiable. We should also add contact information like address, phone numbers and email of the person who has provided information. This will help the users of the Intranet to contact directly for any suggestion or any more information.

4. It is always advisable to add a FAQ (Frequently Asked Questions) section or adding a question and answer forum so that experienced group members can share information with people from outside department.

5. Apply the appropriate level of security and do not hesitate to use password security to restrict certain type of information.

6. Try to make the site as useful as possible. Add links to other sites when it makes good sense to do it.

7. Add buttons and links for the navigation purpose to other departments.

8. In fact in the homepage always try to add links and buttons for navigating to other departments, important information in a position where everybody can see it.

9. Keep announcements, important information and news of the organization where everybody can see it easily. It should not happen that information goes hidden.

10. Help others to help themselves. Post hints and tips that other departments can use when creating their sites.

The corporate intranet is after all only a tool and it's only one of the many ways that can be used to improve internal communications. Creating an effective intranet certainly requires careful planning and a clear understanding of the corporate goals involved, but it can make corporate communications across the entire enterprise cost effective and efficient.

Q5(a). There is a need for user training as browsers change. But, what should technical support staff do in the face of constantly changing browsers? [7]

ANS : Training is an essential part of the intranet setup. Technical staff should always make out schedules and keep lectures, seminars to train the employees to use intranet and in short we can say to use Web Browsers.

But in this face of constantly changing Web Browsers it is a big question for the Technical staff to continuously upgrade employees.

Also on the web while planning contents place training materials, tutorials and informational links to the site to help users answer their own questions and train themselves.

All the new features which have come in the new browsers can be placed on the site only as a new page which will help the employee self train themselves.

A form that asks the users to ask questions and make suggestions can give feed-back on what users want and need to know.

Then a seminar or lectures can be arranged on the new features especially giving those features more emphasize which users have written on the feedback form.

Thus with less effort it will help the employees and technical staff to overcome this difficulty.

(b) What are the various tasks associated with maintaining an Intranet? Explain them. [8]

ANS : Maintenance is one of the most important step in managing or building intranet. Once the Intranet site is running, it has to be properly maintained. The maintenance of the intranet site includes keeping the system free from the errors and bugs, adding new functionality, migrating from old software to new software, migrating from old technology to new technology.

There are many threats to the computer system like threats to Hardware, software and information. The maintenance section of an organization should be capable enough of handling all the threats and keeping intranet free from it.

Threats to Hardware :

The first component of computer system is the hardware used. Some of the common threats to the hardware are:

1. Theft of a computer, printer or other resource.

2. Tampering by a disgruntled employee who interferes with dip switches or cuts a cable.

3. Destruction of resources by fire, flood or electrical power surges. Don't forget those sprinklers in the ceiling which can put out hundreds of gallons of water in a minute; most of the damage to computer systems comes not from the fire but from the water used to put out the fire.

Threats to Software :

The second component of your system is software. Threats to software include the following:

1. Deletion of a program, either by accident or by malicious intent.
2. Theft of a program by one of your users.
3. Corruption of a program, caused either by a hardware failure or by a virus.
4. Bugs in the software. Their effect sometime is immediate and catastrophic and sometimes they come in limelight years later.

Threat to Information :

The third component of your system is the data and data files used by the corporation. Threats to information can include:

1. Deletion of a file or files
2. Corruption, caused either by hardware problems or by a bug in the software
3. Theft of company data files.

Maintenance of the intranet means to deal all the above threats and keep the system free from it. For hardware solution system should be checked continuously, if any hazards occur like fire etc. cease fire should be kept in handy position, electrical power switches, cables and surges should be maintained.

For software solution system and information security should be kept high. For most confidential systems even password protection should be incorporated. For removing bugs continuous testing of the intranet system should be done. Backup should be taken regularly. Anti virus programs should be run continuously.

Q6(a). How are companies using Intranet to distribute information in faster and less expensive ways to communicate with employees in a more timely manner? Give examples. **[7]**

ANS : One of the primary reasons for which Intranet was thought of was to use it as a means of faster communication within an organization having presence at many locations.

Keeping everyone in a corporation up to date about the latest news in the corporation is a never-ending, often impossible task. It is particularly difficult in large corporations with many departments and divisions that are geographically separated.

There are many ways that Intranet can be used to solve the problem and keep everybody in an organization informed about corporate news. Companies can post their company's newsletter on Intranet Web pages. Because Web pages can be updated much more quickly than newsletters printed on papers also these(which are published on intranet) are less inexpensive too.

Intranets can also be used to deliver literally up-to the minute news flashes. The Java language can be used to create news tickers that can flash the breaking news across the top of the newsletter home page. Intranet broadcast technologies can be used that will send out a news flash to everyone connected to the Internet that will run on top of whatever actions they are currently running. And electronic mail can be broadcasted to everyone inside a company with important news, such as press releases, or news about quarterly sales or any other sudden decision which may effect employees at large.

Intranet can also deliver more in-depth information in more involving ways. Audio and video clips can be sent via streaming technologies, so that people can listen to interviews with corporate executives, or see news reports about the company.

A new off-line news readers technology can also be used. With it, corporate news and news from outside world can be delivered to everybody on an Intranet. Off-line news readers work on a client serve model. An off-line news server carries the latest corporate news. Only certain people are allowed to update news on this server. Since people on Intranet may want to read news about the outside word also, the server gets this news from Internet and distributes it on the Intranet.

This news flashes, web page based newsletters, emails, Java tickers, news alerts, and off-line news reader are some of the ways of distributing information to employees in a faster yet less expensive ways.

Here are some examples of how several companies are using an intranet to distribute information in faster and less expensive ways, to communicate with employees in a more timely manner and in general, to run their businesses more effectively:

1. Cargill International employs more than 70,000 people engaged in commodities trading around the world. Even with only 25 percent of company materials on its intranet, Cargill estimates it save tens of thousands of dollars annually by posting electronic updates rather than printing, binding and distributing them through traditional means.

2. Eli Lily, a pharmaceutical firm gives its 30,700 employees the ability to easily access timely information and thus a significant competitive advantage. By using internal web site, employees can find more information in one day than they could find out in several days in the library.

3. McDonnell Douglas distributes some 4 million pages of documentation every year and estimates that distributing this information in paper form costs twice a much as disseminating it via Web. Because manuals for an aircraft can run from 45,000 to 50,000 pages, McDonnell Douglas is experimenting with placing this information on its intranet so it can be accessed by maintenance crews and onboard pilots using Pentium PCs.

(b) What are the four basic steps of your Intranet project? Explain them. [8]

ANS : The four basic steps of the Intranet project are Planning, Constructing (Content), Implementing and Maintaining. Each step is followed by the other.

Following parameters are to be considered when planning your own Intranet:

- **What is the purpose**: One need to make sure that why I want to have an Intranet?
- **Advantages**: What advantages I am going to get if I am replacing my LAN with the Intranet?
- **Save Money**: Does an Intranet save money for me?
- **Security**: What sort of security I need to implement for my Intranet?
- **Software required**: What software do I require to build Intranet I want.
- Hardware should not be forgotten.
- What is going to be on my Intranet? That is content. Content is again a crucial issue.

The purpose of the Internet is simple. It is to corporate all the advantages of the

Internet protocols and technologies which are not possible with LAN.

One need to make sure the security level required and the budget which can be spend for implementing security. Both the things need to be balanced in order to get proper security model for Intranet.

The software required depends upon the field of the company. There is variety of software available which can be used or which is supported by the Intranet protocol stack (TCP/IP protocol stack). To get start with the Intranet, following softwares are required:

- Web Server Software
- HTML authoring Tool
- Browser
- TCP/IP based network

Selection of Hardware is to be done again with the Software being used and Software requirement. For example, an Internet with 1000 clients requires 256 MB of memory and the same server uses Oracle as Back-End tool, which requires additional 256 MB of RAM. Memory requirements increases as number of hosts of the Intranet increases.

Content of the Intranet :

The content that is going to be put on Intranet must serve purpose. One needs to make sure that whatever is going to be put on Intranet is worth or not.

Moreover, good design of the content includes structure as well as appearance. The design, which is created, should reflect the mission defined while planning the Intranet.

Creating each page : Once content is available, it is time to convert the material to a form suitable for display.

It is needed to decide what percentage of existing material can be used and who will be responsible for converting that information.

Testing : Once the content is formatted, test your pages and then test them again!!!! It is a sort of feedback of content. That whatever is worked out really works nicely or not.

Part of content plan should include a test plan detailing:

- What should be tested?
- Who will perform the tests?
- What to do if there are problems?
- When to do retest?

Tracking results and taking feedback : Once Intranet is up and running, emails and comments will start coming. We have to get ready to deal with these comments in an effective manner.

A typical Intranet site may include following Heads as content :

- News
- Organizations under us
- References, Tools & Utilities
- Feedback
- About Us
- Contact Us
- Search
- Go to Home on each
- Go to specific page (when required)

CS-75 : INTRANET ADMINISTRATION
December-2003

Note : There are ***six*** *questions in this paper. Question no. 1 is* ***compulsory*** *and carries 30 marks. Answer any three from the rest.*

Q1(a). Write a short note on the way intranets are being used in various organizations.

ANS : Following are the ways in which Intranets are being used in organizations :

1) Communication
2) Database
3) Email
4) Information
5) Interaction
6) Doc management
7) Bulletin Boards
8) Publishing
9) Discussion
10) Scheduling
11) Desktop conferencing etc.

Communication : Better communication is achieved. Communicating with both the public and staff can change the way people see the company and the product. Employees generally complain about communication, but now cannot. Using the Intranet, they share information very easily.

Database : All the records of an organization is kept in the form of database. It makes the querying, selecting very easy, fast and effective. A lot of filework is reduced. And hence saving of money, time and labor.

E-mail : Used for sending E-mails in or outside the organization. It helps to update the site with the help of suggestions. And increase the information of the employees if they mail any information regarding any difficulty. It helps to increase the communication between the employees and hence better working environment, healthy atmosphere.

Information : Intranet is a source of information for the employees of an organization regarding the organizations. Employees of one department can have knowledge regarding the other departments with the help of intranet. Suppose an employee of the accounts department want to know recent details of the production now he need not to go to the production department and get details from there instead he has to just get connected to the intranet and get details from there. Information regarding the company seminars, entertainment programmes, and announcements all are available on intranet.

Interaction : Faster flow of information and responses are the loveliest thing present on the intranet.

There can be a section on intranet where different employees will place their poems, stories, jokes and funny things which can be read by all just bringing the talent of the employees to the notice of others and making everybody gain something from it.

Discussion, scheduling, bulletin boards, desktop conferencing, doc management are few of the other ways in which intranet is used by the different organizations.

(b) What is the process of customizing Internet Explorer ?

Refer to Chap-3, Q13, Page no.-66.

Q2(a). How can Intranet save money/make money for an organization ?

Refer to Chap-1, Q19, Page no.-22.

(b) What software is needed to set up an intranet ? Also explain the functionality of each software.

Refer to Chap-1, Q11, Page no.-13.

Q3(a). What are the internal issues that are to be addressed before setting up an intranet ? Explain them.

Repeated in Dec 2001, Q5.

Refer to Chap-1, Q20, Page no.-23.

(b) Write a short note on the cost that will be incurred in setting up an Intranet.

Refer to Dec2002, Q1(b), Page no.-178.

Q4(a). What is the process of testing an Intranet ?

Refer to Dec2002, Q3(a), Page no.-180.

(b) How do you develop content for the Intranet ?

ANS : Developing content for the Intranet is very important task. The content which is going to be put on Intranet must serve purpose. One needs to make sure that whatever is going to be put on Intranet is worth or not.

Moreover, good design of content includes structure as well as appearance.

The design which is created should reflect the mission defined while planning the Intranet.

Creating Each Page :

* Once content is available, it is time to convert the material to a form suitable for display.

* It is needed to decide what percentage of existing material can be used and who will be responsible for converting that information.

Testing :

Once the content is formatted, test your pages, and then test them again!!! It is a sort of feedback of content. That whatever is worked out really works nicely or not.

Part of Content plan should include a test plan detailing :

- What should be tested.
- Who will perform the tests.
- What to do if there are problems.

- When to do retest.

Tracking Results and Taking Feedback : Once intranet is up and running, emails and comments will start coming. We have to get ready to deal with these comments in an effective manner.

A typical Intranet site may include following Heads as content:

- News
- Organizations under us
- References, Tools & Utilities
- Feedback
- About Us
- Contact Us
- Search
- Go to Home on each
- Go to specific page (when required)
- Discussion Forum
- Chat Rooms for interaction among professionals / employees

Q5(a). How can you securely configure your Intranet Server ?

ANS : The Intranet server lies inside the firewall and serves clients on the local network. All those services, like mail and file and print, which handle user data and are potential security hazards if exposed to the Internet, are hosted on the Intranet server and are protected behind the firewall. It also makes sense to run services like DHCP and Web proxy on the Intranet server as they are of use only to the LAN they serve.

Unlike the gateway server, the Intranet server should be a fairly powerful machine depending on the number of users who will use its services. For the moment, we'll bunch all the services on a single machine, which is also typical for most small- to medium-sized environments.

Wherever possible, we've tried to implement access control and authentication to reduce abuses. As per our plan of action, the following services will be set up on the Intranet box.

User authentication : All user account management is to be done on the Intranet server using standard Linux tools like useradd, userdel, and passwd. Services like POP, IMAP, proxy, etc, will refer to the flat files (/etc/passwd) for authentication.

Internal DNS : Unlike external DNS, internal DNS will be set up in such a way that it will provide name service for our zone pcquest.com. All hosts inside the LAN will use this server for name resolution. If the internal DNS server receives queries for hosts outside the local domain, it will use the DNS service running on the gateway server as a forwarder.

DHCP : DHCP (Dynamic Host Configuration Protocol) allows for dynamic allocation of network settings to both Windows and Linux clients.

Mail : Here, we'll walk through a typical mail setup using Sendmail for your domain. Dial-up and leased line setups will also be discussed with SMTP relay and spam control, and users will have the choice of using POP3 or IMAP for sending and receiving mail.

Web proxy : How do you share a choked dial-up link among your bandwidth-hungry users? Squid is a very powerful and industrial-strength proxy server, which can do wonders on a saturated link. Squid configuration is discussed with emphasis on access control and authentication.

File and print : Samba is an NT-compatible file and print server for Unix. It can do most of the things an NT server can do and is very robust and stable. Samba is an ideal replacement for NT on most small- and medium-sized networks.

The install : For your convenience, we've provided a 'PCQ Intranet Server' install option on the installation CD, which will install all the necessary packages for setting up the Intranet server.

(b) What are the external threats for an Intranet ? How do you handle them ?

Refer to Jun 2003, Q3(b), Page no-176.

Q6. Write a short note on the following :

(a) Windows NT

Refer to Chap-4, Q12, Page no-89

(b) Unix Servers

Some people use a UNIX computer to connect the LAN to the Internet. The advantage is that UNIX interfaces easily with Internet. UNIX server is a computer which serves / manages the intranet of the organisation, through UNIX operating system installed on it. Also the type of hardware platform for running the WAP usually consists of a Unix server and other networking devices. Most operators use a Unix platform rather than the Windows NT or other such operating systems. Red Hat Linux made its name as a server. As a workstation, Red Hat Linux is easier to install, use, and support than ever before. Because Red Hat Linux is flexible, it plays well with others.

UNIX server's technical options can be configured, including the number of maximum simultaneous requests, listen-queue size, and DNS usage. And all the routine activities can be performed on the UNIX server easily, which are given below:

(i) Enabling Domain Name System lookups : The server can be configured to use Domain Name System (DNS) lookups during normal operation.

(ii) Configuring listen-queue size : The listen-queue size is a socket-level parameter that specifies the number of incoming connections the system will accept for that socket. The default setting is 128 incoming connections.

(iii) Configuring MIME types

(iv) Changing the server's user account

(v) Changing the server name

(vi) Changing the server binding address

(vii) Customizing error responses

(viii) Setting up the response

Etc., UNIX server provide higher security as their counterparts. So, it has become a viable solutions for the companies, which requires high security.

(c) Pacific Internet Web Cube

Refer to June 2003, Q2(b), Page-175.

Special Term-End Examination
June-2004
CS-75 : INTRANET ADMINISTRATION

***Note :** There are **six** questions in this paper. Question number **1** is **compulsory** and carries 30 marks. Answer any three from the rest.*

Q1(a). Discuss the various application areas of Intranet.

ANS : The uses of an Intranet are only limited by imagination. Some of the larger sectors where Intranet can be easily and successfully implemented are as follows:

Education Sector
- ❖Universities
- ❖Colleges
- ❖Institutes

Industry Sector
- ❖Small and large scale manufacturing
- ❖Automation and control

Service Sector
- ❖Hotel
- ❖Tourism
- ❖Travel
- ❖Transportation
- ❖Communication

Research & Development
- ❖Laboratories
- ❖Organizations
- ❖Space

Govt. Sector
- ❖Ministries
- ❖Departments
- ❖States
- ❖Law & order

The following is a partial list of many potential uses of the Intranet, both commonly used and not so commonly used.

Company Documents
- ❖Manuals
- ❖Building Maps
- ❖Airport Directions to other Company locations
- ❖Approved Vendors list
- ❖Procedures library
- ❖Product Manuals
- ❖Daily Bulletins
- ❖History graphs
- ❖Knowledge Base

- ❖Competition products, news and web sites

Customer related

- ❖Controlled Responses
- ❖Feedback Forum
- ❖Company Bulletin Boards
- ❖Company Store
- ❖News Flashes
- ❖Supplies Ordering
- ❖Database queries

General Administration and Management

- ❖Department Budgets
- ❖Departmental FAQs (Frequently Asked Questions)
- ❖Employee Attendance
- ❖Intercompany chatting
- ❖Internal postings
- ❖Employee Orientation
- ❖Online Collaboration Projects
- ❖Organizational Charts
- ❖Security Policies
- ❖Trend Graphs
- ❖Equipment checkouts

Training

- ❖Employee Proficiency Training
- ❖Training Materials
- ❖Video Training

Coordination and control

- ❖Form routing
- ❖Forms Library
- ❖Help Desk submission forms

Meetings related

- ❖Meeting minutes
- ❖Meeting schedules
- ❖Online Meetings
- ❖Meeting Room schedules

(b) List and explain factors which contribute to the selection of computing infrastructure for setting up an intranet.

ANS : There are many primary and secondary factors on which selection of computing infrastructure for an intranet depends. Primarily infrastructure consists of hardware and software. Now the question arises which hardware to choose from, the hardware selection depends on number of factors :

(i) Processing Speed which further depends on the type of activity you want to perform through your intranet, and software you want to install on the systems. E.g. if you need to design graphics or to process highly complex numerical data then you need to install better processing speed in your infrastructure. **(ii) Storage** also depends on the type of activity like graphics need high storage devices, simple data entry work need low capacity storage devices. As images occupy large amount of space due to different colors in the pictures.

(iii) Number of Terminals which depends on the number of users. More the user more will be the terminals.

Scientists also describe how optimal performance of intranets is associated with a number of key hardware factors. In order to optimise performance, servers with fast processors and large amounts of memory are essential. They also noted how good multi-tasking and multi-threading ability is which is also crucial for most of the Web applications. In addition, sufficient memory and disk capacity at the user workstation would improve performance through increased caching. The limitation of large image files can also be considered important to improve performance, but images may be equally important to expand and illustrate data, and pages of text can be discouraging, especially in an educational context. Finally, the database itself, which forms the foundations of almost every intranet, can have a significant effect on performance.

Now the software selection also depends on the activities. Different types of software are available for different tasks. E.g. if you want to do graphics related work then you need image editing tool like Photoshop, CorelDraw etc. And for word processing you need MS-Word, other freeware word processors available on Internet.

Operating System for Server and Clients

On the Server : Since 1994, when the original pair of web servers — **NCSA HTTPd** and **CERN HTTPd**, dozens of commercial and shareware programs have been developed. While the Netscape Enterprise Server defines the commercial high end, the other is Microsoft's Internet Information Server (IIS) Netscape Enterprise Server and lightweight Fast Track Server.

On the Clients : All of the clients running popular operating systems such as Microsoft Windows, MacOS, UNIX, etc. could be used to function as backbone software for the Intranets.

Only one software is sufficient for working with the Intranet viz., the browser software that should be loaded on all the clients. This software serves as a single interface to both the Intranet as well as the Internet. At present, Microsoft Internet Explorer and Netscape Navigator both remain the top web browsers available. Apart for these, various other web browsers are also available to access the information such as NCSA Mosaic.

Language support : Intranet works on the basis of scripts written in any of the following languages, viz., SGML, HTML, DHTML, XML, ASP, CGI, Perl, UML, VRML, etc. Though almost all are variants of the basic markup language or development over it, all provide flexibility to program the needs of the organizations. It is essential to test minutely how the output looks when published on the central server, by using different browsers on different operating systems.

Some organisations need to connect various offices through their Intranet. Those organisations need to have additional hardware device like router to connect to different locations. If oganisation has great security issue, they also need to implement powerful firewall. This firewall can be software based or hardware based, depends on level of security, cost and efficiency.

The Intranet Software and Hardware equipments are available. As an organisation grows, we might want to add a search engine to help user find out information quickly.

Some advanced features like Database support, logging, controlling access, Security etc. requires additional software to manage large Intranets.

If an organisation wants to provide several hundred to thousands of users getting connected to the Intranet server and running applications, use remote login to connect, e-mail distribution software, or serve multimedia - video and audio, then hardware will need to be sophisticated and powerful enough to meet the peak-time demands that will put on the system.

Selection of computing infrastructure also depends on the various functions performed by the intranet in an organization like

1. Communication
2. Database
3. Email
4. Information
5. Interaction
6. Doc management
7. Bulletin Boards
8. Publishing
9. Discussion
10. Scheduling
11. Desktop conferencing

result due to stop which further results in less to the organisation.

(c) List various security concerns and threats for an Intranet. List the various encryption and decryption methods.

ANS : The Intranet requires security because of :

- Hardware causes
- Software causes
- Information

Hardware can be stolen, tampered by frustrated employee, destruction of the resources. Whereas software causes include deletion or theft of a program, corruption of a program, change in program code and thus making it malfunctioning, bugs in the software or virus attack.

Third component of the system liable to be attacked in data which is so important and crucial for an organization/company.

Security should be provided in order to make an Intranet functioning successfully and reliably. There are many ways through which Intranet can be made secured and reliable. Those are :

(1) Certificates
(2) Firewalls
(3) Encryption/Decryption methods
(4) Multiple Level Security
(5) SOCKS

Certificates : Digital Certificates or Digital Signatures are used for securing e-mails, money transactions. Certificates includes a Public Key which is assigned to the users and is required to be sent when user wants to make any transaction. The certificate acts as an evidence of the user's digital identity.

Digital certificates provide excellent means of controlling and monitoring access to the Intranet. The certificate itself acts as a token for access control. The certificate could contain a series of digits and alphabets combined together.

Firewalls : Firewalls provide security by following:

(1) Packet Filtering
(2) Application Gateways for restricting applications
(3) Proxy Servers

Proxy servers are used to isolate IP address range from the Internet. One interface of the Proxy Server is connected to the Internet, whose IP address is known to the Internet (Outside World). This IP address is also called Live IP address.

Whereas other interface is connected to the Intranet where all hosts are assigned unique IP addresses which are independent of the Internet (hidden to the Internet). Firewalls can also be implemented on the proxy server either to give access or deny access based upon Applications or IP addresses.

Encryption :

Public Key Solutions : The Public Key Solutions involves a third party provider which provides key and checks for the authentication based upon the key.

The Architecture is shown in the figure below:

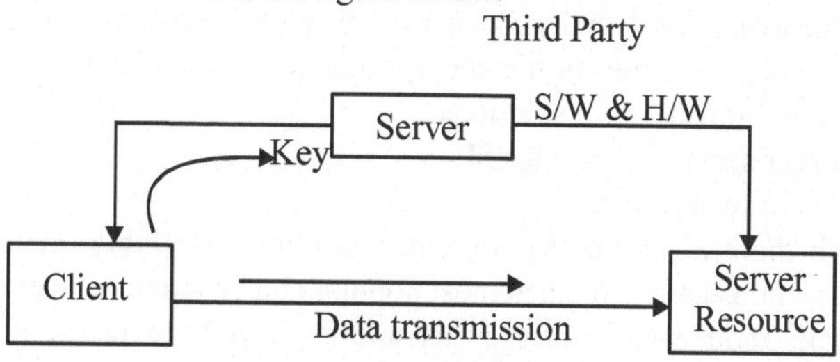

(-Public Key Authentication)

As soon as the third party server authenticates the key, data transmission takes place between the stations on the physical path.

Secured Sockets Layer (SSL) : It is used to secure the web server for authentication of the Users who want to access the resource. Resource requested may be HTTP or FTP or any other protocol supported by the Web Server.

Today, almost all commercial web sites are using SSL to ensure the authenticity of the server and integrity of the data delivered to web site users.

Virtual private Network (VPN) : If an Intranet is extended between two geographically separated locations, VPN is used to secure Intranet data.

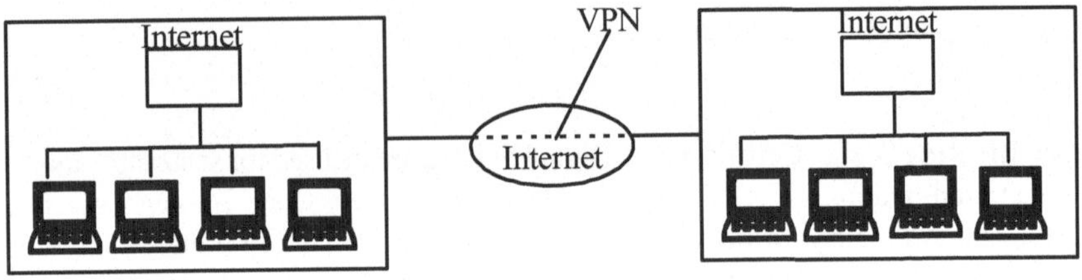

As shown in the diagram, when two geographically separated Intranets are connected using the Internet, VPN is established between the two to secure data of the Intranets. VPN uses IP addresses to differentiate between Internet and Intranet users.

Multiple Level Security : Multiple level security involves more than one type of security mechanisms implemented to secure data. It can be combination of any two described above.

SOCKS : Different types of security can be implemented to secure data. Now these different types of security works at different layers of OSI reference model.

SOCKS works at Transport Layer of OSI and it allows TCP application to access firewalls in a secured and controlled manner.

There are number of products based on SOCKS specifications, latest version is SOCKS 5.

SOCKS implementation requires a change to all existing client-server based software so that all of them use the SOCKS library. This process is known as socksifying".

Encryption and Decryption Methods : One of the best method of ensuring security is to change the form of communication. Let the messages be encoded in such a pattern that it becomes almost impossible to decode for other while the actual user should be able to decode with the use of a simple certificate or key. There are three well known implementations of the encryption/decryption methods:

- ✓ Public key infrastructure solutions
- ✓ Web server security through SSL
- ✓ Virtual private networks

Even though there are a number of other solutions available, the encryption/decryption methods have remained most popular and economical in contrast to the others. Details about each of the security solution have been discussed in detail in the following paragraphs.

Public key infrastructure solutions : The use of public-key based security systems requires great attention and due care in design and management of security features.

The security of entire system is dependent on the security of the key since it is the key that will be used for signing certificates of various messages and documents. This is done at the top of the public key infrastructure also commonly called the root. The encryption and decryption is done by specialized hardware.

Usually, all the keys used for accessing the server are held at a secret location in the primary memory of the server. This area or location is highly prone to attacks (for example, in a server core memory dump). It is obvious that a higher degree of protection is required for this target location.

Specialized hardware such as protected memory or cryptographic memory module for storing and protecting the keys proves to be a good solution. The keys are stored in a highly encrypted format. When loaded for signing, the keys are decrypted using complex encryption/decryption algorithms and loaded into the memory of the secure server, which then performs all the signing operations required on behalf of the server. It should be noted that the keys are never displayed in their unencrypted form to the server or any other user, so even if an intruder manages to access the network, the keys remains safe.

Physical security of the cryptographic modules is also built in order to provide total security of the whole system and protect from unauthorized tampering or any kind of manipulation. The physical security is ensured by use of advanced manufacturing technology wherein strong systems are fabricated to protect the sophisticated security hardware.

Since digital certificates are highly dependent on hardware computations, it is essential that mechanisms are evolved to increase the speed of computing by various means such as parallel processing, provision of additional processors, separate hardware for protection, etc. Assume that a number of users log on to the server, then in such an event it is sure to face a bottleneck at the security gate since it would take considerable time in processing encryption/decryption of the keys or certificates. Nowadays, in order to reduce this kind of difficulty, a separate server called firewall server is placed in front of the main server. Any one willing to access the main server has to get through this gate.

Web server security through SSL : As it is well known that the Intranets and extranets are purely based on use of powerful web servers to deliver information to the users, the username/ password authentication pair has been a highly popular method for preventing access to the web servers. Problem arises with use such pairs when these keys are sent in the form of character/text strings, which are prone to be intercepted, read and converted with simple tools.

A significant enhancement was achieved when communications between the user and the server was sent in encrypted form and later decrypted at the other end. The enhancement went step by step and today it has stood as one of the most secured and popular method of secured communication called the Secure Sockets Layer (SSL). Today, almost all commercial web sites are using SSL to ensure or guarantee the authenticity of the server and integrity of the data delivered to web site users. SSL has become fundamental to the spread of Internet community, and commerce and trade over Internet. Over years, the spread of its use for an increasing range of transactions across the Internet has gone manifold.

Finally, it should be noted that by default most SSL implementations on web servers do not support or authenticate the client web browser. Therefore, SSL is at present best suited to the largely anonymous requirements of retailing and definitely requires lot of enhancements to actually pickup worldwide.

Virtual private networks (VPN) : In order to encrypt/decrypt all the communication network traffic that passes through the Internet or intranet, a VPN uses software or hardware. This kind of implementation is considered the best when limited access to an intranet is needed, for example, when two branches of the same company want to use the same information, or suppliers and customers trying to hook up their supply chains. Best example is that of Maruti Udyog Limited that uses a similar kind of solution.

The greatest disadvantage of a VPN implementation is its non-flexibility to accept unknown locations. VPN works extremely well for two fixed known points, but less well suitable the needs of groups of users and situation becomes worse if they are from unknown locations.

Implementation using the combination of a public key infrastructure, secure web server and virtual private network technologies is considered the most powerful solution for data security. The addition of suitable physical security solutions such as cryptographic keys can further ensure that the security is perfect as well as robust.

(d) Explain the different techniques of Database connectivity.

ANS : Basic connectivity : A number of database management systems are available today such as the Oracle, Sybase, Ingress, Gupta's SQL Base, etc.

Most of the databases that are used to store massive data for use through Internet deploy Relational Database Management System (RDBMS) designed for PC class hardware. They are also available in both server (workgroup) and local engine (stand-alone) configurations, and are usually bundled with the power of Structured Query Language (SQL), transaction processing, and distributed processing for building business applications. By supporting client/server architecture, these software achieve a higher level of scalability, which makes them suitable for a wide range of applications; from a stand-alone, single-user environment to a multi-user workgroup environment.

To build the client side of applications, developers use various tools. Some of the popular software development environments include Visual Basic, C/C++, Power Builder, Java, Delphi, etc. It must be ensured that the databases can connect to these programming languages, or in other words, these database management systems should support these languages by being backend support.

Middleware support : All the connectivity interfaces related tools come under the category of middleware. Middleware provides the link for data exchange between the different points of processing in a distributed application. In an intranet application, the points of processing are the database software, the server software and the client application.

Many of the popular databases also provide support of and to the middleware and consequently, the term middleware has become lesser known. Though software like the ASP, Perl, etc. have got wide popularity, a lot of work is being done to integrate a number of features of the traditional software made available in the middleware also.

During processing of any request, the client/server architecture is maintained and the database and client applications are processed separately even though running on the same platform or machine. For certain middleware, a connectivity interface is not required to support data exchange between the application and middleware or database.

Open Database Connectivity (ODBC) : It happens that in addition to conventional or most popular database management systems, many companies go for proprietary software creating problem for themselves as well as for the clients. It is strongly recommended that companies should use that particular DBMS software which is most popular and widely used.

If this is not followed, a number of difficulties arise with database connectivity and the company may have to shell out enormous amount of money on obtaining proper connectivity tools.

It must also be ensured that whenever any DBMS or middleware is procured, all relevant database connectivity tools are also bundled. Most important of all of the connectivity tools or drivers is the ODBC, which permits connectivity to any type of database from the client application.

Many developers provide not just a simple ODBC driver, but a complete industry standard ODBC database solution for a wide range of operating systems such as Windows, Unix, Linux, MacOS, Sun Solaris, etc.

Java Database Connectivity (JDBC) :

With two different types of technologies available in the market today viz., the Windows and the Java technologies developed by the Microsoft and the Sun Microsystems respectively, it is essential for any company to ensure proper integration of the two technologies so that the customer support is ensured in spite of the technological divide.

Not just ordinary ODBC tools and drivers, it has become almost essential for the companies to obtain the JDBC drivers as well. With JDBC drivers, it would become possible to connect the Java applications with any type of databases and can query as well as update data from any data source across Intranets or the Internet.

(e) Explain the different authoring tools for creating animations on Intranet.

ANS : Authoring tools or softwares are generally used only for the final presentation. Following are the some of the packages with their features :

(i) Photoshop : Photoshop is a software which is a product of Adobe. Adobe Photoshop is an image editing software. It can be used to make layouts, editing images and creating visual effect too. Photoshop is a bitmap image software. It has great options related to masking. One can get different colour modes to work with. One can also create outwork in vector based software like illustrator & edit it out in Photoshop. Another software for graphic creation and manipulation is CorelDraw.

(ii) Sound Forge : Sound forge is a software which is used for digital sound recording and digital sound effects. This software works with sound card and one can have all the features which facilitates in manipulating sound.

(iii) 3DS Max : 3DS Max can be used extensively for 3D animation and special effects. Thus this software can be used to create 3D animation as per our story board. One can apply state of the art effects like camera, light, textures. These effects look very realistic.

(iv) Flash : Flash is a product of Macromedia. It is a vector shape animation product. It is used basically for web animation. But due to its good interactive option and compatibility it is also used in authoring. It also supports action script that gives enhance output as per requirement.

These are the softwares used apart from Authoring Softwares.

(f) How will you configure POP on Microsoft Outlook ? What are the use of POP ?

ANS : POP(also known as the incoming mail server) is the one of the important piece of information needed to configure POP mail accounts in Microsoft Outlook.

Following are the steps to configure POP :

1. Launch your MS Outlook software

2. Under the *Tools* menu, select *Accounts.*

3. Click *Add* button (located in at the top right corner).

4. From the pop-up menu that appears, select *Mail.*

5. Follow the prompts and enter the following information:

<u>Display Name.</u> Your name (i.e. - John Smith) or the name of your business.

<u>Internet E-mail Address.</u> On the page that says "Your e-mail address is the address other people use to send e-mail messages to you", select "I already have an e-mail address that I'd like to use". Beside E-mail Address, enter the e-mail address you want to use as the address outgoing mail will be from. For example, you@yourdomain.com.

<u>E-mail Server Names.</u> Where is asks *My incoming mail server is a ___ server*, select POP3. For the *Incoming mail (POP3, IMAP or HTTP server)*, enter your domain name (i.e. - yourdomain.com). For NT clients, enter mail.yourdomain.com. If your domain name has not been transferred to our servers, use the temporary address provided in your setup letter (i.e. - *some-planet.web-hosting.com*). For NT accounts, use *mailhost.web-hosting.com.*

For the *Outgoing mail (SMTP) server*, enter the SMTP server provided by your ISP (or leave this information as it is).

<u>Internet Mail Logon.</u> For the *Account name*, enter your POP account username. For the *Password*, enter your POP account password. For the *Account name*, enter your POP account username. For the *Password*, enter your POP account password. If you would like Outlook to remember your POP account password, check the *Remember password* box. If you do not save the password, you will be prompted to enter the password each time you check your mail. Make sure you leave the *Log on using SPA* box unchecked (do not check it).

<u>Leave Mail On Server.</u> The "leave mail on server" option should always be disabled. If you leave your mail on the server, you may end up with a corrupt mailbox and you may lose important mail.

6. After you have added new account, you probably would like to make it default one.

To do so, go to "Mail" tab, then select just created account, and then click "Set as

Default" button.

Uses of Post Office Protocol (POP) : A format for storing and retrieving E-mail messages used by mail servers and clients. POP works with Simple Mail Transfer Protocol (SMTP), which enables E-mail messages to be sent from one system to another. Mail servers must run both protocols to be able to receive, send, and store messages. POP functions as a holding area for E-mail messages until it is picked up by software used by the account's owner, who is verified by a login name and password, or in more secure scenarios, a certificate."

Q2(a). Why do we use proxy servers ? Explain Application Level Gateways and Circuit Level Gateways.

ANS : Proxies are store-and-forward caches. When you configure your web browser to use a proxy, it never connects to the URL. Instead, it always connects to the proxy server, and asks it to get the URL for you. Proxies can be used as a sort of firewall, because it isolates you from connecting to the Internet.

Why proxy servers are used : You can use a proxy server if you have a child and wish to restrict the sites they are viewing, you will need to make sure you get the correct type of proxy because not all proxies filter sites. You can use it to protect yourself, it can be used to hide your IP which is useful because it means hackers can not get info about you when using it. They will only get the proxy servers IP. Proxy servers are not hard to set up, no hardware or software is needed, you just need to configure your browser to connect through it.

Some ISPs (Internet Service Providers) make all their users use a proxy server, for example in the United Arab Emirates, the main ISP makes all users use a proxy server which blocks sites with unsuitable material. It does this using the meta tags in the HTML code used to make the web page. Some ISPs may give you a choice so you can use one or not. If you want to use a proxy server there are many around with different functions, you just have to get the one that suits your needs best.

Application level gateways : (also known as *application layer firewalls* and *application proxy firewalls*) are often described as third generation firewalls. They are software applications with two primary modes:

· proxy server

· proxy client

When a user on the trusted networks wishes to connect to a service on the untrusted network (say, Internet), the application is directed to the proxy server on the firewall. The proxy server effectively pretends to be the real server on the Internet. It evaluates the request and decides to permit or deny the request based on a set of rules that are managed for the individual network service.

If the request is approved, the server passes the request to the proxy client, which contacts the *real* server on the Internet. Connections from the Internet are made to the proxy client, which then passes them on to the proxy server for distribution to the *real* client. In this way, inbound connections are always made with the proxy client, while outbound connections are always made with the proxy server. There is no direct connection between the trusted and untrusted networks.

Circuit Level Gateways : This type of proxy server provides a controlled network connection between internal and external systems (i.e., there is no "air-gap"). A virtual "circuit" exists between the internal client and the proxy server. Internet requests go through this circuit to the proxy server, and the proxy server delivers those requests to the Internet after changing the IP address. External users only see the IP address of the proxy server. Responses are then received by the proxy server and sent back through the circuit to the client. While traffic is allowed through, external systems never see the internal systems. This type of connection is often used to connect "trusted" internal users to the Internet

(b) What is SOCKS ? Where do we use it ?

ANS : As it is well known, each different type of network security protects data at a different layer of the OSI model. Built-in at each layer lies the protocol that filters, scans and checks the access. These protocols are usually easily configurable.

SOCKS is an open, industry-standard protocol advanced by the Authenticated Firewall Traversal working group of the IETF (Internet Engineering Task Force). It defines a protocol, which allows TCP applications to access firewalls in a secure and controlled manner, gaining authenticated access through that server to an external network. It can be straightaway used to construct a firewall on a TCP/IP based server.

There a number of products based on SOCKS specifications such as Auto SOCKS available in the market. The latest version is SOCKS 5, which is backward compatible with previous versions as well as supporting key features such as authentication, encryption, the UDP protocol, DNS and IP addressing.

The main problem with SOCKS is that it lacks transparency to software developers and users.

A number of companies, including IBM, DEC, Cyber guard, etc. have commercial firewall products deploying the SOCKS protocol.

Use : SOCKS is a networking middleware: a circuit-level gateway, acting as a proxy and is placed at the session layer to mediate client/server connections. It can be used to connect or establish connections between two hosts and perform transactions on an intranet or the Internet. Since it functions at the lower layer than application layer, it is clearly application-independent.

Implementation requires a change to all existing client-based software so that all of them use the SOCKS libraries. This process of changing the client code is known as "socksifying". This could be extremely cumbersome since it is also expected that at both sides similar level of programming should be available since the entire process takes place at the sessions layer (i.e. at the level of routers).

SOCKS combine powerful features of circuit-level proxies without the programming overhead of traditional application-level firewalls.

Q3(a). What are various Intranet protocols ? Explain the functions of each of them.
(b) Explain the properties of agora .

ANS : Agora : Agora is a simple and inexpensive web protocol for electronic

commerce. The feature that makes the protocol most attractive is that it supports high-volume of transactions with low incurred cost. It has the following properties:
Minimal : The incurred cost of Agora transactions is close to free Web browsing, where cost is determined by the number of messages.
Distributed : Since Agora is fully distributed, traders and merchants can permit customers without access to a central authority. It becomes possible for the customers to purchase from any merchant provided that they have valid accounts.
On-line arbitration : It is obvious that there arise a number of disputes in trade and commerce. With this property, an on-line arbitrator can settle certain customer/ merchant disputes.

The Millicent Protocol : Just as Agora, the Millicent is also a secure protocol for carrying out inexpensive electronic commerce and trading over the Internet. As the name indicates, this protocol was designed to handle purchases and other transactions costing, less than a cent.
This protocol is based on decentralized validation of electronic cash at the vendor's server, and that too without incurring any additional processing for encryption, or communication delays or costs, etc. The greatest application has been from the brokers for taking care of operations during scrip fluctuations. This helps the brokers to check frauds including forgery and double spending. Most notable point is that this protocol is vendor specific.

Q4(a). Explain the process of tuning the performance of a server .
ANS : The process of tuning the performance of a server is being divided into four categories: CPU usage, disk I/O, memory utilization, and network performance. In reality, many times a certain tuning issue can span multiple categories, but if you tend to analyze your server as four distinct processes, you will tend to find more potential areas for improvement than if you had viewed the server as one system. Let's look at some of the potential tuning issues you face when taking this approach.
Try to get a baseline measurement of these four parameters over the course of a week. This gives an idea of when peak load times occur, and an understanding of what resources are being used by the various processes on the server. You will find baseline readings to be particularly useful as a comparison tool when your server starts misbehaving. Most platforms have system accounting and performance monitoring utilities that can log CPU, disk, and memory activity. Although these programs can themselves alter the accuracy of the readings, they are very useful. Other tools, such as netstat, should be employed to gain additional information for snapshots of network performance.
CPU Utilization : has been the least troublesome tuning issue. HTTP services aren't CPU-intensive, so the major focus when addressing CPU issues is to make sure that you have a server fast enough to process the number of HTTP operations per second that your service requires. Closely linked to this is the need to run HTTP server programs that are well designed, and to make sure you are maximizing the efficiency of your CGI, database or other gateway programs.
One area that is often overlooked is the amount of resources that a search and

indexing engine will consume. This is a good argument for baseline measurements which will indicate which processes are responsible for the bulk of resource use.

Disk I/O : requires a close look when optimizing performance. Almost all of the systems with SCSI-based disk subsystems, which give greater flexibility in drive configurations. Use a number of small (typically 10 GB or less) hard drives as opposed to one or two large drives. This is due to the fact that disk I/O can be a substantial bottleneck on fast systems, and having multiple disks seeking and retrieving information can be a much more efficient use of resources.

On heavily-used servers, dedicate a single drive just for log files, as it is the most active file system under load. Databases also fall under this requirement, as the file systems that contain database records may need to be spread among several disks to improve database throughput. When the situation permits, I prefer separating database servers from Web servers, as they tend to have individual tuning requirements that are not always compatible.

Memory : tuning can be both science and art, as it covers a great deal of territory. Memory utilization affects swap space, network buffering, application and OS memory usage and caching. Each one of these areas can impact server performance substantially. The most difficult part of memory tuning is understanding which process, or processes, are responsible for the consumption of memory.

e.g. Unix programs such as swap, sar, ps, and top can help you identify the memory usage requirements for your OS and applications. On Windows NT, the included Performance Monitor is an excellent tool for performance analysis.

The primary rule is to remember that you can never have too much memory. If you are running a Unix system, you must minimize the paging of memory to disk, since server performance will suffer when paged memory is used.

In addition to application and OS memory usage, make sure that you retain sufficient memory for network usage. Your servers are very dependent upon memory to be used as network buffers, which are responsible for the receipt and delivery of data to your server. Network buffer requirements can be identified by running *netstat -m* on Unix hosts. Pay close attention to any indications of memory requests being denied or delayed, which would indicate insufficient memory. It may be more efficient to decrease the size of the buffers servicing requests, as much of the HTTP traffic normally found at Web sites is considerably smaller than typical default buffer sizes.

Another network memory issue that merits notice is the amount of memory used for reverse DNS lookups when logging host names. You can save a considerable amount of memory and network usage by turning off DNS lookups, and possibly reassigning it to another machine that processes the log files offline and does the reverse resolution at that time.

Network performance : is the hardest component to measure consistently, which should come as no surprise when you consider how much the Internet changes. In the same vein as memory, there is no substitute for more capacity when it is needed. As mentioned earlier, it is sometimes beneficial to modify the number of buffers, as well as the buffer size, to improve performance. Make sure you have sufficient memory before you attempt to tweak buffer sizes.

As we undergo growing pains in the Internet infrastructure, you will find that special attention has to be placed on the number of open connections your server maintains. TCP connections start and finish with a 3-way handshake. Unfortunately (due to the fact that many connections are broken off before they are properly closed), you may find that your machine is maintaining a large number of broken connections, which is, in effect, limiting the number of incoming connections that could be serviced.

(b) What are various connectivity interfaces offered by SQLBase 7 for linking client applications with SQLBase databases?

ANS : SQLBase 7 offers five connectivity interfaces for linking client applications with SQLBase databases. One can choose the connectivity interface that best suits the needs based on the development tool/language users are using and application requirements:

SQL/API is a low level, high performance interface suited for use with C and languages that support external functions in DLLs. It provides complete access to the SQLBase feature set, including "administrative" operations.

SAL is the 4GL scripting language used in Gupta's development environments for coding business logic.

SQLBase++ is an object oriented "wrapper" around the SQL/API for use with C++ Applications.

The SQLBase JDBC driver provides a native interface for Java applications and applets.

The SQLBase ODBC driver provides a simple and portable interface via ODBC. SQLBase 7 fully supports multi-threaded ODBC applications. It is also fully compatible with the older ODBC 2.0 API.

Q5(a). What is Virtual Private Network ? How dose it differ from a Firewall ?

ANS : Virtual private Network (VPN) : If an Intranet is extended between two geographically separated locations, VPN is used to secure Intranet data.

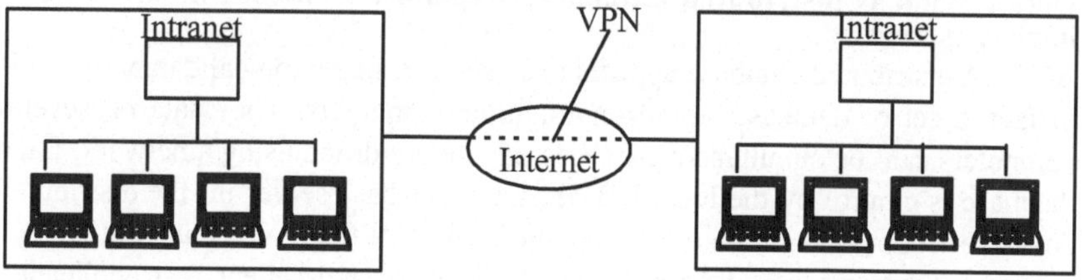

As shown in the diagram, when two geographically separated Intranets are connected using the Internet, VPN is established between the two to secure data of the Intranets. VPN uses IP addresses to differentiate between Internet and Intranet users.

(b) Is there a need for a Firewall when there is a proxy server ? Justify your answer.

Firewalls provide security by following:

(1) Packet Filtering

(2) Application Gateways for restricting applications

(3) Proxy Servers

Proxy servers are used to isolate IP address range from the Internet. One interface of the Proxy Server is connected to the Internet, whose IP address is known to the Internet (Outside World). This IP address is also called Live IP address.

Whereas other interface is connected to the Intranet where all hosts are assigned unique IP addresses which are independent of the Internet (hidden to the Internet). Firewalls can also be implemented on the proxy server either to give access or deny access based upon Applications or IP addresses.

Firewalls also offer additional protection to local users who like to browse or surf out from the intranet to the Internet, by acting as proxy to obtain web pages so that the name and IP number of machines on the network are not revealed to other web sites that the users visit. Not revealing the IP address would help preventing hackers from knowing about the details of the structure of the intranet.

While firewall remains the basic foundation of Internet and intranet security, for many users getting into the corporate intranet would require increasing levels of technology. The intranet technology would need to be expanded beyond those physically present on the same intranet from time to time.

Though there exist a number of definitions of firewall, in simplest terms it can be defined as "a mechanism used to protect a trusted network from an entrusted network". It can also be defined as "A firewall is a system, or group of systems that enforce an access control policy between two networks, and thus should be viewed as an implementation of policy". From the above two definitions, it can be understood that a firewall is only as good as the security policy it supports.

It should be very clear right from the beginning that a firewall is not simply for protecting a corporate network from unauthorized external access via the Internet, but it can also be used internally to prevent unauthorized access to a particular subnet, workgroup or LAN within a corporate network.

Q6(a). What is distributed database? Explain the factors involved in its implementation.

ANS : A distributed database appears to a user as a single logical database, but is in fact, a set of database stored on multiple computers. The data on several computers can be simultaneously accessed and modified using a network. Each database is control by the local DBMS. Each database server in the distributed database cooperates to maintain the consistency of the global database.

A database server is the software managing a database, and a client is an application that requests information from a server. Each computer in a system is a node. A node in a distributed database system can be a client, a server or both.

A Distributed database must also provide the ability to hide the location of the data and the complexity of accessing it access the network. The primary benefits of a distributed database is that the data of physically separate database can be logically combined and potentially made accessible to all users on a network. The database to which a user is directly connected is called the local database. Any additional databases accessed by this user are called remote database.

Factors involved in its Implementations : Atomicity of transactions is an important issue in building a distributed database system. If a transaction runs across two sites, unless the system designers are careful, it may commit at one site and abort at another, leading to an inconsistent state. Transaction commit protocols ensure such a situation cannot arise. The two-phase commit protocol (2PC) is the most widely used of these protocols.

Concurrency control is another issue in a distributed database. Since a transaction may access data items at several sites, transaction managers at several sites may need to coordinate to implement concurrency control. If locking is used (as is almost always the case in practice), locking can be performed locally at the sites containing accessed data items, but there is also a possibility of deadlock involving transactions originating at multiple sites. Therefore deadlock detection needs to be carried out across multiple sites. Failures are more common in distributed system since not only may computers fail, but communication links may also fail. Replication of data items, which is the key of the continued functioning of distributed database when failures occur, further complicates concurrency control.

The standard transaction models, based on multiple actions carried out by a single program unit, are often inappropriate for carrying out tasks that cross the boundaries of database that cannot or will not cooperate to implement protocols such as 2PC. Alternative approaches, based on persistent messaging for communication, are generally used for such tasks.

When the task to be carried out are complex, involving multiple database and/or multiple interactions with humans, coordination of the tasks and ensuring transaction properties for the tasks become more complicated work. Workflow management system are systems designed to help with carrying out such tasks.

In case of organization has to choose between a distributed architecture and a centralized architecture for implementing an application, the system architect must balance the advantages against the disadvantages of distribution of data. The primary disadvantage of distributed database system is the added complexity required to ensure proper coordinations among the sites. This increased complexity takes various forms:

Software-development cost : It is more difficult to implement a distributed system database system; thus, it is more costly.

Greater potential for bugs : Since the sites that constitute the distributed system operate in parallel, it is harder to ensure the correctness of algorithms, especially operation during failures of part of the system, and recovery from failures. The potential exist for extremely subtle bugs.

Increased processing overhead : The exchange of messages and the additional computation required to achieve intersite coordination are a form of overhead that does not arise in centralized systems.

There are several approaches to distributed database design, ranging from fully distributed designs to ones that include a large degree of centralization.

(b) What are the various cost factors involved in setting up of an Intranet ?

ANS : The cost of the Intranet depends on many parameters, as well as there are many variables. Mainly cost depends on the requirement / facilities we want with out intranet. As the facilities / requirement increases the cost also increases. Requirement are of three types :

(1) Hardware Requirements.

(2) Software Requirements.

(3) Use Training Requirements, like how much efficient your hardware should be to handle the activities you want to perform. Software requirement also depends on the activities you want to run on the intranet. User training is also necessary to develop "feel good" factor among the employees of the organisation.

For example, if network is large, better hardware configuration is required, which results in high cost of Server itself.

With 100 clients running a small Intranet requires one server with 100 MHz, 16 MB of RAM and 2 GB of IDE Hard Disk.

But if Intranet is having 1000 clients, with Database Support, it requires 3 Servers of 200 MHz, 32 MB of RAM and 4.3 GB Hard Disk with Disk Mirroring implemented (it means 6 Hard Disks are required). 2 servers will be used to share the overall load of the Intranet and hence the cost of the Intranet increases in this regard.

Similarly, if your Intranet requires software for Database, for Server side Scripting (ASP, ISAPI or any other), all this counts in terms of high cost as well as high resources in terms of Hardware.

Following are some approximate prices for Intranet Tools:

Server (133 MHz Pentium, 32 MB RAM, two 2 GB Hard Drives – Rs.2 Lacs to 3 Lacs.

Network Server – Rs. 1 Lac

Communications Server – Rs. 50000

Editors – Rs.10000

Search Engine – Rs. 0

Database – Rs. 1 to 2 Lacs

Proxy Server – Rs. 50000

Other Software – Rs. 100000

Client Hardware – Rs. 25000 per terminal

So, if we calculate for an Enterprise Network, it requires approximately Rs. 7 lacs just for intranet.

Feedback is the breakfast of Champions.

Ken Blanchard

You can Help other students.
"Inform any error or mistake in this book."

We and Universe
will reward you for Your Kind act.

Email at : feedback@gullybaba.com
or
WhatsApp on 9350849407

CS-75 : INTRANET ADMINISTRATION
DEC 2004

Note : *There are* **six** *questions in this paper. Question number 1 is* **compulsory** *and carries 30 marks. Answer any* **three** *from the rest.*

1(a) How does Intranet work ? Explain this with the help of an example. [5]

An Intranet can be defined as a private network, which uses Internet tools. The principal tool is the Web browser, but there are other Internet tools such as ftp and telnet that are useful. The resources defined as private may be protected physically (with a firewall or a separate physical network), geographically (by restricting access to computers with a network address on the local network), or personally (by username and password).

Typically, resources will be private either because they are confidential to the organization (for example, an internal telephone directory), or because they are covered by restrictive licenses (for example, if the Library subscribes to a bibliography whose license restricts its use to members of the University).

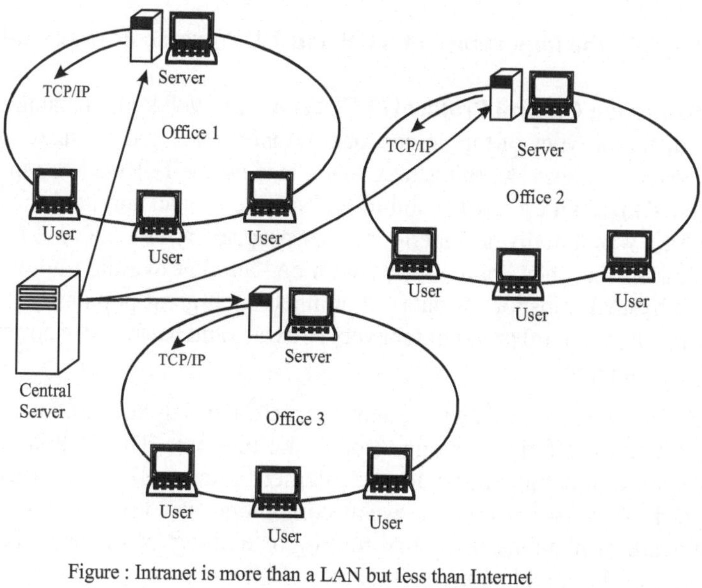

Figure : Intranet is more than a LAN but less than Internet

For an Intranet to work, all computers connected together in a network must speak and understand the same language, or protocol. The language used is Hypertext Mark-up Language (HTML) and the protocol that both intranets and the Internet uses are called Transmission Control Protocol/Internet Protocol or TCP/IP. A network server supports all the activities of an intranet. On the clients' side, is software known as a browser is used, usually Netscape Navigator or Internet Explorer.

The browser when invoked seeks a server computer through the communication medium that has the first or Home Page of the Intranet, which is usually seen in the folders as 'index.htm'. This is the default page for accessing the intranet from any computer attached to an internal network. This is what automatically appears on the screen when a user logs in and clicks on the browser icon on the desktop for accessing Internet also. The hyperlinks to specific files or databases requests for files send the control from anywhere on the network to the browser. The server accesses the file and sends back a copy of what it contains to the computer or client that has requested for it.

It is the simplicity of TCP/IP that makes Intranets so easy to set-up. Web browsers can be used to connect to virtually any information source, from Structured Query Language (SQL) databases to highly proprietary information systems. With simple HTML pages one can view only information related to library placed on the intranet site while with SQL support user can place different queries based upon which he can get results displayed after processing on the server.

(b) Explain the importance of TCP and UDP protocols in the Intranet. [5]

Transmission Control Protocol (TCP) :- As it is well known that the Internet uses different types of topologies, data transfer rates, packet sizes, and other related technologies. Keeping these issues in view, the TCP has been specifically designed to provide a reliable end-to-end service over an unreliable connection. The TCP was initially designed for either proprietary or Unix based operating systems so that they communicate with one another avoiding unreliable and slow physical transport of data. It attained such great popularity that it has become the standard protocol for every software and hardware to communicate with one another.

The entire message or data to be sent over Internet is divided into various units or packets for efficient routing through the Internet. The TCP is a protocol that is used in conjunction with the Internet Protocol (IP) to send the data in the form of message units between computers over the Internet. While IP takes care of handling the actual routing or delivery of the data, TCP keeps track of each individual units of data.

Even though every packet has the same destination IP address, they arrive at the destination through different routes over the Internet and finally reassembled at the at destination to make it a complete message or data as was sent. This breaking of message or data into packets before transmission and then rearranging at the destination in proper order after receipt of all packets is called disassembling and assembling respectively and done by a specific portion of TCP called the packet assembler and disassembler (PAD).

TCP falls under the category of connection-oriented protocols, which means that a connection or session is established and maintained until the message or messages has been exchanged totally.

User Datagram Protocol (UDP) :- The User Datagram Protocol, or UDP as it is known, is a connectionless transport level protocol supported by the IP. It offers a limited service as compared to the conventional TCP and can be used for transferring messages between computers in a IP based network.. In short, it can be said that UDP is more or less an alternative to the TCP and, it functions in a suite like TCP/IP called the UDP/IP. Unlike the TCP where the basic unit of data is called packet, under UDP a data unit is called a datagram.

```
0         7 8        15 16      23 24       31
+----------+----------+----------+----------+
| Source   | Destination
|   Port   |   Port   |
+----------+----------+----------+----------+
|          |          |
|   Length |Checksum|
+----------+----------+----------+----------+
|
|      data octets ...
+-------------------- ...
```

Figure: User Datagram Header Format

UDP does not divide a message into small packets (or datagram's) and then reassemble them after receipt as it is done with TCP/IP. The basic philosophy behind use of UDP is that the entire message is sent and ensured that the receiver has received the message properly without any errors. UDP is highly useful in those network based applications that aim at saving lot of processing time spent on breaking and reassembling them.

(c) What are the software and hardware requirements for the installation of an Intranet ? **[5]**

Hardware :- An Intranet is simply a standard Wide Area Network (WAN). The use of the term Intranet recently to describe using software developed for the Internet on the company's WAN. Web servers are an example.

To setup a WAN, one will need to have some type of communications between the different sites. National ISDN, Very Small Aperture Terminal (VSAT) connectivity or a long distance Frame Relay could be the best choice. It will be essential to install a router at each site. Each router would connect back to a central site over dedicated phone lines. Note that the hardware should be configured for the following protocols/ services.

Protocol/Service	To be installed on
IP	Network
HTTP	Server
SMTP/POP3/IMAP4	Server
LDAP	Server
X509 Certificate	Server
Java	ORB
Document Server	Server

Scientists also describe how optimal performance of intranets is associated with a number of key hardware factors. In order to optimise performance, servers with fast processors and large amounts of memory are essential. They also noted how good multi-tasking and multi-threading ability is which is also crucial for most of the Web applications. In addition, sufficient memory and disk capacity at the user workstation would improve performance through increased caching. The limitation of large image files can also be considered important to improve performance, but images may be equally important to expand and illustrate data, and pages of text can be discouraging, especially in an educational context. Finally, the database itself, which forms the foundations of almost every intranet, can have a significant effect on performance.

Operating System for Server and Clients

On the Server : Since 1994, when the original pair of web servers — **NCSA HTTPd** and **CERN HTTPd**, dozens of commercial and shareware programs have been developed. While the Netscape Enterprise Server defines the commercial high end, the other is Microsoft's Internet Information Server (IIS) Netscape Enterprise Server and lightweight Fast Track Server.

On the Clients :- All of the clients running popular operating systems such as Microsoft Windows, MacOS, UNIX, etc. could be used to function as backbone software for the Intranets.

Only one software is sufficient for working with the Intranet viz., the browser software that should be loaded on all the clients. This software serves as a single interface to both the Intranet as well as the Internet. At present, Microsoft Internet Explorer and Netscape Navigator both remain the top web browsers available. Apart for these, various other web browsers are also available to access the information such as NCSA Mosaic.

Language support :- Intranet works on the basis of scripts written in any of the following languages, viz., SGML, HTML, DHTML, XML, ASP, CGI, Perl, UML, VRML, etc. Though almost all are variants of the basic markup language or development over it, all provide flexibility to program the needs of the organizations. It is essential to test minutely how the output looks when published on the central server, by using different browsers on different operating systems.

Some organisations need to connect various offices through their Intranet. Those organisations need to have additional hardware device like router to connect to different locations. If organisation has great security issue, they also need to implement powerful firewall. This firewall can be software based or hardware based, depends on level of security, cost and efficiency.

The Intranet Software and Hardware equipments are a variable. As an organisation grows, we might want to add a search engine to help user find out informations quickly.

Some advanced features like Database support, logging, controlling access, Security etc. requires additional software to manage large Intranets.

If an organisation wants to provide several hundred to thousands of users getting connected to the Internet server and running applications, use remote login to connect, e-mail distribution software, or serve multimedia - video and audio, then hardware will need to be sophisticated and powerful enough to meet the peak-time demands that will put on the system.

(d) List the operating systems that may be used in Intranet. Explain the important features of any operating system. [5]

Operating System for Server and Clients

On the Server :- Since 1994, when the original pair of web servers — **NCSA HTTPd** and **CERN HTTPd**, dozens of commercial and shareware programs have been developed. While the Netscape Enterprise Server defines the commercial high end, the other is Microsoft's Internet Information Server (IIS) Netscape Enterprise Server and lightweight Fast Track Server.

On the Clients :- All of the clients running popular operating systems such as Microsoft Windows, MacOS, UNIX, etc. could be used to function as backbone software for the Intranets.

Only one software is sufficient for working with the Intranet viz., the browser software that should be loaded on all the clients. This software serves as a single interface to both the Intranet as well as the Internet. At present, Microsoft Internet Explorer and Netscape Navigator both remain the top web browsers available. Apart for these, various other web browsers are also available to access the information such as NCSA Mosaic.

The most popular network system in the PC world is Novell **NetWare.** It was designed to be used by companies downsizing from a mainframe to a network of PCs. In such systems, each user has a desktop PC functioning as a client. In addition, some number of powerful PCs operate as servers, providing file services, database services, and other services to a collection of clients. In other words, Novell NetWare is based on the client-server model.

NetWare uses a proprietary protocol stack illustrated in Fig. It is based on the old Xerox Network System, XNS™ but with various modifications. Novell NetWare predates OSI and is not based on it. If anything, it looks more like TCP/IP than like OSI.

Layer			
Application	SAP	File server	. . .
Transport	NCP		SPX
Network	IPX		
Data link	Ethernet	Token ring	ARCnet
Physical	Ethernet	Token ring	ARCnet

Fig : The Novell NetWare reference model.

(e) Give any five differences in the features of IIS and the Samba Server. [5]

Samba Server	Internet Information Server
1. It can run as a Windows NT System Service by executing the file ntserver.exe	It has replaced Windows NT LAN Managers authentication with stronger Kerberos 5.0 authentication protocols used in Windows 2000
2. Supports Windows NT based system	Now bundled with Windows 2000 to support new tool as WebDAV
3. No addition of wizards	Three new wizards added
4. Slower restarts of Web and FTP services	Faster restarts of Web and FTP services
5. Basic Samba Production Server is available free	It is not the case with IIS

(f) What are the tasks that are to be properly synchronized for the proper functioning of Intranet? [5]

Since an Intranet can be defined as simply a standard WAN limited to an organization, powerful hardware should be made available for web server. The computing equipment must be selected in such a manner that they do not get obsolete very quickly or become too costly for the company.

It is also important that other points such as the following along with their specifications should essentially be considered and drawn carefully:

Communication medium/services that provide connectivity between different locations of the company should use technologies such as ISDN, leased line, etc.

Network equipment and connectivity should address various networking equipment such as routers, types of cables, as well as the topology behind the network

It is a must that the hardware should be configured for protocols such as IP, HTTP, SMTP, POP, X509 Certification, etc. in order to provide security to the intranet server.

For an intranet to work smoothly, the following tasks should be properly synchronized:

- All computers connected together in a network must communicate using the same language and protocol. Inability to do so may leave the users disconnected to the repository of information and resources

- It must be always remembered that the language used is Hyper Text Markup Language (HTML) and every thing that is developed for and intended to be hosted on the intranet must follow HTML invariably.

- The protocol suite applicable for both intranets and Internet are called Transmission Control Protocol/ Internet Protocol (TCP/IP) and every computer should be compatible to TCP/IP. Though, TCP/IP evolved initially on UNIX based computers, it became a standard for data communication and more recently for every type of communication across intranet and internet, especially supported by every major operating system in use.

- The intranet is driven by a network server that uses a browser, like Netscape Navigator or Internet Explorer.

2(a) Explain the multiple layers of Intranet Security, with the help of an example. [8]

Security requirements vary from organization to organization, and also vary based on the content organization's intends to place on its servers. While for certain intranets simple security solutions are enough, for many organizations solution could be in the form of implementing more than a firewall or multi-layered security architecture.

A company can implement a wide range of security models but the most useful ones are those that are organized in multiple levels. Implementation of a multi-layered or multi-tiered scheme is easier and flexible than using all or no security approach in which a user allows either total access or provides a total denial.

In addition to not just access, security methods also protect information from accidental or intentional modification, manipulation or destruction. Most security experts tells that a security breach is more likely to come from within a company's own staff rather than from outside. These may be frustrated employees, or enthusiasts who are after the thrill of breaking the code.

As one can see that in the physical world, there are many layers of security. For example, a bank maintaining lockers has strong vaults, good locks, alter guards, and highly sensitive alarms, etc. Each security measure tries to compensate the limitations of others. Similarly, assuming information is cash, Intranets also follow the same suite and have a similar layered approach.

Most commercial servers use a powerful operating system as base that provides good methods of file-system security. Some servers require additional software to control access to server resources and files. The immediately next higher level is the software tool that monitors the system logs, serious looking out for any suspicious activity. When any intrusion is detected, the software generates an alert message. The response could be spontaneous and automatic, with an option to generate the alert message manually. The history recorded in the server logs is usually used to assess damage and for planning restoration from the damage.

Use of firewalls and proper alarm systems can act as complement to above security measures, which can be added to network routers to detect or block potential threats. There devises help in filtering, detecting and then permitting the user requests and have tendency to scan the IP packets for blocking suspicious behaviour or patterns. A proxy server also helps a lot since it hides the real IP addresses of users requesting resources outside the firewall.

Finally, software run outside the firewall tries all known security tricks of hackers, thus scanning for vulnerability points. The security implementation also should be supplemented with regular process audits by an independent security expert.

(b) Define any seven 'security policy' principles for Intranet. **[7]**

As you begin to formulate your security policy, consider the following:
Look at exactly what you are trying to protect-network hardware, software, company-confidential data, and network operations.
Look at who you need to protect it from-current users, previous employees, and outsiders trying to break into your system.
Look at what you need to protect it from-fire, smoke, floods, extremes of temperature and humidity, power outages, earthquakes, and theft.
Determine the likelihood of these potential threats.
Implement measures that will protect your assets in a way that you or your firm can afford.
Review your processes and procedures continuously, and improve them every time you find a weakness or a new security mechanism becomes available.
Your security policy should minimize all types of threats and ensure network compromise or security breaches are as infrequent as impossible. It should also minimize the affect of any security breach once it occurs.

As you develop your security policy, focus on the following goals:

- Preventing malicious damage to files and systems.
- Preventing accidental damage to files and systems.
- Limiting the results of any deletions or damage to files that do over.
- Protecting the integrity and confidentiality of data.
- Preventing unauthorized access to the system.
- Providing appropriate disaster-recovery systems so the server can be restored and be back online again quickly.
- Information is an asset. It has value to the organization and needs to be suitably protected.
- Whatever form, information should always be protected to its value.

3(a) Assume a network of a university with four departments and having 20 computers in each department. Configure an Intranet for the specifications of the university defined above. Make any necessary assumptions. [8]

Intranet configuration basically involves

1.Planning

2.Construction(Content)

3.Implementation and,

4.Maintenance

1.Planning-We will access the needs of the university i.e. type of services needed.

The university will typically want separate servers, printers for each department in order to avoid chaos of data access & also to isolate working thereby maintaining security levels. University can have separate departments for Admissions, Examination settings, Schedule of courses & Sports Department. It is recommended that all the 4 servers are connected & bound by ID and passwords for access to allow communication among departments when needed

We should ideally have a main server that prohibits access between departments as long as authentication is invalid.

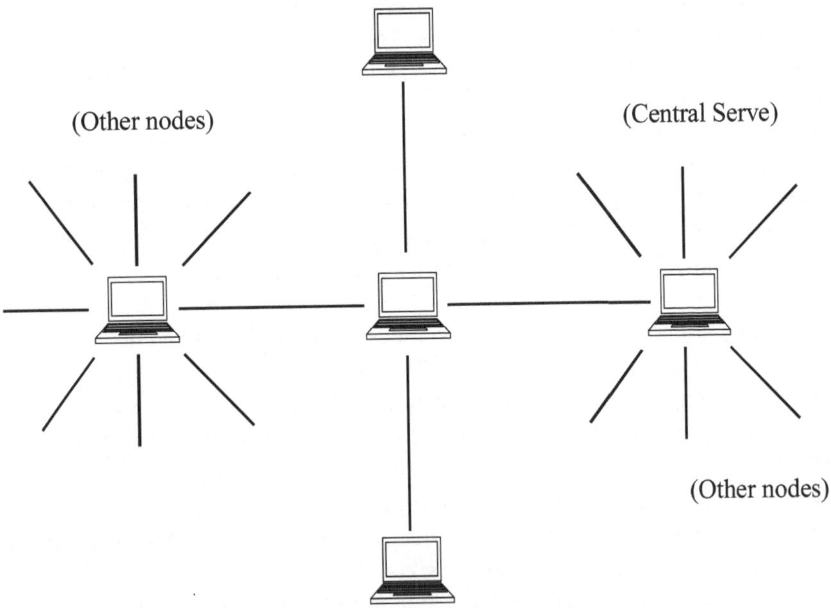

While setting up intranet university has to decide upon

a.Purpose of intranet-i.e. enhanced performance and communication.
b.Money & time saved-that will go vis-a-vis.
c.Security tools-depending upon threats(internal or external) encryption and decryption techniques are determined.
d.Software required-Web Server typically IIS will be ideal. Browser-Netscape Navigator is the ideal choice. Network protocol-TCP/IP suits best due to reliability.
2.Construction-Involves good structure formation.Here structure shown above is the recommended one.Proper cabling must be laid down to have communication clarity.
3.Implementation-Involves determining percentage of existing material that can be distributed among departments & percentage of work to be developed by systems(removing redundant information).
4.Maintenance- Should be done by communication with various department system professionals after implementation has been done. Various tests as real time test must be performed. All the tests must be feedback based.

(b) In a small organisations, the Intranet is comprised of 28 computers, 2 printers and 2 Fax machines. Give the hardware/software specifications of the Server and the Clients. **[7]**

We have 28 computers, 2 printers and 2 fax machines.
Ideally to share the workload two servers can be there handing one printer and one fax machine each.
Thus we will have 2 servers and 13 clients for each one .
SERVER—As far as server is concerned handling 13 clients doesn't build up lot of load so we can have
A Pentium III Xeon based server(dual processor recommended)
2*40 GB HDD(one extra recommended for backup)
128 MB RAM(256 MB recommended)
The basic software required should be capable of handling NCSA HTTP & CERN HTTP.
Products like Netscape Enterprise Server,MS IIS,FastTrack Server etc. are well known products in this line.The are available for a variety of OS as UNIX,Windows NT,MacOS etc.

CLIENT—The client can be based on any architecture as Intel,AMD,Motorola or any other well known processor and OS as Unix,Windows NT ,MacOSetc.

In addition to OS, a client will require only a browser as MS Internet Explorer, Netscpe Navigator, NCSA Mosaic, Lynx, Emacs, Midas WWW etc. Browser must be

- **Of latest version**

- Supporting TCP/IP
- Compatible to Microsoft and Java technologies.

4(a) Explain the following E-Commerce protocols : [9]
(i) Agora
(ii) Millicent Protocol
(iii) Secure Electronic Transactions Protocol

(i) Agora :- Agora is a simple and inexpensive web protocol for electronic commerce. The feature that makes the protocol most attractive is that it supports high-volume of transactions with low incurred cost. It has the following properties:

Minimal :- The incurred cost of Agora transactions is close to free Web browsing, where cost is determined by the number of messages.

Distributed :- Since Agora is fully distributed, traders and merchants can permit customers without access to a central authority. It becomes possible for the customers to purchase from any merchant provided that they have valid accounts.

On-line arbitration :- It is obvious that there arise a number of disputes in trade and commerce. With this property, an on-line arbitrator can settle certain customer/merchant disputes.

(ii) Millicent Protocol :- Just as Agora, the Millicent is also a secure protocol for carrying out inexpensive electronic commerce and trading over the Internet. As the name indicates, this protocol was designed to handle purchases and other transactions costing less than a cent.

This protocol is based on decentralized validation of electronic cash at the vendor's server, and that too without incurring any additional processing for encryption, or communication delays or costs, etc. The greatest application has been from the brokers for taking care of operations during scrip fluctuations. This helps the brokers to check frauds including forgery and double spending. Most notable point is that this protocol is vendor specific.

(iii) Secure Electronic Transactions Protocol :- The SET based purely on the science of cryptography that speaks of encoding and decoding messages for communication. This science is not new to us rather it has been in use since the evolution of human. Preserving the secrecy of transactions through strong encryption algorithms, especially for applications like the military, trade and banking has been described infinite number of times in the history books. There has been tremendous advance in the field of encryption with the advancement in computing and mathematics.

Secure Electronic Transactions (SET) is a protocol developed jointly by Visa and MasterCard, involving other computing majors like IBM. SET is an open standard for protecting the privacy, and ensuring the authenticity, of electronic transactions, especially applicable to the banking sector where the transactions could be in terms of few cents to multi-million dollars.

Since the customer/consumer as well as the traders interest has to be protected, methods such as privacy, authentication, encryption, etc. evolved to provide back to back support for carrying out electronic commerce over the Internet.

(b) Write any two differences between the basic, ODBC and the distributed databases, in the context of Intranet management tools. [6]

Basic Database	ODBC	Distributed database
1. Centralised specific database access thus permissible to heavy load on the server.	Access to any type of database in a centralized environment.	Data of physically separate database can be logically combined.
2. Development cost is fair & overhead is less.	ODBC allows clean connection making overhead problems minimal but ODBC drives are a bit expensive due to functionality they provide.	Development cost & communication overhead is considerable. Atomicity of transactions needed.

5(a) Explain the various steps involved in network installation and administration of Intranet. [10]

The four basic steps of the Intranet project are Planning, Constructing (Content), Implementing and Maintaining. Each step is followed by the other.

Following parameters are to be considered when planning your own Intranet:

- **What is the purpose :** One need to make sure that why I want to have an Intranet?
- **Advantages :** What advantages I am going to get if I am replacing my LAN with the Intranet?
- **Save Money :** Does an Intranet save money for me?
- **Security :** What sort of security I need to implement for my Intranet?
- **Software required :** What software do I required to build Intranet I want.
- Hardware should not be forgotten.
- What is going to be on my Intranet? That is content. Content is again a crucial issue.

The purpose of the Internet is simple. It is to corporate all the advantages of the Internet protocols and technologies which are not possible with LAN.

One need to make sure the security level required and the budget which can be spend for implementing security. Both the things need to be balanced in order to get proper security model for Intranet.

The software required depends upon the field of the company. There is variety of software available which can be used or which is supported by the Intranet protocol stack (TCP/IP protocol Stack). To get started with the Intranet, following software are required:

- Web Server Software
- HTML authoring Tool
- Browser
- TCP/IP based network

Selection of Hardware is to be done again with the Software being used and Software requirement. For example, an Internet with 1000 clients requires 256 MB of memory and the same server uses Oracle as Back-End tool, which requires additional 256 MB of RAM. Memory requirements increases as number of hosts of the Intranet increases.

Content of the Intranet :- The content that is going to be put on Intranet must serve purpose. One needs to make sure that whatever is going to be put on Intranet is worth or not.

Moreover, good design of the content includes structure as well as appearance. The design, which is created, should reflect the mission defined while planning the Intranet.

Creating each page :- Once content is available, it is time to convert the material to a form suitable for display.

It is needed to decide what percentage of existing material can be used and who will be responsible for converting that information.

Testing :- Once the content is formatted, test your pages and then test them again!!!! It is a sort of feedback of content. That whatever is worked out really works nicely or not.

Part of content plan should include a test plan detailing :

- What should be tested?
- Who will perform the tests?
- What to do if there are problems?
- When to do retest?

(b) What is the process of configuring a maximum simultaneous request and listen queue size? **[5]**

Lets take an example of FastTrack Server to understand **"the process of configuring a maximum simultaneous request and listen queue size".** One can improve the FastTrack Server's performance by configuring these options: Maximum Simultaneous Request, Domain Name System Lookups, Listen-Queue Size, and http Persistent Connection Timeout.

Maximum Simultaneous Request :- If your FastTrack Server is processing client request slowly, you can change this parameter (the number of active request allowed for the server at one time) to improve performance, default is 48. It will defer processing new requests until the number of active request drops below the maximum amount, it waits 30 sec or more for the data before timing out. To change the maximum simultaneous request - Server Manager - Server Preferences - Performance Tuning - Type number of request.

Listen-Queue Size :- Is a socket-level parameter that specifies the number of incoming connections the system will accept for that socket. The default is 100 incoming connections. If you manage a heavily used Web site, you should make sure your system's listen-queue size is large enough to accommodate the listen-queue size setting specified in the Server Manager form. If you change the listen-queue size, make sure your system supports the new size. The listen-queue size in the Server Manager form changes the listen-queue size requested by the server. If the server requests a listen-queue size larger than the system's maximum listen-queue size, the size defaults to the system's maximum. Setting the listen-queue size to high can degrade server performance. The listen-queue size was designed to prevent the server from becoming overloaded with connections it cannot handle.

6(a) Explain the following Basic Intranet Protocols : [8]
(i) ARP
(ii) SMTP
(iii) POP, and
(iv) IMAP

(i) Address Resolution Protocol (ARP) :- One of the basic communication protocols is the ARP that resolves the IP addresses used by various networking equipment into network usable format that used by LANs. ARP addresses two basic services to the clients viz., it obtains the media access control address for the requesting device and recording of the media access control address in a table called the ARP cache for future use.

The Address Resolution Protocol (ARP) is situated at the bottom half of the Network layer. It can be considered as a mechanism for mapping or translation of addresses between the Network logical addresses and MAC (Media Access Control) layer physical addresses. For instance, the MAC layer uses a 48-bit address whereas the Ethernet uses a 32-bit address. ARP provides the mechanism to translate the MAC addresses to IP addresses and vice versa using a lookup table like data structure called the ARP cache.

The greatest advantage of using an ARP is its simplicity since it does not have to perform any kind of computations or otherwise, except then to use the look up table and assign each machine an IP address and decide about subnet masks ARP does the rest.

(ii) Simple Mail Transfer Protocol (SMTP) :- The SMTP protocol is used in the TCP/IP based networks for transferring mail messages between user computers. Most popular freeware for Unix based SMTP mail programs are Elm and Pine. The other Windows based software also such as Netscape or Eudora that have become very popular. The Microsoft Outlook that comes with the Windows operating system also uses SMTP to transfer messages and is very popular.

The most notable aspect is that the SMTP works only when both the mail sender and receiver are ready to transact at the same time. Suppose that the receiver computer is not connected or available at that moment, then the messages are stored in a temporary server (may be the nearest gateway or hub). A post office protocol (such as IMAP or POP) must then be used to retrieve the mail.

Since the mail messages cannot have control characters in them, the binary files must first be converted into ASCII. A program called Unicode usually does the process of this conversion. Once the mail is sent to the other end, it is converted back to binary or ASCII or whatever format required using another utility program

called the Unicode.

It should be clear that two separate protocols are used for sending and receiving email (or mail messages). For sending messages, the SMTP is used whereas for receiving at the other end either POP or IMAP is used at their local server. While configuring the email accounts, certain addresses are exclusively declared, viz., the addresses of an SMTP server, a POP server, address where returned messages are to be sent, and the basic server where the user has his email account.

There are two main difficulties using the SMTP protocol, i.e., the message of size more than 64 KB cannot be handled and the second is the timeout. Whereas the first problem could be overcome with newer implementations of the operating systems as well as attaching files as attachments to the main messages, the second problem continued as both the client and server can have different timeouts, and quite naturally, one of them may timeout very quickly keeping the other busy or unexpectedly terminate the connection.

(iii) Post Office Protocol (POP) :- As the name indicates, the POP delivers all the messages stored on the server to the user's email account. It can be configured in such a manner that the user can obtain emails from his multiple email accounts into his only email software installed on the computer such as the Microsoft Outlook or Outlook Express. This facility is also available on almost all the Internet based email web sites such as Hotmail, Yahoo, etc.

Like the SMTP, the POP is also a very simple protocol and can be easily written for a command-line-based application. With the advent of a number of Windows based applications, the difficulty of writing such command-line based applications has totally vanished and the work of user has become much easier. Similar applications have evolved over the Unix based implementations as well.

Note that it is easy to write code for simulating a client by use of telnet to connect to the server, and then enable the client to do email-related tasks such as logging into the account, logging off, downloading the emails, deleting them, etc.

The transactions begins with the initiation of a session when newly logged in and it is possible to do only three things viz., get the username, password or quit the session. Once logged into the mail server, the transactions allow doing the following tasks:

STAT	Gives the number of messages in the box as well as total size of those messages in bytes
LIST	Gives the list of messages in the mailbox
RETR **msg**	RETR retrieves a message. It uses the message number as generated using the LIST command
DELE **msg**	Deletes a message. Message would be permanently deleted with the sessions ended using the quit command. Message can be undeleted using RSET command
TOP **msg n**	Returns the headers of desired message and also **n** lines of its body

(iv) Internet Message Access Protocol (IMAP) :- Internet Message Access Protocol (IMAP) is a standard protocol for accessing e-mail from the local server. The method of functioning of IMAP is very much similar to POP but there is a little difference between the two.

While both POP and IMAP deal with the receiving of e-mail from the local server, POP just stores and then sends the messages whereas IMAP acts totally as a remote file server.

IMAP is more popular for the Internet based email services but the POP is gradually taking up the lead. IMAP acts more or less like a client/server type protocol wherein the messages are kept on a server and the user connects to it for viewing. In order to download the mail message, the user has to decide it by viewing only the header part and name of the sender. The only interesting part of the IMAP services is the creation and use of folders (also called mailboxes), delete messages, or search for certain parts. The downside is that the IMAP requires continuous access to the mail server while the user is session in order to keep the content and connection alive.

IMAP has the ability to view the mail messages not only by arrival number but by using attributes as well. In this kind of output the folder or the mailbox looks like a relational database table rather than just a collection of messages.

(b) What is WAP ? Write any five applications of WAP. [7]

The Wireless Application Protocol (WAP) is client/server architecture based technology and has been one of the landmark developments in the communications industry because of the attempt to develop an open standard for wireless protocols, independent of vendor and air link.

The WAP is developed for micro-browser of the mobile or cell phone. These phones can be considered as hand-held terminals. The WAP servers are programmed to provide simple services to the users since it is not possible to provide complete flexibility of an ordinary browser. Limited services such as providing result of examination, amount balance in the bank account, temperature and humidity of the day, simple message service, etc. can be easily provided on the phones. Day-by-day, new services are being added to the features.

Applications of WAP : Corporate applications on requirements that are being enhanced and enabled with a WAP interface include:

- ✓ Remote Point of Sale
- ✓ Customer Service
- ✓ Remote Monitoring such as Meter Reading
- ✓ Vehicle Positioning
- ✓ Corporate Email

Consumer Applications that are being enhanced and enabled with a WAP interface include:

- ✓ Simple Person to Person Messaging
- ✓ Voice and Fax Mail Notifications
- ✓ Unified Messaging
- ✓ Internet Email
- ✓ Prepayment

CS-75 : INTRANET ADMINISTRATION
JUNE 2005

*Note : There are **six** questions in this paper. Question number 1 is **compulsory** and carries 30 marks. Answer any **three** from the rest.*

1(a) Give five reasons why Intranet is preferred over a set of stand-alone computers in an organisation. [5]

The real-world benefits and applications of intranets can be many in number. One major benefit of intranets is that it could be used to enhance communication, which in turn could lead to improved linkages within the organization. This communication could happen between various workgroups, departments, or even within entire organization, simply by hosting the contents on the intranet server.

Intranet can largely eliminate paper-based documents, which otherwise become outdated over passage of time. Increased communication will also lead to tremendous reduction in expenditure for numerous publishing services such as creating, printing, and distributing information for internal use. Besides these benefits, Web and conferencing technologies can be easily provided to improve synergy amongst the employees; still further, collaboration can be enhanced by use of internal newsgroups and mailing lists. Information posted to the newsgroups and distributed via mailing lists can be made available to selected groups within the organization and archived as a repository of information.

Using Internet technologies on an intranet means that organizations can deploy integrated applications that connect public and private networks using the same applications and data. Hence, straightaway standardization of activities or process will find its place. It could be possible that all users have to use the same environment in such an event thereby causing a fear for loss of freedom or creativity, but it has its own advantages.

Broadly speaking, the benefits can be enumerated as follows:

Cheaper :- Use of client browsers with one standard Window interface, offers easy integration with a number of other applications, such as electronic mail, faxes, videoconferencing, calendaring, and linkages within messages. As a single interface to a variety of information sources, the browser is cost-effective, highly efficient, uses minimal resources, and very easy to use.

Versatile :- An Intranet server eliminates the need to replicate database by providing users with easy access to source data. A single WWW server platform can support both internal and external applications for both internal information

- sharing and external marketing on the Internet. In contrast, the Lotus Notes application is costlier and purely an internal application.

Flexible :- The Intranet provides the users with access to centralized information resources on a single point-and-click basis through the browser, which is available on a variety of client platforms (Windows, Mac, Unix, etc.), at any location. With Notes, data distribution is in real-time, on an as-requested basis, over a public (or private) network.

Intranets obviously have many advantages to both the organisation and its personnel.

The most obvious advantage is that everyone with access to a computer terminal can obtain the entire store of information that can be easily updated at regular intervals. It is essential to note that even a simple database like an organization telephone directory gets outdated quickly, sometimes even before it is printed on paper whereas an on-line directory can be updated immediately whenever there is a change needed.

(b) What is the need of distributed databases ? Write four main features of distributed databases to justify its need. [5]

NEED :- A database server is the software managing a database, and a client is an application that requests information from a server. Each computer in a system is a node. A node in a distributed database system can be a client, a server or both.

A Distributed database provides the ability to hide the location of the data and the complexity of accessing it across the network. The primary need of a distributed database is that the data of physically separate database can be logically combined and potentially made accessible to all users on a network. The database to which a user is directly connected is called the local database. Any additional databases accessed by this user are called remote database.

Features of Distributed Databases

1. Fault tolerance through redundancy – if data is lost on one site, it can be gathered from the other site.

2. Autonomous Systems – that permits security to be applied via user authentication.

3. Less workload on the server due to distribution of work.

4. Masking out irrelevant communication – It is done by limiting communication to case where some coordination is needed. Otherwise, one site can completely handle its data.

(c) Write the purpose of IP addressing schemes. Explain all the classes of IP addressing schemes. [5]

Every host and router on the Internet has an IP address, which encodes its network number and host number. The combination is unique: no two machines have the same IP address. All IP address are 32 bits long and are used in the Source address and destination address fields of IP packets. The formats used for IP address are shown in Fig. Those machines connected to multiple networks have a different IP address on each network.

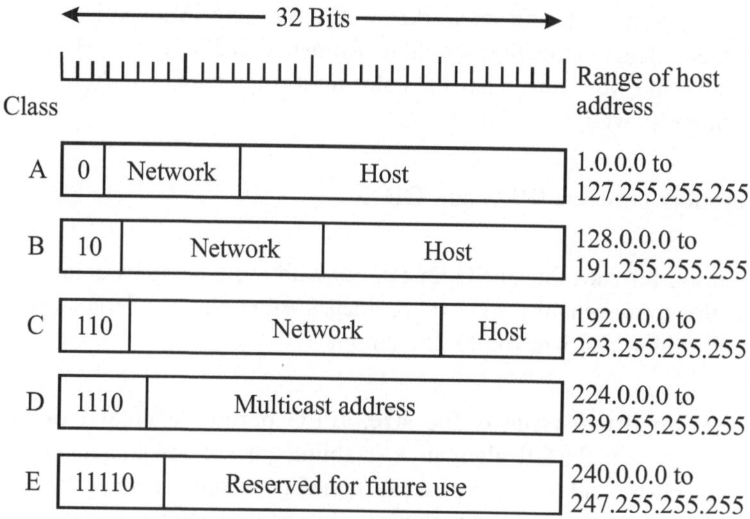

Fig : IP address formats.

The class A, B, C, and D formats allow for up to 126 networks with 16 million hosts each, 16, 382 networks with up to 64K hosts, 2 million networks, (e.g., LANs), with up to 254 hosts each, and multicast, in which a diagram is directed to multiple hosts Address beginning with 11110 are reserved for future use. Tens of thousands of networks are now connected to the Internet, and the number doubles every year. Network numbers are assigned by the NIC **(Networks Information Center)** to avoid conflicts.

(d) Why are GIF and JPEG used in the Web pages ? Give any four differences between the JPEG and GIF formats. **[5]**

When you're ready to add graphics to your Web pages, you'll immediately be confronted with a question: How should you format your images? Graphics in their natural state are too big to be quickly downloaded over the Web, so you have to compress them. The standard compression formats are GIF and JPEG (compression, by the way, doesn't shrink the dimensions of your graphics, it just reduces the size of the file).

But is GIF or JPEG the better format to use? The resounding answer to this question is: It depends. It depends on the type of image you're working with, how small you want your image file to be, and the way you want your graphic to download.

One of your primary considerations is the type of image you're working with. Photographs and graphics with lots of color fields, and particularly colors that blend and fade into one another, are best served by JPEG. For example, an unnerving picture of your co-worker waiting to sing "Yankee Doodle" in a Club Med talent competition should be formatted in JPEG (see below). If, on the other hand, your image has flat color fields, like the talent show poster, it will compress well in the GIF format.

Differences between JPEG and GIF :

The reason for choosing JPEG for images with more complex color patterns is that this format enables you to save images with millions of colors, whereas the GIF option restricts you to 256 colors.

Another important issue is file size. JPEG permits a greater degree of compression than the GIF alternative, enabling quicker downloading times for larger graphics. And JPEGs appear to retain almost complete image quality for most photographs. As a demonstration, this photo showing the producer of Webmonkey at a staff meeting has been compressed as a JPEG (above) and as a GIF (below). Those dots you see in the GIF are called "dithering," and they come from that format's characteristic adjusting of pixels within a graphic to simulate the display of colors not in the GIF's color palette.

But don't write off the GIF just yet. For one thing, the JPEG format does not work well for graphics that contain large fields of color - these color fields can break up and fragment and look terrible.

Furthermore, an image's compression format shapes the way a browser can download it, and browsers can do several things with GIFs that JPEGs don't support. One of the advantages to a GIF is that you can interlace it. Interlaced GIFs appear first with poor resolution and then improve in resolution until the entire image has arrived, allowing the viewer to get a quick idea of what the picture will look like while waiting for the rest. JPEGs can only arrive linearly, from the top row to the bottom row.

Another plus is that the background of a GIF can be made transparent, so you see the background color of the browser window you're in.

Finally, GIFs can also be animated, like the little fellow you see below. Poor old JPEGs just have to stand still.

(e) What are the different measures for selecting servers (hardware) in a large scale organisation? [5]

Hardware forms the greatest asset of the company, but it reaches the obsolescence rate very quickly. Normally, it is said that every six months technology in the electronics, telecommunication and computing discipline changes. With such rapid rate of obsolescence, it is very important how the professionals select hardware equipment including the server, clients, peripherals, etc. while maintaining a proper balance between cost and the obsolescence rate.

Care must be taken to ensure that proper spare parts are available even after about five years of commissioning. In addition to this it should also be ensured that proper and reliable service backup is available throughout for keeping the intranet at maximum uptime.

Whenever any component of the entire intranet system breaks down or any extra component of higher capacity is required to be added, proper compatible component must be selected.

Besides this one has to consider in mind that what type of activities our intranet is going to handle. According to that hardware is chosen.

(f) Explain the need and working of a Public Key based Security System. [5]

One of the best method of ensuring security is to change the form of communication. Let the messages be encoded in such a pattern that it becomes almost impossible to decode for other while the actual user should be able to decode with the use of a simple certificate or key. There is well known implementation of the encryption/decryption method:

✓ Public key infrastructure solution

Public key infrastructure solutions :- The use of public-key based security systems requires great attention and due care in design and management of security features. The security of entire system is dependent on the security of the key since it is the key that will be used for signing certificates of various messages and documents. This is done at the top of the public key infrastructure also commonly called the root. The encryption and decryption is done by specialized hardware.

Usually, all the keys used for accessing the server are held at a secret location in the primary memory of the server. This area or location is highly prone to attacks (for example, in a server core memory dump). It is obvious that a higher degree of protection is required for this target location.

Specialized hardware such as protected memory or cryptographic memory module for storing and protecting the keys proves to be a good solution. The keys are stored in a highly encrypted format. When loaded for signing, the keys are decrypted using complex encryption/decryption algorithms and loaded into the memory of the secure server, which then performs all the signing operations required on behalf of the server. It should be noted that the keys are never displayed in their unencrypted form to the server or any other user, so even if an intruder manages to access the network, the keys remains safe.

Physical security of the cryptographic modules is also built in order to provide total security of the whole system and protect from unauthorized tampering or any kind of manipulation. The physical security is ensured by use of advanced manufacturing technology wherein strong systems are fabricated to protect the sophisticated security hardware.

Since digital certificates are highly dependent on hardware computations, it is essential that mechanisms are evolved to increase the speed of computing by various means such as parallel processing, provision of additional processors, separate hardware for protection, etc. Assume that a number of users log on to the server, then in such an event it is sure to face a bottleneck at the security gate since it would take considerable time in processing encryption/decryption of the keys or certificates. Nowadays, in order to reduce this kind of difficulty, a separate server called firewall server is placed in front of the main server. Any one willing to access the main server has to get through this gate.

2(a) Explain the types of database connectivity supported on Intranet, with the help of a suitable example of each. [8]

Basic connectivity : A number of database management systems are available today such as the Oracle, Sybase, Ingress, Gupta's SQL Base, etc.

Most of the databases that are used to store massive data for use through Internet deploy Relational Database Management System (RDBMS) designed for PC class hardware. They are also available in both server (workgroup) and local engine (stand-alone) configurations, and are usually bundled with the power of Structured Query Language (SQL), transaction processing, and distributed processing for building business applications. By supporting client/server architecture, these software achieve a higher level of scalability, which makes them suitable for a wide range of applications; from a stand-alone, single-user environment to a multi-user workgroup environment.

To build the client side of applications, developers use various tools. Some of the popular software development environments include Visual Basic, C/C++, Power Builder, Java, Delphi, etc. It must be ensured that the databases can connect to these programming languages, or in other words, these database management systems should support these languages by being backend support.

Middleware support :- All the connectivity interfaces related tools come under the category of middleware. Middleware provides the link for data exchange between the different points of processing in a distributed application. In an intranet application, the points of processing are the database software, the server software and the client application.

Many of the popular databases also provide support of and to the middleware and consequently, the term middleware has become lesser known. Though software like the ASP, Perl, etc. have got wide popularity, a lot of work is being done to integrate a number of features of the traditional software made available in the middleware also.

During processing of any request, the client/server architecture is maintained and the database and client applications are processed separately even though running on the same platform or machine. For certain middleware, a connectivity interface is not required to support data exchange between the application and middleware or database.

Open Database Connectivity (ODBC) :- It happens that in addition to conventional or most popular database management systems, many companies go for proprietary software creating problem for themselves as well as for the clients. It is strongly recommended that companies should use that particular DBMS software which is most popular and widely used.

If this is not followed, a number of difficulties arise with database connectivity and the company may have to shell out enormous amount of money on obtaining proper connectivity tools.

It must also be ensured that whenever any DBMS or middleware is procured, all relevant database connectivity tools are also bundled. Most important of all of the connectivity tools or drivers is the ODBC, which permits connectivity to any type of database from the client application.

Many developers provide not just a simple ODBC driver, but a complete industry standard ODBC database solution for a wide range of operating systems such as Windows, Unix, Linux, MacOS, Sun Solaris, etc.

Java Database Connectivity (JDBC) :- With two different types of technologies available in the market today viz., the Windows and the Java technologies developed by the Microsoft and the Sun Microsystems respectively, it is essential for any company to ensure proper integration of the two technologies so that the customer support is ensured in spite of the technological divide.

Not just ordinary ODBC tools and drivers, it has become almost essential for the companies to obtain the JDBC drivers as well. With JDBC drivers, it would become possible to connect the Java applications with any type of databases and can query as well as update data from any data source across Intranets or the Internet.

(b) What are the "threats" on Intranet? Give an example of each to describe them. Explain any three solutions for minimizing these threats. [7]

The Intranet requires security because of :

- Hardware causes
- Software causes
- Information

Hardware can be stolen, tampered by frustrated employee, destruction of the resources.

Whereas software causes include deletion or theft of a program, corruption of a program, change in program code and thus making it malfunctioning, bugs in the software or virus attack.

Third component of the system liable to be attacked in data which is so important and crucial for an organization/company.

Security should be provided in order to make an Intranet functioning successfully and reliably. There are many ways through which Intranet can be made secure and reliable. Those are :

(1) Certificates

(2) Firewalls

(3) Encryption/Decryption methods

(4) Multiple Level Security

(5) SOCKS

Certificates :- Digital Certificates or Digital Signatures are used for securing e-mails, money transactions. Certificates includes a Public Key which is assigned to the users and is required to be sent when user wants to make any transaction. The certificate acts as an evidence of the user's digital identity.

Digital certificates provide excellent means of controlling and monitoring access to the Intranets. The certificate itself acts as a token for access control. The certificate could contain a series of digits and alphabets combined together.

Firewalls :

Firewalls provide security by following:

(1) Packet Filtering

(2) Application Gateways for restricting applications

(3) Proxy Servers

Proxy servers are used to isolate IP address range from the Internet. One interface of the Proxy Server is connected to the Internet, whose IP address is known to the Internet (Outside World). This IP address is also called Live IP address.

Whereas other interface is connected to the Intranet where all hosts are assigned unique IP addresses which are independent of the Internet (hidden to the Internet).

Firewalls can also be implemented on the proxy server either to give access or deny access based upon Applications or IP addresses.

NAT performs mapping between IP range of the Internet and IP addresses (resources such as web sites) of the Internet.

Encryption :

Public Key Solutions :- The Public Key Solutions involves a third party provider which provides key and checks for the authentication based upon the key.

The Architecture is shown in the figure below:

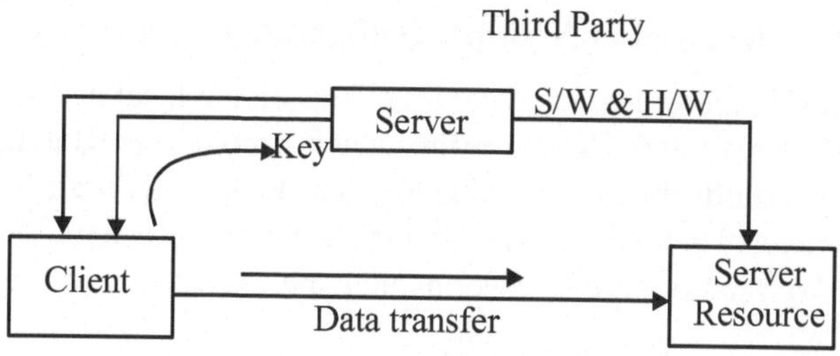

(-Public Key Authentication)

As soon as the third party server authenticates the key, data transmission takes place between the stations on the physical path.

Secured Sockets Layer (SSL) : It is used to secure the web server for authentication of the Users who want to access the resource. Resource requested may be HTTP or FTP or any other protocol supported by the Web Server.

Today, almost all commercial web sites are using SSL to ensure the authenticity of the server and integrity of the data delivered to web site users.

Virtual private Network (VPN) : If an Intranet is extended between two geographically separated locations, VPN is used to secure Intranet data.

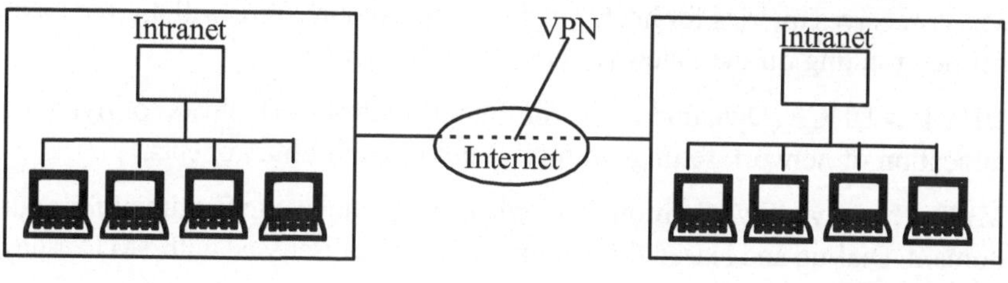

As shown in the diagram, when two geographically separated Intranets are connected using the Internet, VPN is established between the two to secure data of the Intranets. VPN uses IP addresses to differentiate between Internet and Intranet users.

Multiple Level Security :- Multiple level security involves more than one type of security mechanisms implemented to secure data. It can be combination of any two described above.

Interaction :- Where there are means of communication between the members of the company interaction becomes very easy. Hence the flow of information and responses are the loveliest thing present on the intranet. There can be a section on intranet where different employees will place their poems, stories, jokes and funny things which can be read by all just bringing the talent of the employees to the notice of others and making everybody gain something from it.

Discussion, scheduling, bulletin boards, desktop conferencing, doc management are few of the other benefits which are provided by the intranet.

3(a) List the steps involved in Network configuration of a server. [8]

The server lies inside the firewall and serves clients on the local network. All those services, like mail and file and print, which handle user data and are potential security hazards if exposed to the Internet, are hosted on the Intranet server and are protected behind the firewall. It also makes sense to run services like DHCP and Web proxy on the server as they are of use only to the LAN they serve.

Wherever possible, we've tried to implement access control and authentication to reduce abuses. As per our plan of action, the following are the steps involed in Network Configuration of a Server :

User authentication :- All user account management is to be done on the Intranet server using standard Linux tools like useradd, userdel, and passwd. Services like POP, IMAP, proxy, etc, will refer to the flat files (/etc/passwd) for authentication.

Internal DNS :- Unlike external DNS, internal DNS will be set up in such a way that it will provide name service for our zone pcquest.com. All hosts inside the LAN will use this server for name resolution. If the internal DNS server receives queries for hosts outside the local domain, it will use the DNS service running on the gateway server as a forwarder.

DHCP :- DHCP (Dynamic Host Configuration Protocol) allows for dynamic allocation of network settings to both Windows and Linux clients.

Mail :- Here, we'll walk through a typical mail setup using Sendmail for your domain. Dial-up and leased line setups will also be discussed with SMTP relay and spam control, and users will have the choice of using POP3 or IMAP for sending and receiving mail.

Web proxy :- How do you share a choked dial-up link among your bandwidth-hungry users? Squid is a very powerful and industrial-strength proxy server, which can do wonders on a saturated link. Squid configuration is discussed with emphasis on access control and authentication.

File and print :- Samba is an NT-compatible file and print server for Unix. It can do most of the things an NT server can do and is very robust and stable. Samba is an ideal replacement for NT on most small- and medium-sized networks.

The install :- For your convenience, we've provided a 'PCQ Intranet Server' install option on the installation CD, which will install all the necessary packages for setting up the Intranet server.

(b) Consider any seven protocols that are related to Intranet or Internet. State the requirements based on which each of these protocols is to be used. **[7]**

Internet Protocol (IP) :- The Internet Protocol (IP) is responsible for sending data from one point to another (may be through different routes) on the Internet and is also used for intranets. Every point or computer must have a unique IP address that gives an identity to that particular computer on the Internet. This unique address of the sender as well as the destination machine is put on the data packet before sending and the Internet gateway decides where to send this packet based on this IP address.

TELNET :- When it is required to develop and test software for another operating system such as Sun Solaris or SCO Unix when working on a Windows NT based computer, it is preferable to connect to a computer that actually runs on Sun Solaris or SCO Unix and run all the commands on that while viewing the output at this Windows based computer. This situation resembles something like a terminal emulation kind of working and is possible through the telnet protocol. It is possible to work on the ISP's server by connecting to it as a regular user (from a remote computer) and run all the Unix based commands on it even though the user might not be having Unix installed at his location.

The Telnet protocol is used to establish an on-line connection (or connection oriented service) to a remote machine. It gives an impression that the user can access someone else's computer (also called a host computer) and that all the required permission have been given.

User Datagram Protocol (UDP) :- The User Datagram Protocol, or UDP as it is known, is a connectionless transport level protocol supported by the IP.

It offers a limited service as compared to the conventional TCP and can be used for transferring messages between computers in a IP based network.. In short, it can be said that UDP is more or less an alternative to the TCP and, it functions in a suite like TCP/IP called the UDP/IP. Unlike the TCP where the basic unit of data is called packet, under UDP a data unit is called a datagram.

```
0       7 8       15 16      23 24      31
+--------+--------+--------+--------+
| Source | Destination
|  Port  |  Port  |
+--------+--------+--------+--------+
|        |        |
| Length |Checksum|
+--------+--------+--------+--------+
|
|    data octets ...
+---------------- ...
```

Figure: User Datagram Header Format

UDP does not divide a message into small packets (or datagram's) and then reassemble them after receipt as it is done with TCP/IP. The basic philosophy behind use of UDP is that the entire message is sent and ensured that the receiver has received the message properly without any errors. UDP is highly useful in those network based applications that aim at saving lot of processing time spent on breaking and reassembling them.

The Wireless Application Protocol (WAP) is client/server architecture based technology and has been one of the landmark developments in the communications industry because of the attempt to develop an open standard for wireless protocols, independent of vendor and air link.

The WAP is developed for micro-browser of the mobile or cell phone. These phones can be considered as hand-held terminals. The WAP servers are programmed to provide simple services to the users since it is not possible to provide complete flexibility of an ordinary browser. Limited services such as providing result of examination, amount balance in the bank account, temperature and humidity of the day, simple message service, etc. can be easily provided on the phones. Day-by-day, new services are being added to the features.

Wireless Transaction Protocol (WTP) :- Responsible for ensuring proper wireless enabled transaction using protocols such as Wireless Datagram Protocol or standard suite of TCP/IP protocols. WTP offers three types of services:

unreliable one way request, reliable one way request and reliable two way request respond.

Wireless Datagram Protocol (WDP) :- This is a protocol very much similar to the UDP except that the WDP uses the wireless communication techniques.

The SMS, CSD and the USSD are three most important of the WAP's underlying bearers:

✓ Short Message Service: Supports a maximum length of 160 characters per short message.

✓ Circuit Switched Data: Since CSD has very few users as of today, the WAP could not have a good start with the CSD as well.

✓ Unstructured Supplementary Services Data: USSD is a means of transmitting information or instructions over a GSM network.

Secure Electronic Transactions (SET) Protocol :- The SET based purely on the science of cryptography that speaks of encoding and decoding messages for communication. This science is not new to us rather it has been in use since the evolution of human. Preserving the secrecy of transactions through strong encryption algorithms, especially for applications like the military, trade and banking has been described infinite number of times in the history books. There has been tremendous advance in the field of encryption with the advancement in computing and mathematics.

Secure Electronic Transactions (SET) is a protocol developed jointly by Visa and MasterCard, involving other computing majors like IBM. SET is an open standard for protecting the privacy, and ensuring the authenticity, of electronic transactions, especially applicable to the banking sector where the transactions could be in terms of few cents to multi-million dollars.

Since the customer/consumer as well as the traders interest has to be protected, methods such as privacy, authentication, encryption, etc. evolved to provide back to back support for carrying out electronic commerce over the Internet.

4(a) Explain the following in the context of user management : [8]
(i) User authentication

User authentication :- This refers to authentication by username and password and is often provided by the operating system. Some operating systems, such as Windows NT, have robust security systems; some have relatively fragile security, l and Windows 3.1 has none to speak of.

(ii) Process of logging on :- 'Logging on' is the basic terminology used to indicate the process of accessing a distant sit via and address of it .The term came up with 'intranets' and 'internet' coming to the front and users accessing the various documents and web pages by typing in the address in the browser.

Telnet is the protocol, or set of procedures, that enables a user of one computer on the Internet to log on remotely to any other computer on the Internet, provided the user has a password for the distant computer or the distant computer provides publicly available files. Telnet is also the name of a computer program that uses these rules to make connections between computers on the Internet. Many computers that provide large electronic databases, like library catalogues, often allow users of Telnet in to search the databases. Many resources that were once available only through Telnet have now become available on the World Wide Web.

(iii) User properties :- The properties representing the pieces of useful user information: like personal data, demographic data, or something of equal importance that can be logically grouped together into something called a property set. These property set is specific to the user is later used to manage users. E.g. Windows 2000 server maintains property set for all the users created.

(iv) File and folder permission.

Here we have taken example of Windows 2000/XP systems that have NTFS formatted disks to have complete understanding of File and folder persmission in the context of user management :

You can set File and Folder permissions when you want to share files with others. You can allow others to view your files, modify your files, create new files, and even delete files. You can even restrict access to your files.

Permissions can be set on folders and files. If permissions are set on folders, then by default all subfolders and files inherit those permissions. More information about inherited permissions is located below. Permissions can be given to users or groups.

The permissions that can be set include:

Full Control :- Be careful granting someone full control permissions. Do this only if you do not want to own the files anymore because someone with Full Control permissions can deny permissions to you. Granted Full Control for a folder, users can delete files and subfolders within that folder regardless of the permissions protecting them. If you select this permission, the other permissions are also selected. The other permissions are listed below.

Modify :- If you select Modify, then Read & Execute, Read, Write, and List Folder Contents (if the permission is set on a folder) are also selected. This permission gives others the rights to read, write, create and also delete files.

Read & Execute :- If you select Read & Execute, then Read and List Folder Content (for folders) are also selected. Read & Execute permissions on folders will allow someone to traverse a folder. Executable files are programs that you run such as Word and Excel. For the most part, you will not own any executable files. But if you do, then you'll need to give people the Read & Execute permissions.

List Folder Contents :- These permissions are only valid for folders not files. These permissions allow people to see the files listed in a directory. It does not give permissions to open files, just to see what files are in the directory. To allow others to view the files, use the Read & Execute permission.

Read :- Read permissions will give users permission to open files and view contents within a folder.

Write :- If you wish to give someone Write permissions, you must also select Read permissions. Write permissions will allow others to modify files, and create new files.

Special Permissions

Inherited Permissions

Permissions are inherited this means that if permissions are set on folders, then by default all subfolders and files inherit those permissions. This is the default setting, and you can tell if it is in effect if the check boxes under the permissions are shaded (or greyed-out).

(b) In which layer is the Address Resolution Protocol (ARP) situated in the OSI reference model? Draw and explain the format of an ARP message. [7]

ARP is situated of the bottom left of the Network layer. It can be considered as mechanism for mapping or translation of addresses below the network logical addresses & MAC (Media Access Control) layer physical addresses.

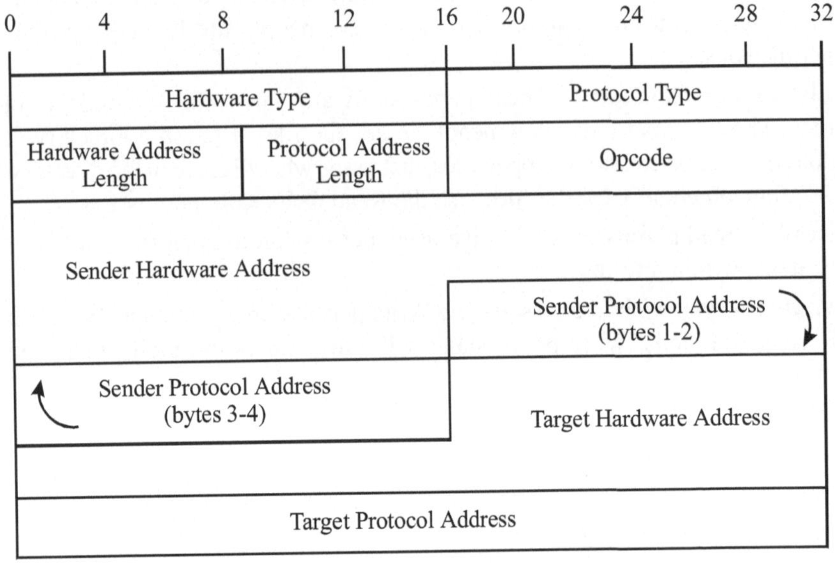

Figure : Address Resolution Protocol (ARP) Message Format

The ARP message format is designed to accommodate layer two and layer three addresses of various sizes. This diagram shows the most common implementation, which uses 32 bits for the layer three ("Protocol") addresses, and 48 bits for the layer two hardware addresses.

Explanation of ARP message format :

Field Name **Size (bytes)**

HRD ***2***

Description → Hardware Type : This field specifies the type of hardware used for the local network transmitting the ARP message; thus, it also identifies the type of addressing used.

Field Name **Size (bytes)**

PRO 2

Description → ***Protocol Type:*** This field is the complement of the *Hardware Type* field, specifying the type of layer three addresses used in the message. For IPv4 addresses, this value is 2048 (0800 hex), which corresponds to the EtherType code for the Internet Protocol.

Field Name **Size (bytes)**

HLN 1

Dexcription → ***Hardware Address Length:*** Specifies how long hardware addresses are in this message. For Ethernet or other networks using IEEE 802 MAC addresses, the value is 6.

Field Name **Size (bytes)**

PLN 1

Description → ***Protocol Address Length:*** Again, the complement of the preceding field; specifies how long protocol (layer three) addresses are in this message. For IP(v4) addresses this value is of course 4.

Field Name **Size (bytes)**

OP ***2***

Description → Opcode : This field specifies the nature of the ARP message being sent. The first two values (1 and 2) are used for regular ARP. Numerous other values are also defined to support other protocols that use the ARP frame format, such as RARP.

Field Name **Size (bytes)**

SHA (Variable, equals value in *HLN* field)

Description → ***Sender Hardware Address:*** The hardware (layer two) address of the device sending this message (which is the IP datagram source device on a request, and the IP datagram destination on a reply).

Field Name **Size (bytes)**

SPA (Variable, equals value in *PLN* field)

Description → ***Sender Protocol Address:*** The IP address of the device sending this message.

Field Name **Size (bytes)**

THA (Variable, equals value in *HLN* field)

Description → ***Target Hardware Address:*** The hardware (layer two) address of the device this message is being sent to. This is the IP datagram destination device on a request, and the IP datagram source on a reply)

Field Name **Size (bytes)**

TPA (Variable, equals value in *PLN* field)

Description → ***Target Protocol Address:*** The IP address of the device this message is being sent to.

5(a) Explain the importance and usage of the following : [8]
(i) Firewall
(ii) LDAP

(iii) DNS

(iv) HTTP

(i) Firewall :- For intranet developers, restricting access of unauthorized users to the web site has been the greatest challenge. In addition to preventing external users, a watchful eye on the users within the company may also have to be maintained. There are various tools to provide protection against unwanted intruders into the corporate wide networks, but the most popular amidst all security measures is the firewall.

The simplest way to restrict the users to peek inside the internals of the web site is to use firewalls, where the information cannot be seen or accessed from the Internet at large. Simple firewalls consist of software that prevents access to internal networks from the Internet. While general traffic such as email is allowed in to the mail server, programs such as FTP clients, telnet users or search engine queries cannot access machines beyond the safety premises of the firewall.

Firewalls also offer additional protection to local users who like to browse or surf out from the intranet to the Internet, by acting as proxy to obtain web pages so that the name and IP number of machines on the network are not revealed to other web sites that the users visit. Not revealing the IP address would help preventing hackers from knowing about the details of the structure of the intranet.

(ii) LDAP :- Stands for Lightweight Directory Access Protocol. LDAP is preferred for creating directories. LDAP provides a standard way for Internet clients, applications, and servers to access directory services using TCP/IP, regardless of the hardware/software platform.

(iii) DNS :- Programs rarely refer to hosts, mailboxes, and other resources by their binary network addresses. Instead of binary numbers, they use ASCII strings, such ass *info@gullybaba.com.*

Way back in the ARPANET, there was simply a file, hosts,txt, that listed all the hosts and their IP addresses.

However, when thousands of workstations were connected to the net, everyone realized that this approach could not continue to work forever. For one thing, the size of the file would occur constantly unless names were centrally managed, something unthinkable in a huge international network to solve these problems, **DNS (the Domain Name System)** Was invented.

To map a name onto an IP address, an application program calls a library procedure called the resolver, passing it the name as a parameter. The resolver sends a UDP packet to a local DNS server, which then looks up the name and returns the IP address to the resolver, which then returns it to the caller. Armed with the IP address, the program can then establish a TCP connection with the destination, or send it UDP packets.

(iv) HTTP Hypertext Transfer Protocol :- The Hypertext Transfer Protocol (HTTP) is an application level protocol and has become the standard Web service protocol. It enables transfer of files that may include text, graphic images, sound, video, and other multimedia files on the World Wide Web. Essential concepts that are part of HTTP include (as its name implies) the idea that files can contain references to other files whose selection will elicit additional transfer requests.

The concept of HTTP is based purely on Request-Response combination, with the client "requesting" and the server "responding" to the requests. The server straightaway processes the request, generates a response, and closes the connection. Thereafter, the server keeps waiting for other requests.

The HTTP protocol consists of two distinct items viz., the set of requests from browsers to server and the set of responses going back to them.

Although HTTP was designed for use on the Web, most widely known methods are GET, PUT and POST. There are other methods also that offer greater flexibility of usage and have been put keeping in view the future applications.

(b) Explain the working of the following Web servers : [6]
(i) AOL
(ii) Samba
(iii) Internet Information Server

(i) AOL :- AOLpress and AOLserver were formerly known as GNNPress and GNNServer (and much before they were popularly known as NaviPress and NaviServer) respectively. America Online combined or bundled the features of web authoring tools and web server into one.

The basis of AOL's complete web development service is known as PrimeHost, which combines the fineness of the HTML editor and web server. Joining the PrimeHost service, as a member will allow the user to have own domain name, a web site space of 20 MBs or more, counter programs, SSL support, and CGI capabilities.

Using PrimeHost user accounts can be easily set up with appropriate and moderate inexpensive monthly rates. Also offered are membership categories such as an individual, commercial, or dedicated user. Using the AOLserver software, whenever any a page is saved through AOLpress, it gets automatically hosted on the site. This cuts out the time and efforts required for saving files locally, transferring them to the remote server using FTP, and then making additional changes for maintenance thereafter.

In addition to seamless integration with the AOLpress client, the AOLserver offers the following services:

- Secure Sockets Layer (SSL) support (40-bit encryption)
- Multithreading and multi-homing capabilities with the ability to configure hundreds of virtual servers in a single process
- An integrated search engine
- Hierarchical access control (for restricting access to parts of the web site)
- Built-in TCL scripting language capabilities (for quickly building custom Web applications)
- Internal image map support
- SQL database services
- A complete C API for writing custom functions, drivers, and applications
- Support for AOLserver Dynamic Pages (ADPs) which make it easier to create dynamic content
- An integrated nsftp module (a fully-functioning FTP server that uses the AOLserver's permission system)
- Support for server-parsed HTML
- HTML caching (allows pages to be served more efficiently)
- An nsvhost module for virtual hosting (non-SSL only)

(ii) Samba :- Samba is excellent web server software and had taken a lead further by being functional, reliable, and free. Samba 5.0 is the latest version and provides the following:

- It is functional that means Samba not only works like the server but also works very well in a wide variety of applications. At any time , if it is found that the server does not work according to the desired pattern, the system administrator can program APIs using languages like C and C++.
- A web-based step-by-step guidelines for configuration of Samba
- Supports ASP Web pages via the Samba Server CScript language so that the system administrators can create dynamic and database-driven web pages
- Samba uses the HTTP protocol in both 40- and 128-bit versions. Also, the OpenSSL libraries are supported
- Samba is reliable. When matched with a Windows-NT-based system, Samba's reliability can come very close to that of a Unix/Apache-based system, so long as the supporting, custom APIs are programmed properly.
- Samba can run as a Windows NT System Service by executing a file named ntserver.exe binary in the "bin" directory
- Provides features similar to Unix daemons, i.e., the use of a system program without the need to log on to a machine and keep it connected.
- Provides a module called the Watcher Daemon that will try to restart the Web server and build up the system status automatically, and also arrange to send e-mail the administrator if server crashes.

It would be interesting to note that the basic Samba Production Server is available free. The professional version of Samba (that is priced at few thousand rupees) features such as DNS, mail, telnet, and proxy capabilities are offered.

(iii) Internet Information Server :- Microsoft's IIS 5.0 is a great improvement over the existing versions of web servers and now bundled with the Windows 2000 Server operating system. This version contains many new features along with enhanced performance and reliability. Notable improvements include

- Better and clearly documented security policies
- Support for the new WebDAV publishing standards
- Faster restarts of both Web and FTP services.
- Support of clustering, Microsoft has significantly improved the configuration and setup to enable multiple machines to share the load and deliver more reliable web services

Microsoft has also added a few new wizards to perform common tasks much easily. Three important wizards are

- The Permissions Wizard (to synchronize and align Web and NTFS security settings)
- The Web Server Certificate Wizard (to obtain and install server certificates)
- The CTL Wizard (to create and modify certificate trust lists)

There is a strong support of a number of standards in IIS 5.0 including:

- Fortezza (a new U.S. government security standard)
- Transport Layer security using SSL 3.0
- Digest Authentication (a method of hashing authentication information introduced in IE 5.0)
- Replacing NT LAN Manager authentication with the stronger Kerberos 5.0 authentication protocols used in Windows 2000.

(c) What is the need of SSL ? **[1]**

As it is well known that the Intranets and extranets are purely based on use of powerful web servers to deliver information to the users, the username/ password authentication pair has been a highly popular method for preventing access to the web servers. Problem arises with use such pairs when these keys are sent in the form of character/text strings, which are prone to be intercepted, read and converted with simple tools.

A significant enhancement was achieved when communications between the user and the server was sent in encrypted form and later decrypted at the other end. The enhancement went step by step and today it has stood as one of the most secured and popular method of secured communication called the

Secure Sockets Layer (SSL). Today, almost all commercial web sites are using SSL to ensure or guarantee the authenticity of the server and integrity of the data delivered to web site users.

SSL has become fundamental to the spread of Internet community, and commerce and trade over Internet. Over years, the spread of its use for an increasing range of transactions across the Internet has gone manifold.

Finally, it should be noted that by default most SSL implementations on web servers do not support or authenticate the client web browser. Therefore, SSL is at present best suited to the largely anonymous requirements of retailing and definitely requires lot of enhancements to actually pickup worldwide.

CS-75 : INTRANET ADMINISTRATION
DEC-2005

Note: Question number 1 is compulsory. Answer any three questions from the rest.

1(a). What is the purpose of proxy server ? How does it provide security in intranet ? [5]

Refer to June-04, Q.No-2(a), Page No-155

(b). How many class a network can we have in Internet ? How does the fragmentation and reassembly of packets take place in intranet ? [5]

First Refer to Dec-2001, Q.No-6(2), Page No-189

Fragmentation and Reassembly refers to the process used to fragment and reassemble packets so as to allow them to be transported across networks.

TCP protocol along with the IP protocol ensures the secure and correct transmission of data. TCP manages the flow of data and also manages the error in data transmission from one machine to another machine. On the other network the TCP checks for the transmission of packets from one node to another node. If it finds any error in data transmitted then it retransmits the data again. The TCP is at the transport layer. TCP has the responsibility to make connection with the destination machine and then to send the data packets one by one. TCP is connection oriented protocol . The whole message or data that is to be sent on the network is divided into smaller fragments and sent from the machine to another machine in the form of packets. The size of packets is decided. These different data packets reaches the destination machine through different paths and when they reach the destination machine they need to be reassembled correctly. The TCP/IP does this job with good responsibility.

(c). What is the difference between active static and dynamic documents in www ? How does CGI work? [5]

Static documents are fixed-content documents that are created and stored in a server. The client can get a copy of the document only. In other words, the contents of the file are determined when the file is created not when it is used. Of course, the contents in the server can be changed but the user cannot change them. When a client accesses the document, a copy of the document is sent. The user can then use a browsing program to display the document.

A **dynamic document** is created by a web server whenever a browser requests the document. When a request arrives, the web server runs an application program or a script that creates the dynamic document. The server returns the output of the program or script as a response to the browser that requested the document. Because a fresh document is created for each request, the contents of a dynamic document can vary from one request to another.

For many applications, we need a program or a script to be run at the client site. These are called **active documents**. For example, suppose we want to run a program that creates animated graphics on the screen or a program that interacts with the user. The program definitely needs to be run at the client site where the animation or interaction takes place. When a browser requests an active document, the server sends a copy of the document or a script. The document is then run at the client site.

Now Refer to Chapter-6, Q7, Page No-125

(d). Which of the following services should be enabled in a secure workstation connected in an Ethernet LAN? Give reasons for your answer.

Anacron, ftp, netfs, nfs, telnet sendmail, SSH, syslog, SNMP, time (assume the LAN is connected to the Internet but is not connected via Firewall nor is Kerberos used). [5]

NFS service is must for the given situation. The Network File System (NFS) is a client/server application that lets a computer user view and optionally store and update file on a remote computer as though they were on the user's own computer. The user's system needs to have an NFS client and the other computer needs the NFS server. Both of them require that you also have TCP/IP installed since the NFS server and client use TCP/IP as the program that sends the files and updates back and forth. (However, the User Datagram Protocol, UDP, which comes with TCP/IP, is used instead of TCP with earlier versions of NFS.) Its protocol uses the Remote Procedure Call (RPC) method of communication between computers. Using NFS, the user or a system administrator can mount all or a portion of a file system (which is a portion of the hierarchical tree in any file directory and subdirectory, including the one you find on your PC or Mac). The portion of your file system that is mounted (designated as accessible) can be accessed with whatever privileges go with your access to each file (read-only or read-write). While all other services provide more facility but without all of them the given objective can be achieved so nfs must be enabled in a secure workstation connected in an Ethernet LAN.

(e). What is a Socket? Write two difference between a TCP Socket and UDP Socket. [3]

An Internet socket (or commonly, a socket or network socket), is a communication end-point unique to a machine communicating on an Internet Protocol-based network, such as the Internet.

An Internet socket is composed of the following:

Protocol (TCP, UDP, raw IP)

Local IP address

Local port

Remote IP address

Remote port

The remote address can be either any valid IP address, or 0.0.0.0 for listening sockets and 255.255.255.255 for broadcasting sockets.

Operating systems associate sockets with a running process or processes (which use the socket to send and receive data over the network), and a transport protocol (i.e. TCP or UDP) with which the process(es) communicate to the remote host.

Usually sockets are implemented over TCP but this is not required. They can be implemented over any transport protocol, such as SNA. The concept of a socket is an entity that implements an API, regardless of the implementation.

Two widely used Internet socket types are,

1. Datagram Sockets use UDP (User Datagram Protocol) for transmission. UDP is an unreliable, connection-less protocol.

2. Stream Sockets use TCP (Transmission Control Protocol), which is a reliable, connection-oriented protocol. TCP treats communications as a continuous stream of characters.

(f). What are the standard port number for

(i) Web server (ii) Mail server (iii) FTP server (iv) Telnet? [2]

(i) Web server

80

(ii) Mail server

25

(iii) FTP server

21

(iv) Telnet?

23

(g). Why is the ARP protocol necessary? What is the significance of the field's hardware type protocol type and operation in the ARP header? [5]

Refer to June-05 ,Q.No-4(b), Page No-209

2(a). On what basis would you choose between public key algorithm or symmetric key algorithm in an application? Explain with the help of an appropriate example, the use of each. [6]

Public key cryptography, also known as **asymmetric cryptography,** is a form of cryptography in which a user has a pair of cryptographic keys - **a public key** and a **private key**. The private key is kept secret, while the public key may be widely distributed. The keys are related mathematically, but the private key cannot be practically derived from the public key. A message encrypted with the public key can only be decrypted with the corresponding private key.

Conversely, **Secret key cryptography,** also known as **symmetric cryptography** uses a single secret key for both encryption and decryption.

The two main branches of public key cryptography are:

Public key encryption — a message encrypted with a user's public key cannot be decrypted by anyone except the user possessing the corresponding private key. This is used to ensure confidentiality.

digital signatures — a message signed with a user's private key can be verified by anyone who has access to the user's public key, thereby proving that the user signed it and that the message has not been tampered with. This is used to ensure authenticity.

An analogy for public key encryption is that of a locked mailbox with a mail slot. The mail slot is exposed and accessible to the public; its location (the street address) is in essence the public key. Anyone knowing the street address can go to the door and drop a written message through the slot. However, only the person who possesses the key can open the mailbox and read the message.

An analogy for digital signatures is the sealing of an envelope with a personal wax seal. The message can be opened by anyone, but the presence of the seal authenticates the sender.

A central problem for public key cryptography is proving that a public key is authentic, and has not been tampered with or replaced by a malicious third party. The usual approach to this problem is to use a public key infrastructure (PKI), in which one or more third parties, known as certificate authorities, certify ownership of key pairs. Another approach, used by PGP, is the "web of trust" method to ensure authenticity of key pairs.

Public key techniques are much more computationally intensive than purely symmetric algorithms. The judicious use of these techniques enables a wide variety of applications. In practice, **public key cryptography** is used in combination with secret key methods for efficiency reasons. For encryption, the message may be encrypted with secret key algorithm using a randomly generated key, and that key encrypted with the user's public key. For digital signatures, a message is hashed (using a cryptographic hash function) and the smaller "hash value" is signed; before verifying the signature, the recipient computes the hash of the message himself, and compares this hash value with the signed hash value to check the message has not been tampered with.

(b). What is network address translation (NAT)? Give any two advantages and two disadvantages of Nat. [5]

Refer to Chapter-3, Q.No-6, Page No-59

(c). What is VPN? How is it useful for an organization? [5]

Refer to Chapter-2, Q.No-6, Page No 47

3(a). What is a search engine ? How is it useful for Internet/Intranet? Give the names of any four search engines. [4]

A search engine is an information retrieval system designed to help find information stored on a computer system, such as on the World Wide Web, inside a corporate or proprietary network, or in a personal computer. The search engine allows one to ask for content meeting specific criteria (typically those containing a given word or phrase) and retrieves a list of items that match those criteria. This list is often sorted with respect to some measure of relevance of the results. Search engines use regularly updated indexes to operate quickly and efficiently.

A search engine usually refers to a Web search engine, which searches for information on the public Web. Other kinds of search engine are enterprise search engines, which search on intranets, personal search engines, and mobile search engines. Different selection and relevance criteria may apply in different environments, or for different uses.

Some search engines also mine data available in newsgroups, databases, or open directories. Unlike Web directories, which are maintained by human editors, search engines operate algorithmically or are a mixture of algorithmic and human input

A search engine operates, in the following order

Web crawling

Indexing

Searching

Web search engines work by storing information about a large number of web pages, which they retrieve from the WWW itself. These pages are retrieved by a Web crawler (sometimes also known as a spider) — an automated Web browser which follows every link it sees. Exclusions can be made by the use of robots.txt. The contents of each page are then analyzed to determine how it should be indexed (for example, words are extracted from the titles, headings, or special fields called meta tags). Data about web pages are stored in an index database for use in later queries. Some search engines, such as Google, store all or part of the source page (referred to as a cache) as well as information about the web pages, whereas others, such as AltaVista, store every word of every page they find. This cached page always holds the actual search text since it is the one that was actually indexed, so it can be very useful when the content of the current page has been updated and the search terms are no longer in it. This problem might be considered to be a mild form of linkrot, and Google's handling of it increases usability by satisfying user expectations that the search terms will be on the returned webpage. This satisfies the principle of least astonishment since the user normally expects the search terms to be on the returned pages. Increased search relevance makes these cached pages very useful, even beyond the fact that they may contain data that may no longer be available elsewhere.

When a user comes to the search engine and makes a query, typically by giving key words, the engine looks up the index and provides a listing of best-matching web pages according to its criteria, usually with a short summary containing the document's title and sometimes parts of the text. Most search engines support the use of the boolean terms AND, OR and NOT to further specify the search query. An advanced feature is proximity search, which allows users to define the distance between keywords.

The usefulness of a search engine depends on the relevance of the result set it gives back. While there may be millions of webpages that include a particular word or phrase, some pages may be more relevant, popular, or authoritative than others. Most search engines employ methods to rank the results to provide the "best" results first. How a search engine decides which pages are the best matches, and what order the results should be shown in, varies widely from one engine to another. The methods also change over time as Internet usage changes and new techniques evolve.

List of search engines:

Google

Alta vista

Yahoo

Excite

(b). What is an Intranet authority tool? Give the name of any three tools with their uses. **[4]**

Refer to Chapter-5, Q.No-1, Page No-100

(c). What is WAP? Give any two advantages and two limitations of WAP

also explain it's layered architecture. **[7]**

Refer to Chapter-6, Q.No-11, Page No-129

4(a). Write the main function of each of the following: **[4]**

(i) Telnet

TELNET (TELetype NETwork) is a network protocol used on the Internet or local area network (LAN) connections. The term telnet also refers to software which implements the client part of the protocol. TELNET clients have been available on most Unix systems for many years and are available for virtually all platforms. Most network equipment and OSs with a TCP/IP stack support some kind of TELNET service server for their remote configuration (including ones based on Windows NT). However with recent advancements SSH has become more dominant in remote access for Unix-based machines.

(ii) Rlogin

Rlogin is a Unix software utility that allows users to log in on another host via a network, communicating via TCP port 513. It was first distributed as part of the 4.2BSD release. rlogin is also the name of the application layer protocol used by the software, part of the TCP/IP protocol suite. Logged-in users can act as if they were physically present at the computer. RFC 1258, in which it was defined, states that: "the rlogin facility provides a remote-echoed, locally flow-controlled virtual terminal with proper flushing of output." rlogin communicates with a daemon, rlogind, on the remote host. rlogin is similar to the Telnet command, but has the disadvantage of not being as customizable and being able to connect only to Unix hosts.

(iii) SSH

In computing, Secure Shell or SSH is a set of standards and an associated network protocol that allows establishing a secure channel between a local and a remote computer. It uses public-key cryptography to authenticate the remote computer and (optionally) to allow the remote computer to authenticate the user. SSH provides confidentiality and integrity of data exchanged between the two computers using encryption and message authentication codes (MACs). SSH is typically used to log into a remote machine and execute commands, but it also supports tunneling, forwarding arbitrary TCP ports and X11 connections; it can transfer files using the associated SFTP or SCP protocols. An SSH server, by default, listens on the standard TCP port 22.

(iv) RSH

rsh (remote shell) is a command line computer program which can execute shell commands as another user, and on another computer across a computer network. The remote system on which the rsh executes the command needs to be running the rsh daemon.

The rsh protocol is not secure for network use, because it sends unencrypted information over the network

(b). Explain how a message sent by an application to another application travels on a different network via one or more routers using TCP/IP. [5]

The Internet is one of the 20th century's greatest communications developments. It allows people around the world to send e-mail to one another in a matter of seconds, and it lets you read, among other things. We're all used to seeing the various parts of the Internet that come into our homes and offices — the Web pages, e-mail messages and downloaded files that make the Internet a dynamic and valuable medium. But none of these parts would ever make it to your computer without a piece of the Internet that you've probably never seen. In fact, most people have never stood "face to machine" with the technology most responsible for allowing the Internet to exist at all: the router.

Routers are specialized computers that send your messages and those of every other Internet user speeding to their destinations along thousands of pathways. When you send e-mail to a friend on the other side of the country, how does the message know to end up on your friend's computer, rather than on one of the millions of other computers in the world? Much of the work to get a message from one computer to another is done by routers, because they're the crucial devices that let messages flow between networks, rather than within networks. Let's look at what a very simple router might do. Imagine a small company that makes animated 3-D graphics for local television stations. There are 10 employees of the company, each with a computer. Four of the employees are animators, while the rest are in sales, accounting and management. The animators will need to send lots of very large files back and forth to one another as they work on projects. To do this, they'll use a network.

When one animator sends a file to another, the very large file will use up most of the network's capacity, making the network run very slowly for other users. One of the reasons that a single intensive user can affect the entire network stems from the way that Ethernet works. Each information packet sent from a computer is seen by all the other computers on the local network. Each computer then examines the packet and decides whether it was meant for its address. This keeps the basic plan of the network simple, but has performance consequences as the size of the network or level of network activity increases. To keep the animators' work from interfering with that of the folks in the front office, the company sets up two separate networks, one for the animators and one for the rest of the company. A router links the two networks and connects both networks to the Internet.

Directing Traffic

The router is the only device that sees every message sent by any computer on either of the company's networks. When the animator in our example sends a huge file to another animator, the router looks at the recipient's address and keeps the traffic on the animator's network. When an animator, on the other hand, sends a message to the bookkeeper asking about an expense-account check, then the router sees the recipient's address and forwards the message between the two networks.

One of the tools a router uses to decide where a packet should go is a configuration table. A configuration table is a collection of information, including:

1) Information on which connections lead to particular groups of addresses

2) Priorities for connections to be used

3) Rules for handling both routine and special cases of traffic

A configuration table can be as simple as a half-dozen lines in the smallest routers, but can grow to massive size and complexity in the very large routers that handle the bulk of Internet messages.

A router, then, has two separate but related jobs:

(i) The router ensures that information doesn't go where it's not needed. This is crucial for keeping large volumes of data from clogging the connections of "innocent bystanders."

(ii) The router makes sure that information does make it to the intended destination.

In performing these two jobs, a router is extremely useful in dealing with two separate computer networks. It joins the two networks, passing information from one to the other and, in some cases, performing translations of various protocols between the two networks. It also protects the networks from one another, preventing the traffic on one from unnecessarily spilling over to the other. As the number of networks attached to one another grows, the configuration table for handling traffic among them grows, and the processing power of the router is increased. Regardless of how many networks are attached, though, the basic operation and function of the router remains the same. Since the Internet is one huge network made up of tens of thousands of smaller networks, its use of routers is an absolute necessity.

Transmitting Packets

When you make a telephone call to someone on the other side of the country, the telephone system establishes a stable circuit between your telephone and the telephone you're calling. The circuit might involve a half dozen or more steps through copper cables, switches, fiber optics, microwaves and satellites, but those steps are established and remain constant for the duration of the call. This circuit approach means that the quality of the line between you and the person you're calling is consistent throughout the call, but a problem with any portion of the circuit — maybe a tree falls across one of the lines used, or there's a power problem with a switch — brings your call to an early and abrupt end. When you send an e-mail message with an attachment to the other side of the country, a very different process is used.

Internet data, whether in the form of a Web page, a downloaded file or an e-mail message, travels over a system known as a packet-switching network. In this system, the data in a message or file is broken up into packages about 1,500 bytes long. Each of these packages gets a wrapper that includes information on the sender's address, the receiver's address, the package's place in the entire message, and how the receiving computer can be sure that the package arrived intact. Each data package, called a packet, is then sent off to its destination via the best available route — a route that might be taken by all the other packets in the message or by none of the other packets in the message. This might seem very complicated compared to the circuit approach used by the telephone system, but in a network designed for data there are two huge advantages to the packet-switching plan.

(iii) The network can balance the load across various pieces of equipment on a millisecond-by-millisecond basis.

(iv) If there is a problem with one piece of equipment in the network while a message is being transferred, packets can be routed around the problem, ensuring the delivery of the entire message.

The Path of a Packet

The routers that make up the main part of the Internet can reconfigure the paths that packets take because they look at the information surrounding the data packet, and they tell each other about line conditions, such as delays in receiving and sending data and traffic on various pieces of the network.

(c). How are PPP and SLIP used in an Intranet? Also write any two differences between them. [5]

In computing, the Point-to-Point Protocol, or PPP, is commonly used to establish a direct connection between two nodes. It can connect computers using serial cable, phone line, trunk line, cellular telephone, specialized radio links, or fiber optic links. Most Internet service providers use PPP for customers' dial-up access to the Internet. An encapsulated form of PPP, called Point-to-Point Protocol over Ethernet (PPPoE), is commonly used in a similar role with Digital Subscriber Line (DSL) Internet service.

PPP is commonly used to act as a data link layer (layer two of the OSI model) protocol for connection over synchronous and asynchronous circuits, where it has largely superseded the older, non-standard Serial Line Internet Protocol (SLIP), and telephone company mandated standards (such as Link Access Protocol, Balanced (LAPB) in the X.25 protocol suite). PPP was designed to work with numerous network layer protocols, including Internet Protocol (IP), Novell's Internetwork Packet Exchange (IPX), and AppleTalk.

The Serial Line Internet Protocol (SLIP) is a mostly obsolete encapsulation of the Internet Protocol designed to work over serial ports and modem connections. It is documented in RFC 1055. On PCs, SLIP has been largely replaced by the Point-to-Point Protocol (PPP), which is better engineered, has more features and does not require its IP address configuration to be set before it is established. On microcontrollers, however, SLIP is still the preferred way of encapsulating IP packets due to its very small overhead.

SLIP modifies a standard Internet datagram by appending a special "SLIP END" character to it, which allows datagrams to be distinguished as separate. SLIP requires a port configuration of 8 data bits, no parity, and either EIA hardware flow control, or CLOCAL mode (3-wire null-modem) UART operation settings.

SLIP does not provide error detection, being reliant on other higher-layer protocols for this. Therefore SLIP on its own is not satisfactory over a particularly error-prone dial-up connection. It is however still useful for testing OS' real-time capabilities under load (by looking at flood-ping statistics).

(d). How is SSL used to provide security is an intranet? **[2]**

Refer to June-05, Q.No-5(c), Page No-215

5(a). Explain the FTP connection mechanism between client and server, with the help of a suitable diagram. **[5]**

Refer to Chapter-6, Q.No-5, Page No-123

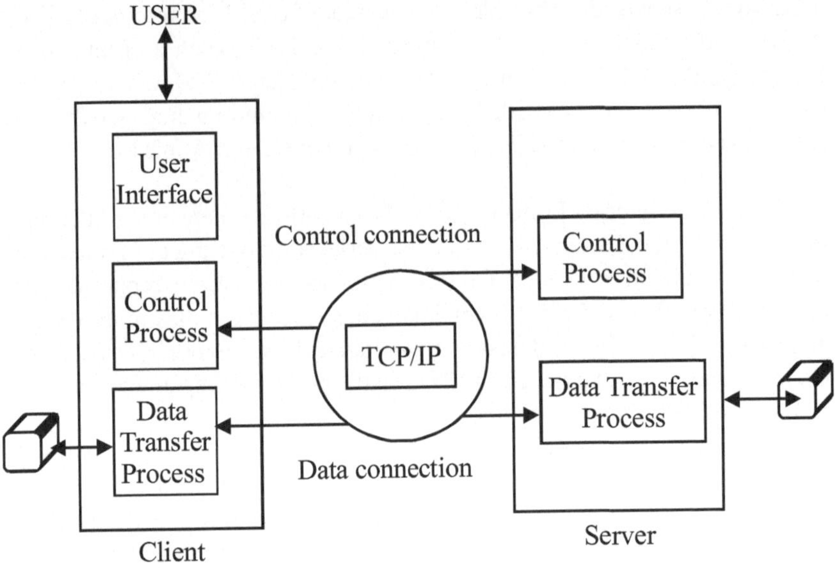

FTP

(b). How are SMTP and POP3 servers useful in Internet/ Intranet? What is the difference between IMAP and POP3? [5]

SMTP (Simple Mail Transfer Protocol) is a TCP/IP protocol used in sending and receiving e-mail. However, since it is limited in its ability to queue messages at the receiving end, it is usually used with one of two other protocols, POP3 or IMAP, that let the user save messages in a server mailbox and download them periodically from the server. In other words, users typically use a program that uses SMTP for sending e-mail and either POP3 or IMAP for receiving e-mail. On Unix-based systems, sendmail is the most widely-used SMTP server for e-mail. A commercial package, Sendmail, includes a POP3 server. Microsoft Exchange includes an SMTP server and can also be set up to include POP3 support.

SMTP usually is implemented to operate over Internet port 25.

Post Office Protocol ,version 3(POP3) is simple protocol and limited in functionality.

The client POP3 software is installed on the recipient computer , the server POP3 software is installed on the mail server.

Mail access starts with the client when the user needs to download its email from the mailbox on the mail server (POP3 server). The client opens a connection to the server on TCP port 110. It then sends its user name and password to access the mailbox. The user can then list and retrieve the mail messages, one by one.

Figure shows an example of downloading using POP3

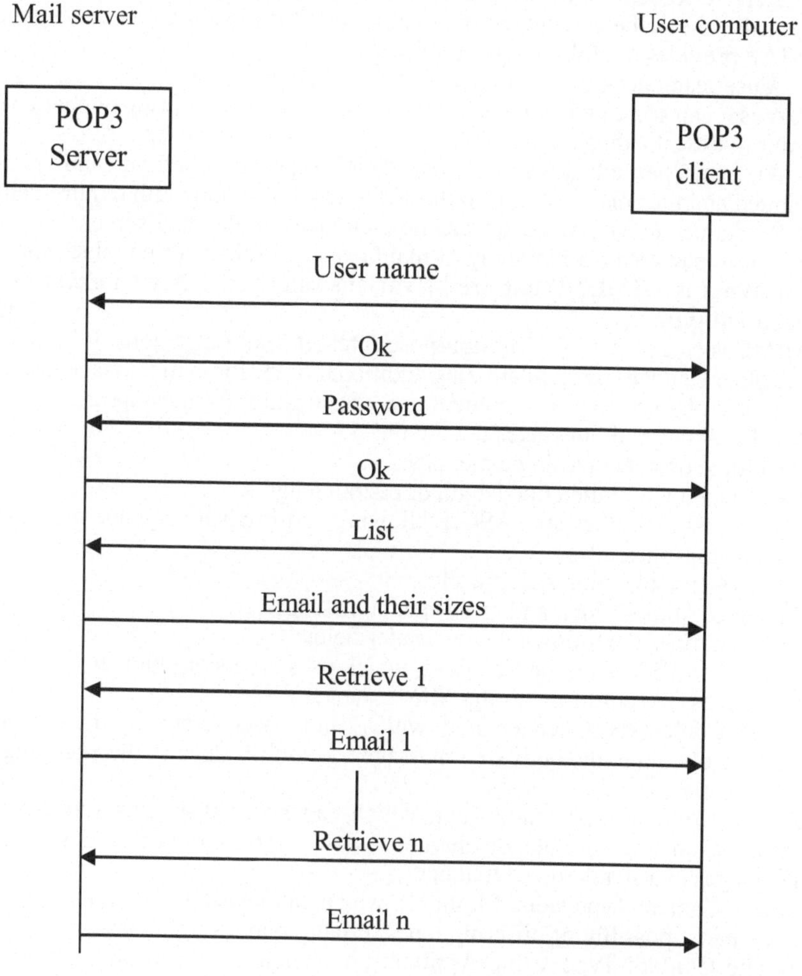

POP3 has two modes: the delete mode and the keep mode . In the delete mode , the mail is deleted from the mailbox after each retrieval. In the keep mode , the mail remains in the mailbox after retrieval. The delete mode is normally used when the user is working at her permanent computer and can save and organize the received mail after reading or replying. The keep mode is normally used when the user accesses her mail away from her primary computer(e.g., a laptop). The mail is read but kept in the system for later retrieval and organizing.

Difference between POP3 and IMAP

Internet Mail Access Protocol (IMAP) is similar to POP3, but it has more features. IMAP is more powerful and more complex.

POP3 is deficient in several ways. It does not allow the user to organize her mail on the server; the user cannot have different folders on the server (user can create folders on her own computer) . POP3 does not allow the user to partially check the contents of the mail before downloading.

IMAP provides the following extra functions:

1. A user can check the email header prior to downloading.
2. A user can search the contents of the email for a specific string of characters prior to downloading.
3. A user can partially download email. This is especially useful if bandwidth is limited and the email contains multimedia with high bandwidth requirements.
4. A user can create, delete or rename mailboxes on the mail server.
5. A user can create a hierarchy of mailboxes in a folder for email storage.

(c). What is MIME? What are its various subtypes? Give an example of each subtype. [5]

MIME is an acronym for Multipurpose Internet Mail Extensions. It builds on the older standard by standardizing additional fields for mail message headers that describe new types of content and organization for messages.

MIME allows mail messages to contain:

· Multiple objects in a single message.
· Text having unlimited line length or overall length.
· Character sets other than ASCII, allowing non-English language messages.
· Multi-font messages.
· Binary or application specific files.
· Images, Audio, Video and multi-media messages.

MIME defines the following new header fields:

1. The MIME-Version header field, which uses a version number to declare that a message conforms to the MIME standard.

2. The Content-Type header field, which can be used to specify the type and subtype of data in the body of a message and to fully specify the encoding of such data.

a. The Content-Type value Text, which can be used to represent textual information in a number of character sets and formatted text description languages in a standardized manner.

b. The Content-Type value Multipart, which can be used to combine several body parts, possibly of differing types of data, into a single message.

c. The Content-Type value Application, which can be used to transmit application data or binary data.

d. The Content-Type value Message, for encapsulating a mail message.

e. The Content-Type value Image, for transmitting still image (picture) data.

f. The Content-Type value Audio, for transmitting audio or voice data.

g. The Content-Type value Video, for transmitting video or moving image data, possibly with audio as part of the composite video data format.

3. The Content-Transfer-Encoding header field, that specifies how the data is encoded to allow it to pass through mail transports having data or character set limitations.

4. Two header fields that can be used to further identify and describe the data in a message body: the Content-ID and Content-Description header fields.

CS-75 : INTRANET ADMINISTRATION

JUNE-2006

Note: Question number 1 is compulsory. Answer any three questions from the rest.

1(a). Give any two differences between intranet and Internet. Also, list any three advantages of intranet. **[5]**

Refer to Chapter-1, Q.No-4, Page No-3

Refer to Chapter-1, Q.No-6, Page No-5

(b). Differentiate between internal and external security threats in an intranet.

Refer to Chapter-2, Q.No-2, Page No-39

(c). Explain the purpose of the following : **[6]**

(i) Kerberos v5

Kerberos V5: An Internet standard authentication protocol which is the default protocol for Windows 2000 computers within a domain.

(ii) Windows NT LAN Manager (NTLM)

Windows NT LAN Manager (NTLM): used to authenticate users from Windows 95, 98 and NT systems. Windows 2000 Active Directory must be operated in mixed mode to use this authentication method.

(iii) Secure Socket Layer/Transport Layer Security

Secure Socket Layer/ Transport Layer security (SSL/TLS): Requires certificate servers and is used to authenticate users that are logging onto secure web sites.

(d). Differentiate between intranet authoring and management tool. Give one example of each type of tool also. **[6]**

With the active involvement of major developers such as Microsoft, Netscape, Macromedia, Adobe, Trellix, Sun, etc, there are a number of tools ranging from small applications such as image animation up to powerful e-mail response handling application available to everyone. Most of them are even free on the web and those available commercially can be obtained at reasonable low cost.

It is essential to know almost all the HTML tags and take case of every tag and parameter of the HTML syntax this need has led to the development of appropriate tools to take care of relevant activities. These tools are being updated very quickly to suit to the requirement of various newly added features, integrated with other tools as well as to allow users platform functionality.

Examples: Adobe Page Mill, Microsoft front Page Tools, other than the ones used for intranet authoring fall under the category of Intranet Management they include tools ranging from simple solutions to massive deployment tools.

Groupware can be considered as one good solution for Intranet Management but there are other tools also which help in accomplishing this task. Database, application servers and other software tools for controlling the operations such as tools for discussion forum, emailing, chatting, etc come under this category.

These tools are sophisticated and require higher expertise to tackle. e.g.: Application servers like bluestone, cyber prise.

(e). What is the difference between local and domain account types ? Write the steps for creating these accounts. **[6]**

Local account is for local computer access. Domain account is for access to network resources in the domain.

Administrators and power users can create and modify accounts in the domain. Administrators on local computer can create and modify accounts locally.

Account creation

Local account: use the "Local users and groups" tool.

1. Right click "My Computer", select "Manage"

2. Click the t next to " Local users and Groups" in the "Computer Management" box.

3. Enter user information into the "New user" dialog box.

To modify the user properties, right click on the user and select" Properties".

User Property tabs include:

1) General –Set up when user must change password and disable the account here. Indication of account lockout is here.

2) Member of-Set up local groups the user is a member of.

3) Profile – Set up the environment variables, set a network path to the user profile folder and use home folder. This profile includes desktop settings.

4) Dial-in (only on server computer) - Set remote access permission, callback policy, and IP address and routing information.

Domain Account: use the "Active directory users and computers" tool.

1. From the Active Directory users and computer tool click t next to the domain name.

2. Highlight the "Users" folder and select "Active", "New", and "User".

3. Enter user information into the "New User" dialog box. To modify user properties, right click on the user and select "Properties".

User Property tabs include:

1) General: Set up when user must change password and disable the account here. Indication of account lockout is here.

2) Address: Set mail address or physical address information.

3) Account: Set hours that the user can logon during and restrict computers the user can use.

4) Profile: Set up the environment variables, set a network path to the user profile folder and user home folder. A logon script file can be set.

Domain user logon scripts are in the NETLOGON share on the Domain controller in the system Root/ SYSVOL / sysvol / domain name / SCRIPTS folder. The profile includes desktop settings. Default profile file location is c:\ documents and settings\ username on the computer that the user logged on to.

4) Other aspects such as Telephones, mobile, fax phone number etc and about the organisation consisting of the user title, department, massager, and company could be entered.

5) Member of –used to assign users to groups and remove user from groups.

6) Dial In- Dial in privileges can be granted or denied and callback options are set here.

7) Published Certificates – can add or remove user Internet certificates.

8) Object – view information about the user account object such as when the account was modified last.

9) Security – can set users and groups that can modify this domain user account properties.

(f). What is a Virtual Private Network (VPN) ? Give one advantage and disadvantage of VPN. **[3]**

Refer to Chapter-2, Q.No-6, Page.No-47

2(a). Explain the public key infrastructure solution, with the help of an example. **[4]**

Refer to Chapter-2, Q.No-6, Page.No-45

(b). What is Agora ? Explain any two of its properties that make it useful for E-commerce. **[5]**

Refer to Dec-04, Q.No- 4(a) (i), Page. No-228

3(a). Give any two uses of intranet authoring tools. Also list any three features of these tools. [5]

Refer to Chapter-5, Q.No-1, Page.No-100

(b). What is distributed database? Give two benefits of using a distributed database for an organisation. Give two differences between a distributed database and a file server model. [5]

Distribution database can be defined as consisting of a collection of data with different parts under the control of separate DBMSs, running on independent computer systems. All the computers are interconnected and each system has autonomous processing capability, serving local applications. Each system participates, as well, in the execution of one or more global applications. Such applications require data from more than one site.

A database server is the software managing a database, and a client is an application that requests information from a server. Each computer in a system is a node. A node in a distributed database system can be a client, a server or both.

A Distributed database must also provide the ability to hide the location of the data and the complexity of accessing it. The primary benefits of a distributed database is that the data of physically separate database can be logically combined and potentially made accessible to all users on a network. The database to which a user is directly connected is called the local database. Any additional databases accessed by this user are called remote database.

Benefits of using a distributed database for an organisation

1) There is a difficulty of communicating massive data and application across the network on-line. In such a scenario, the organisation plans to implement distributed databases and connects them into an integrated network. For instance, look at the railways or airline ticketing which cannot be easily communicated over the expensive network, lines for hours. Visually all processing is done at local level and are connected to the control server only when there is a need.

2) That the organisation may like to keep the information centralized but applications remain distribution in order to attain greater reliability, availability, safety or performance, or all of the above.

Differences between distributed database and a file server model

1) Less workload on the server due to distribution of work in distributed database

2) If data is lost on one site, it can be gathered from the other site in case of distributed database.

4(a). What is the importance of an Internet Information Server? Give any two differences between an Internet information server and a personal web server. **[4]**

Refer to Chapter-5 Q.No-8, Page No-110

Refer to Chapter-5, Q.No-9, Page No-111

(b). What are the different classes of IP address? Explain each class, with an example. **[6]**

Refer to Dec-01, Q.No-6(2), Page No-189

5(a). What are the different firewall technologies ? Explain the working of the packet filter firewall technology. **[5]**

Refer to Dec-02, Q.No-5 (a), Page No-182

(b). What are the uses of the following commands in an Intranet/Internet ? Write their complete syntax also. **[5]**

(i) Unlink in HTTP

Unlink in HTTP –Breaks and existing connection between two resources

(ii) TOP msg n in POP

Top msg n in POP- Returns the headers of desired message and also n lines of its body.

CS-75 : INTRANET ADMINISTRATION
DEC-2006

Note: Question number 1 is compulsory. Answer any three questions from the rest.

1(a). "An Intranet uses the Internet technologies within an organization to achieve better results than the conventional means of data access and transfer." Give comments in support of the above statement. [5]

Refer to Chapter-1, Q.No-7&8, Page No-6

(b). Write and explain any five benefits of implementing Intranet in any organization. [5]

Refer to Chapter-1, Q.No-6, Page No- 5

(c). List any five security threats in an Intranet and also mention what can be the solution (s) for each of them. [10]

Refer to Chapter-1, Q.No-10, Page No-11

(d). Mention the role of the following with example (s) for each of the following with respect of intranet : [10]

(i) Servers

Refer to Chapter-3, Q.No-3, Page No-56

(ii) Clients

Refer to Chapter-3, Q.No-3, Page No- 56

(iii) Security systems

Refer to Chapter-3, Q.No-4, Page No-57

(iv) Protocols

Refer to June-05, Q.No-3(b), Page No-205

2(a). What is Groupware ? List any five broad range of applications associated with hem. [5]

Refer to Chapter-3, Q.No-7, Page No 59

(b). Mention the context where a database is required in the intranet applications. List any five databases (Internal databases or external databases) which can be used as Backend for the applications. Also mention about the database connectivity required to connect respective

databases with the front end application. **[5]**

Refer to Chapter-3, Q.No-8, Page No-61

A database system is required in the organization(intranet) to provide centralized control of its data. The situation that prevails in many enterprise is that each application has its own private files in its own tapes and disks so the data is widely dispersed and therefore difficult to control.

But a database is organized in such a way that a computer program can quickly select desired pieces of data .The following are the examples of database applications:

1. computerized library systems

2. Automated teller machines

3. Flight reservation systems

Having complete authority over the operational data , enables Database administrator (DBA) in ensuring that the only means of access to the database is through proper channels.

centralized control of its data helps in permitting the administrator to define integrity constraints to the data in the database. The existing applications can share the data in a database.

Examples of databases:

1. Microsoft SQL Server

2. Microsoft Access

3. Microsoft Foxpro

4. Oracle

5. dBase

All the above database can use ODBC for connectivity.

For application to communicate with the database ,it needs to have the following information:

1. The RDBMS/DBMS product using which the database is created.

2. The location of the database.

3. The name of the database.

Microsoft provides a standard for the application to communicate with the database called open database connectivity(ODBC).

1. Open database connectivity (ODBC) : ODBC API is a set of library routines that enable programs to access a variety of databases.All you need to do is to install a DBMS-specific ODBMS driver and write the program to interact with the specified ODBC driver.

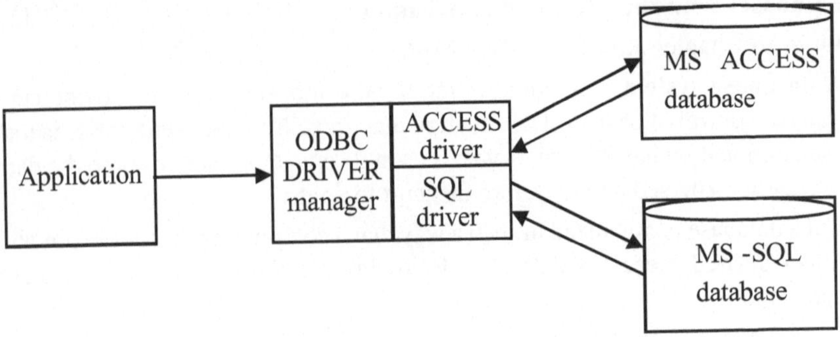

ODBC Application Architecture

Java database connectivity (JDBC) provides a database programming for API for java programs.

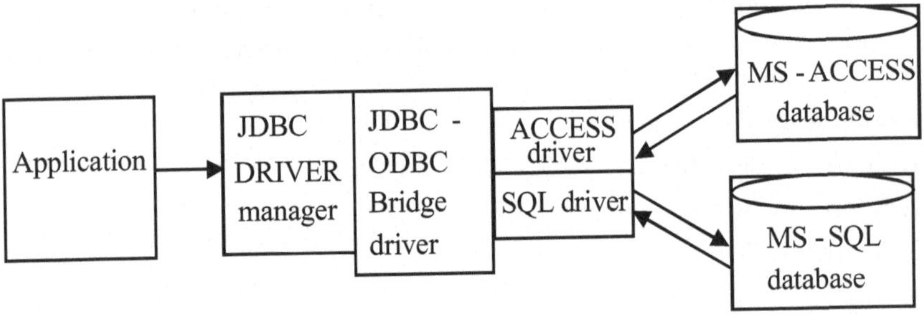

JDBC Application Architecture

3(a). What is encryption and decryption ? How can these be achieved using the SSL ? [5]

In cryptography, encryption is the process of obscuring information to make it unreadable without special knowledge, sometimes referred to as scrambling. Encryption has been used to protect communications for centuries, but only organizations and individuals with an extraordinary need for secrecy had made use of it. In the mid-1970s, strong encryption emerged from the sole preserve of secretive government agencies into the public domain, and is now used in protecting widely-used systems, such as Internet e-commerce, mobile telephone networks and bank automatic teller machines.

Encryption can be used to ensure secrecy, but other techniques are still needed to make communications secure, particularly to verify the integrity and authenticity of a message; for example, a message authentication code (MAC) or digital signatures. Another consideration is protection against traffic analysis.

Encryption or software code obfuscation is also used in software copy protection against reverse engineering, unauthorized application analysis, cracks and software piracy used in different encryption or obfuscating software.

The process of converting encrypted data back into its original form, so it can be understood is called decryption. To easily recover the contents of an encrypted signal, the correct decryption key is required. The key is an algorithm that "undoes" the work of the encryption algorithm. Alternatively, a computer can be used in an attempt to "break" the cipher. The more complex the encryption algorithm, the more difficult it becomes to eavesdrop on communications without access to the key.

Refer to June-05, Q.No-5(c), Page No-215

(b). What is Authentication ? List and explain any three types of authentication mechanisms supported by WINDOWS 2000 Operating System. **[5]**

Authentication is a process that is performed by the system automatically to ensure that the user is genuine. Authentication may be done at a local computer or at a global level for a domain using domain controllers across the network. Windows 2000 support the following types of authentication.

(i) Kerberos V5 : An Intranet standard authentication protocol which is the default protocol for Windows 2000 computers within a domain.

(ii) Windows NT LAN Manager (NTLM): Used to authenticate users from Windows 95,98, and NT systems. Windows 2000 Active directory must be operating in mixed mode to use this authentication method.

(iii) Secure Sockets Layer / Transport Layer Security (SSL/TLS): Requires certificate servers and is used to authenticate users that are logging onto secure websites.

(c). What is an Internet Authoring tool ? List any four authoring tools. **[5]**

Refer to Chapter-5, Q.No-1, Page-No-100

4(a). Assume a network of an organization with departments (HR, Manufacturing, Marketing, Finance, Sales) and having sufficient number of computers in each. Configure an Intranet for the specifications of the company defined above. Also, list the applications which can be launched on the Intranet. Make any necessary assumptions. **[5]**

Refer to Chapter-1, Q.No-11, Page No-13

(b). Give five reasons why an organization should implement the distributed database. **[5]**

1.The primary need of a distributed database is that the data of physically separate database can be logically combined and potentially made accessible to all users on a network.

2. Fault tolerance through redundancy–if data is lost on one site, it can be gathered from the other site

3. Autonomous systems- that perinets security to be applied via user authentication.

4. Less workload on the server due to distribution of work.

5. Masking out irrelevant communication- It is done by limiting communication to case where some coordination is needed otherwise, one site can completely handle its data.

5(a). What is an Application Server ? List any four application servers that are available in the market. [5]

Application servers allow serving information about the organisation, its services and products over the Intranet or Internet. At the most fundamental level, it uses the HTML for presentation of the content. Application servers accept request from browsers like Netscape and Internet Explorer generated by users at the client end and then return the appropriate HTML documents.

With the advancement of technology, thousands of new features are being added day in and day out. A combination of many server side computing techniques and technologies can be used to enhance the power of the server beyond its ordinary capabilities, which may include implementation of CGI scripts, server side includes, SSL security and Active server pages (ASPs)

Application server are

1) Bluestone

2) Cyber prise

3) Fast Track

4) Persistence

(b). What is an IP address? Into how many classes the static IP address divided? Give their purpose of use and the respective address structure. [3]

Refer to Dec-01, Q.No-6(2), Page No-189

(c). Write the full forms for the following : [2]

(i) CGI

CGI – Common Gateway Interface

(ii) UDP

UDP – User Database Protocol

(ii) IIS

IIS- Internet Information Server

(iv) IMAP

IMAP –Internet Message Access Protocol

CS-75 : INTRANET ADMINISTRATION
June, 2007

Note : Question number 1 is **compulsory.** Answer any **three** questions from the rest.

1. (a) Explain the term threats. Differentiate between Internal and External threats.

Ans. Refer to Chapter-2, Q.No.-2, Page No.-39

(b) (i) What are Service Protocols?

Ans. Refer to Chapter-6, Q.No.-2, Page No.-119

(ii) Define the term Gateway.

Gateway (in telecommunications), it is a computer or a network that allows or controls access to another computer or network. And Gateway (in computer networking), it is a node that serves as an entrance to another network, and vice-versa. The meaning of this term has altered subtly in recent years, however.

(c) Write short notes on:

(i) HTTPd

Ans. Refer to Chapter-1, Page No.-18

(ii) Webmaster

Ans. Refer to Chapter-4, Q.No.-10, Page No.-84

(iii) Telnet

Ans. Refer to Chapter-4, Page No.-93

(d) What is WAP (Wireless Application Protocol)? Explain the WAP layered architecture and write any four applications of WAP.

Ans. Refer to Chapter-6, Q.No.-11, Page No.-129,
Refer to Chapter-6, Q.No.-12, Page No.-132
& Refer to Chapter-6, Q.No.-13, Page No.-132

(e) Explain the following:

Ans. (i) Address Resolution Protocol (ARP)

Ans. Refer to Chapter-6, Q.No.-1, Page No.-116

(ii) Internet Message Access Protocol (IMAP)

Ans. Refer to Chapter-6, Page No.-118

(f) How does Intranet work? Also, explain its advantage over Internet.

Ans. First Refer : Chapter-1, Q.No.-2, Page No.-2

Advantages of Intranet over Internet :

(i) Secure connections : Intranet provides private internal networks such as local area network(LAN) or wide are network (WAN), which are protected from outside Internet users by a firewall.

(ii) Easier Control : Intranet is much easier to handle in terms of protocols and connections.

(iii) Higher data transfer speed per unit (bandwidth) : Intranet provides higher and broader bandwidth per unit cost than the Internet.

2. (a) What is Groupware ? Give advantages and disadvantages of

Groupware.
Ans. Refer to Chapter-3, Q.No.-7, Page No.-59

(b) Explain the terms Encryption and Decryption. How is it relevant to Intranet?
Ans. In cryptography, encryption is the process of transforming information (referred to as plaintext) using an algorithm (called cipher) to make it unreadable to anyone except those possessing special knowledge, usually referred to as a key. The result of the process is encrypted information (in cryptography, referred to as ciphertext). In many contexts, the word encryption also implicitly refers to the reverse process, decryption (e.g. "software for encryption" can typically also perform decryption), to make the encrypted information readable again (i.e. to make it unencrypted). Encryption has long been used by militaries and governments to facilitate secret communication over their Intranet also. Encryption is also used in digital rights management to prevent unauthorized use or reproduction of copyrighted material and in software also to protect against reverse engineering. Some organisations need to connect various offices through their Intranet. Those organisations need to have additional hardware device like router to connect to different locations. If organisation has great security issue, they also need to implement encryption/decryption to communicate. If the important / sensitive message is exchanged over the Intranet then encryption/decryption must be used.

3. (a) Explain different classes of IP Address. Give suitable example of each.
Ans. IP address is also called dynamic IP address and it changes every time the user logs on to the ISP's server.
The IP address are divided into four classes since networks vary in size, which the organizations decide when applying for a static IP address:
(i) Class A addresses are for extremely large networks or gateways, usually given at the level of one per country
(ii) Class B addresses are for large networks, or extremely large organizations
(iii) Class C addresses are for small networks (fewer than 256 devices) or may be for those at the level of organization
(iv) Class D addresses are also called multicast addresses, normally for representing devices and computers on the networks
The class of addresses used by a device or network is identified by the first few bits of each IP address. The address structures look like this:

Class A 0	Network (7 bits)	Local address (24 bits)
Class B 10	Networks(14 bits)	Local address (16 bits)
Class C 110	Networks(21 bits)	Local address (8 bits)
Class D 1110	Multicast address (28 bits)	

The IP address is usually expressed as a combination of four octal numbers with each number representing eight bits, all of them separated by periods, such as 202.64.15.30. The number 202 represents the class A network (usually for India), the second number would represent a large organization or a service provider (in this case it is VSNL), third number represents a server (here it indicates a server of the VSNL at New Delhi) and finally the fourth number would indicate a particular user connected to that server.

(b) Differentiate between CDMA and GSM technology.

Ans. GSM's high-speed wireless data technology, GPRS (General Packet Radio Service), usually offers a slower data bandwidth for wireless data connection than CDMA's high-speed technology (1xRTT, short for single carrier radio transmission technology), which has the capability of providing ISDN (Integrated Services Digital Network)-like speeds of as much as 144Kbps (kilobits per second). However, 1xRTT requires a dedicated connection to the network for use, whereas GPRS sends in packets, which means that data calls made on a GSM handset don't block out voice calls like they do on CDMA phones.

GSM's real benefit for domestic business use is in its SIM (subscriber identity module) card, the onboard memory device that identifies a user and stores all of his information on the handheld. You can swap GSM SIM cards between handsets when a new one is necessary, which enables you to carry all of your contact and calendar information over to a new handset with no hassle.

4. (a) Explain the different types of firewall architecture.

Ans. Following are the types of Firewall Architectures:

(i) Packet filter firewalls : They remain the most common type of firewall in use as of today. They were the earliest firewalls developed and were capable of permitting or denying traffic based on certain simple field-level filters which could determine such things as source or destination packet address, or the protocol being used. The greatest advantage is that they are fast since they have minimum processor overheads, and are transparent as well as highly inexpensive. On the down side, they are not strong enough at the application level. This is because these firewalls work purely at the level of network layer, making them difficult to configure and manage effectively.

Most of the present day routers include capabilities of such firewalls as a standard feature in their system. This kind of packet filtering can be found in almost every major firewall available today.

(ii) Proxy servers : These types of firewalls have been further classified into two types: application level gateways and circuit level gateways.

The application level gateways establish a connection to a remote system on behalf of specific applications. This type of firewall is usually a collection of application proxies, with a one-to-one relationship between the application used and its proxy. Whereas the circuit level gateways provide the proxy or relay capabilities in a much-generalized form, which is not limited to specific applications. The primary advantage of such firewalls over application level gateways is that they do not require a specific application proxy for each new application that needs to be communicated outside the internal network.

Although in terms of security measure the proxy servers are very secure, they require a lot of programming which can result in a delay in release of new proxies for application level gateways as well as tend to be highly CPU intensive, thereby directly having impact on the overall network performance.

(iii) Stateful multi-layer inspection (SMLI) : They are considered as the third generation of firewall technology and usually combines the facilities of

the above two. They are further classified into two types.
The Stateful multi-layer inspection (SMLI) firewall is similar to application level gateways in the sense that all levels of the OSI model are inspected carefully right from the network wire to the IP application layer.
The SMLI firewalls are different from the conventional "stand in" proxies in a way that the stand-in proxies are used for the applications when communicating to the outside world, thus putting a heavy processing load on the processors. In contrast, the SMLI firewall just examines each packet and compares them against the known states (i.e. bit patterns) to know about the behaviour pattern of the acceptable packets. The term stateful implies that the firewall is wakeful and is capable of remembering the state of each session of packet exchange across it, allowing it to monitor all the packets for unauthorized access while maintaining high level of security, even with connectionless service protocols such as UDP, SMTP, etc.

(b) Discuss the term "Intranet Authoring Tools" with example.
Ans. Refer to Chapter-5, Q.No.-1, Page No.-100

5. (a) What is e-commerce? How is Agora used for electronic commerce?
Ans. Refer to Chapter-6, Q.No.-15, Page No.-133

(b) How do you tune applications over Intranet? Explain.
Ans. Tuning Applications Over Intranet involves.
SQL/API : The Structured Query Language/Application Programming Interface (SQL/API) is a function library designed for use with the C Programming language, and development environments that support C-style external function calling conventions. SQL/AI is a call level interface (CLI) analogous to SQL Net in Oracle environments and CT-LIB in Sybase environments.One can make calls to SQL/API functions throughout the application to interact with SQL Base. Typical function calls include connecting and disconnecting to a database, passing SQL statements to the server for compilation and execution, providing bind variable data, and retrieving result sets. Additionally, the SQL/API provides functions to perform administrative tasks such as performing database backups and restorations.
ODBC : Not just an ODBC driver, Recital ODBC Developer provides a complete industry standard ODBC database solution for Unix, Linux, or Open VMS. Consisting of an ODBC driver, and an Application Server, which has a complete SQL-92 database engine, Recital ODBC Developer can create, query and update Recital databases from Windows applications. If Recital applications are running on Unix, Linux or Open VMS, one can provide full read and update access to the databases from Microsoft Windows clients with Recital ODBC Developer. Using Recital ODBC Developer one can use industry standard management reporting tools such as Crystal Reports to generate high quality reports against live data in a Recital based application.
JDBC : Not just a JDBC driver, Recital JDBC Developer provides a complete industry standard JDBC database solution, consisting of an all-Java type 3 driver, and an Application Server that implements a complete SQL-92 database engine. With JDBC Developer, Java applications can query and update data from any data source across Intranets or the Internet.

CS-75 : INTRANET ADMINISTRATION
December, 2007

Note : Question number 1 is **compulsory.** Answer any **three** questions from the rest.

1. (a) "An Intranet can be defined as a private network which uses Internet tools." Comment on the above statement and differentiate between an Internet and an Intranet.
Ans. Refer to Chapter-1, Q.No.-1, Page No.-2
& Refer to Chapter-1, Q.No.-4, Page No.-3

(b) Describe Encryption/Decryption as a method of ensuring security. Discuss any three implementation of Encryption/Decryption methods.
Ans. Refer June-2007, Q.No.-2(b), Page No.-260
Now Refer to Chapter-2, Q.No.-6, Page No.-45

(c) What are the points to be considered while selecting the hardwares for an Intranet? Also, mention the tasks that should be properly synchronized for smooth working of an Intranet.
Ans. Hardware : An Intranet is simply a standard Wide Area Network (WAN). The use of the term Intranet recently to describe using software developed for the Internet on the company's WAN. Web servers are an example.
Scientists describe how optimal performance of intranets is associated with a number of key hardware factors. In order to optimise performance, servers with fast processors and large amounts of memory are essential. They also noted how good multi-tasking and multi-threading ability is which is also crucial for most of the Web applications. In addition, sufficient memory and disk capacity at the user workstation would improve performance through increased caching. The limitation of large image files can also be considered important to improve performance, but images may be equally important to expand and illustrate data, and pages of text can be discouraging, especially in an educational context. Finally, the database itself, which forms the foundations of almost every intranet, can have a significant effect on performance.
Following are the points to be considered while selecting the hardwares for an Intranet :
(i) Communication medium/services that provide connectivity between different locations of the company should use technologies such as ISDN, leased line, etc.
(ii) Network equipment and connectivity should address various networking equipment such as routers, types of cables, as well as the topology behind the network.
(iii) It is a must that the hardware should be configured for protocols such as IP, HTTP, SMTP, POP, X509 Certification, etc. in order to provide security to the intranet server.

Following are the tasks that should be properly synchronized for smooth working of an Intranet :

(i) All computers connected together in a network must communicate using the same language and protocol. Inability to do so may leave the users disconnected to the repository of information and resources.

(ii) It must be always remembered that the language used is Hyper Text Markup Language (HTML) and every thing that is developed for and intended to be hosted on the intranet must follow HTML invariably.

(iii) The protocol suite applicable for both intranets and Internet are called Transmission Control Protocol/Internet Protocol (TCP/IP) and every computer should be compatible to TCP/IP. Though, TCP/IP evolved initially on UNIX based computers, it became a standard for data communication and more recently for every type of communication across intranet and internet, especially supported by every major operating system in use.

(iv) The intranet is driven by a network server that uses a browser, like Netscape Navigator or Internet Explorer.

(d) Explain the steps for configuring a web server. You can assume any common web server as an example.

Ans. The first step of setting up intranet is to configure a web server. Many web servers are available some of them are commercial and some are free. One of the popular web server is Apache, the current version of Apache web server is 1.3.3-x. It is available free with Red Hat Linux 5.2, and can also be downloaded from http://www.apache.org. It set up and ready to run automatically at boot as soon as the Linux installation is completed. Apache web server is extremely powerful, and can be configured to handle any kind of environment from a lightly loaded Intranet to a commercial heavily loaded Intranet Web server taking more than 100,000 hits a day.

It is very simple to test the working of Apache web server, simply point the browser to the URL http://localhost. The Apache's default "It Worked" page starts up. The index.html file in the /home/httpd/html directory can be changed to start publishing pages on the Intranet. The default configuration file/etc/httpd/conf/httpd.conf is suitable for simple configurations, though one might want to edit it if there is an unusually heavy load, or wish to configure a different machine name, port, or address to send error messages.

(e) What is UDP? At what layer of OSI is it present? Depict its header format, explaining the purpose of various fields

Ans. User Datagram Protocol (UDP) : The UDP is the simpler of the two standard TCP/IP transport protocols. It is an end-to-end transport level protocol that adds only port addresses, checksum error control, and length information to the data from the upper layer.

UDP present at transport layer(4th layer) in OSI.

The packet produced by the UDP is called a user datagram. A brief description of fields is :

Source port address : The Source port address is the address of the application program that has created the message .

Destination port address : The destination port address is the address of the application program that will receive that message.

Total length : The total length field defines the total length of the user datagram in bytes.

Checksum : The checksum is a 16-bit field used in error detection.

Header specification and fields:-

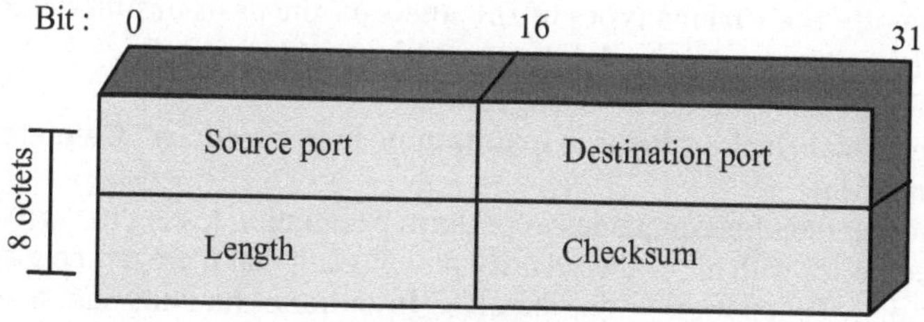

Fig : UDP Header

UDP provides only the basic functions needed for end-to-end delivery of a transmission. It does not provide any sequencing or reordering functions, and cannot specify the damaged packet when reporting an error (for which it must be paired with ICMP). UDP can discover that an error has occurred; ICMP can then inform the sender that a user datagram has been damaged or discarded. Neither, however, has the ability to specify which packet has been lost. UDP contains only a checksum; it does not contain an ID or sequencing number for a particular data segment.

2. (a) What are distributed databases? Explain their advantages over the centralized databases.

Ans. Now Refer : June-2004, Q.No.-6(a), Page No.-160

Advantages of Distributed Databases over the centralized databases :

Increased reliability/availability

Local control over data

Modular growth

Lower communication costs

Faster response for certain queries

Disadvantages of Distributed Database Compared to Centralized Databases :

Software cost and complexity

Processing overhead

Data integrity exposure

Slower response for certain queries

(b) Differentiate between the following:

(i) Internal and External threats

Ans. Refer June-2007, Q.No.-1(a), Page No.-259

(ii) FTP and Telnet

Ans. Telnet to allows remote logins to computers over networks. FTP is nothing to do with log into a remote computer, but it allows us to *transfer files* between two different computers on the Internet. It is named "File Transfer Protocol", but is usually just called FTP. Telnet is a program that allows an Internet host computer to become a terminal of another host on the Internet. Ftp opens a connection solely for transfer of files either way from terminal to host computer (uploading) or from host to terminal (downloading), however, Telnet allows you to become a user on a remote machine. You can run the Internet computer program available on that machine. Downloading and Uploading of files can be performed through both ftp and Telnet.

3. (a) Classify the various types of Intranets on the basis of functionality and applications. Also explain each category with suitable examples.

Ans. Refer to Chapter-1, Q.No.-8, Page No.-9

(b) "Intentional Hacking helps in maintaining better security" Comment on the above statement.

Ans. It is common for companies to perform penetration testing to verify that the system complies with all of the security policies and that there are no exploitable securityholes. Penetration testing involves **intentional hacking** into a system to find failures and/or mis-configurations that enable users to open a valid session on the PortalServer or to gain illegal access to the system. This testing must be done by someone who is very familiar with hacking tools and is able to analyze the output of the tools. Even though most, if not all, of the tools are available on the Internet, the planning, execution, and result analysis must be done by a certified security consultant. Thus, as per above description we can say that intentional hacking helps in maintaining better security. But if done by any unauthorised person then it can be disastrous also.

4. (a) What are the two graphic formats supported by web browsers? Compare them, listing the features of each :

Ans. Refer to June-2005, Q.No.-1(d), Page No.-197

(b) Explain any three protocols used for Electronic Commerce.

Ans. Refer to Dec-2004, Q.No.-4(a), Page No.-228

5. Write short notes on the following, giving suitable examples, if any:

(a) Client/Server Architecture

Ans. Client-server is a computing architecture which separates a client from a server, and is almost always implemented over a computer network. Each client or server connected to a network can also be referred to as a node. The most basic type of client-server architecture employs only two types of nodes: clients and servers. This type of architecture is sometimes referred to as two-tier. It allows devices to share files and resources. Each instance of the client software can send data requests to one or more connected servers. In turn, the servers can accept these requests, process them, and return the requested information to the client. Although this concept can be applied for a variety of reasons to many different kinds of applications, the architecture remains fundamentally the same.

(b) Internet Information Server

Ans. Refer to Chapter-5, Q.No.-8, Page No.-110

(c) SMTP

Ans. Refer to Chapter-6, Page No.-117

(d) CGI

Ans. Refer to Chapter-6, Q.No.-7, Page No.-125

(e) GPRS

Ans. Refer to Chapter-6, Q.No.-14, Page No.-133

CS-75 : Intranet Administration
June, 2008

Note : Question number 1 is **Compulsory.** Answer any **three** questions from the rest.

Q1. (a) Explain the similarities and difference between Intranet and Internet. Is there any difference between the softwares used for Internet and Intranet? If yes, explain. If no, give justification.

Ans. There are many similarities and differences between the Internet and the intranet. They both use the same technology regarding clients, servers and IP. One may find email, HTTP, and FTP as well in an intranet. Although the link between the two is obvious it does not need to be linked. An intranet can exist without Internet connection available. If connection to the WWW is available, the local network will usually be protected by a firewall and the process of connecting to the Internet will be done through a Gateway. In most cases the intranet is used by companies to make it easier for employees to share information. Tools and applications can also be shared and the possibility of network support is also useful in many occasions.

There are three main advantages when talking about using intranet :

(i) Communication – Intranets provide users with a fast and reliable way to communicate with every needed person in the network

(ii) Time – Using the Intranet saves time because of the fast information gathering and communication possibility

(iii) Productivity – A company that is taking advantage of the Intranet increases its workforce productivity. A database can easily be created and accessed. It saves time and eventually money, making it possible for employees to work faster and better.

Yes, there is difference between the software used for Internet and Intranet.

Justification : Sometimes it may be same e.g. we can create a website which can work same on Intranet and Internet. But Internet is used as an global entity while intranet is used as local i.e. within an organisation.

Platform compatibility : The Internet consists of a wide variety of hardware platforms and operating systems. When publishing information, platform compatibility should be taken into account to ensure smooth accessibility to a wide variety of users. When users need to use a special helper application to view a file at your Web site, provide URLs for downloading helper applications that run on several platforms. At a minimum, Windows and Macintosh users should be able to view information published at your Web site, as should those who use widely used flavors of UNIX. This implies separate softwares is to be made depending on the platform used in your intranet.

(b) Explain the functioning of the following Internet tools :

Ans. (i) Discovery Agent : Processes that retrieve information about devices on the network. They are also capable of reporting the existence of new devices by virtue of the connections found to other devices.

(ii) Push Agent : The network push agent has two primary functions. It helps lock the end user desktops and/or allows you to create a push for any file on application that you need to update on the workstation. It provides a cost effective, vendor independent and extremely easy solution to the issue of controlling end user windows 95 desktops and distributing software to large numbers of networked PC's.

(iii) Search Agents : Search agents use advanced search engine to constantly monitor the content coming in on your channels and alert you to things that you are interested in.

(iv) Subscription Agents : Subscription agents and intermediaries help libraries and publishers to save money. They reduce the amount of time spent on the many detailed administrative tasks in acquiring and accessing journals, thus allowing librarians and publishers to focus their attention on other important matters. In the process they perform these administrative tasks more cheaply than would otherwise be the case.

(c) How is Security Configuration and Analysis Tool used to analyse the Computer Security? List its important features.

Ans. The 'Security configuration and analysis' tools used to analyze a computer security configuration. To get ready to use this tool, do the following :

- The MMC "Security Templates" snap-in must be previously installed. Once installed, it is the administrative tool called "Security Console"
- The MMC "Security configuration and analyze" snap-in must be installed to the "Security Console" by starting it from "Administrative Tools" selecting "Console" and "Add/Remove snap-in"
- A database in the snap-in must be created by selecting "Administrative Tools", "Security Console", select "Action" and "open database"
- To perform the analysis against a template, open a database and then select "Action" and "Analyze computer now".
- To apply setting from a template, open a database that has the setting user intend to apply to the computer then select "Action" and "Configure computer now".

Its important features are:

- Reduce deskside visits for software and hardware problems up to 56 percent.
- Conduct hardware and software inventory up to 94 percent faster.
- Decrease energy requirement without compromise to performance.
- Enjoy broad industry support
- Remain compliant with next generation management standards.

(d) How many TCP connections are used in Telnet? Explain the process of remote login in TELNET.

Ans. A machine offering Telnet service can support multiple simultaneous sessions with different users, keeping each distinct by identifying it using the IP address and port number of the client. The TCP connection is maintained for the duration of the Telnet session, which can remain alive for hours, days, or even weeks at a time.

Process of remote login in TELNET : The user (say Gullybaba) has an account on both the local and remote machines.

For example, Gullybaba on *farkas.gphindia.com* types *telnet optlab.cas.gphindia.com* at his user prompt. Here, *farkas.gphindia.com* is the client and *optlab.cas.gphindia.com* is the server. The Telnet client would perform a *methotrexate()* call to determine the IP address of *optlab.cas.gphindia.com*. Then the client would create a socket to communicate with the Telnet server. The server prompts Gullybaba for a login identifier - the name of the user's account on the remote server followed by a password. The Telnet users interact with the remote machine in the same way they would interact with their local machine. The client relays Gullybaba's keystrokes to the remote server, and the remote server displays them on its pseudo terminal (which is actually the display screen on the client machine).

(e) What are the different protocols available in Wireless Application Protocol (WAP) Stack? Explain the purpose of each protocol.

Ans. Refer to Page No. 131

Q2. (a) Define the following :

(i) Network service access policy : A high level, issue specific policy which defines those services that are allowed or denied from the restricted network. It also contains clear guidelines giving instruction detailing the way in which these services will be used and the conditions for exceptions to this policy.

(ii) Firewall design policy Refer to Q5, Page No.-44.

(iii) Virtual private network Refer to Page No.-47

(iv) Web server security Refer to Page No.-46

(b) Differentiate between internal and external threat.

Ans. Refer to Q2, Page No.-39

Q3. (a) How is address translation done in a network in order to locate a particular web site? Explain the process of address translation with an example.

Ans. Refer to Q6, Page No.-59

(b) Explain the purpose and use of following HTTP methods :

Ans. (i) POST : Sends some information from client to server. It appends the data to the existing document.

(ii) LINK : Connects two existing resources.

(iii) PUT : Sends a document from to server. It replaces the existing document.

(iv) GET : Request to read a web page.

Q4. (a) Make the format of RARP message. Explain the purpose of its various fields.

Ans. First Refer to Q(b), Page No.-209

RARP : reverse address resolution protocol (RARP) is used for diskless computers to determine their IP address using the network. The RARP message format is very similar to the ARP format. When the booting computer sends the broadcast ARP request, it places its own hardware address in both the sending and receiving fields in the encapsulated ARP data packet. The RARP server will fill in the correct sending and receiving IP addresses in its response to the message. This way the booting computer will know its IP address when it gets the message from the RARP server.

(b) What are the parameters that are considered while designing the security of a network? Explain.

Ans. Refer to Q(b), Page No.-225

Q5. Differentiate between the following :

(a) IMAP and POP3 Refer to Page No.-246

(b) Primary web server and AOL server Refer to Page No.-107

(c) CDMA and GSM technology

Ans. CDMA : The CDMA technology spreads the information contained in a particular signal of interest over a much greater bandwidth than the original signal. This technology offers a number of benefits to the cellular operators as well as to subscribers. To name a few, the following benefits of CDMA:

- Capacity increases of 8 to 10 times that of an analog system
- Improved call quality
- Reduced installation time
- Enhanced privacy

GSM : GSM is a cellular network, which means that mobile phones connect to it by searching for cells in the immediate vicinity. GSM network operate in four different frequency ranges. Most GSM networks operate in the 900 MHz or 1800 MHz bands.

(d) Interior Gateway Protocol and Exterior Gateway Protocol

Ans. The Interior Gateway Routing Protocol : Open shortest path first has become standard interior gateway routing protocol. It supports many advanced features to meet a long list of requirements.

- The protocol specification should be publicly available.
- It is a dynamic algorithm one that adopts to changes in the topology automatically and quickly.
- Load distribution: when multiple paths to a destination have the same cost
- OSPF allows multiple paths to be used.
- Support for hierarchy within a single routing domain.
- Security : All exchanges between OSPF routers are authenticated and allows only trusted routers to participate.

The Exterior Gateway Routing Protocol : The purpose of Border Gateway Protocol is to enable two different areas to exchange routing information so that IP traffic can flow across the AS border. A different protocol is needed between the Areas because the objectives of an interior gateway and exterior gateway routing protocols are different. Exterior gateway routing protocol such as BGP is related to policy matters. BGP is fundamentally a distance vector protocol but, it is more appropriately characterized as path vector protocol.

CS-75 : Intranet Administration
December, 2008

Note : Question number 1 is **Compulsory.** Answer any **three** questions from the rest.

Q1. (a) What is an IP address? Explain various classes of IP addresses.

Refer to Dec-01, Q.No-6(2), Page No-189

(b) Define an Intranet. With the help of a diagram, explain its various components.

Refer to Q.No-1, 2, Page No-2

(c) What is Encryption and Decryption? Explain any two implementations of Encryption/Decryption methods.

Refer to Q.No-3(a), Page No-256

Refer to Q.No-2(a), Page No-238

(d) What are Web Servers? Describe any two Web Servers.

Refer to Q.No-4, Page No-106

(e) Write short notes on the following:

Ans. (1) Types of Communication Cables

There are numerous types of Communication Cables available in the market today, but some types of Cables like Coaxial Cables, Drop Cables, UTP Cables and Fibre Optic Cables are used more often. These Cables are applicable in different types of data transfer in our day to day life.

(i) Coaxial cable is called "coaxial" because it includes one physical channel that carries the signal surrounded (after a layer of insulation) by another concentric physical channel, both running along the same axis. The outer channel serves as a ground. Many of these cables or pairs of coaxial tubes can be placed in a single outer sheathing and, with repeaters, can carry information for a great distance.

(ii) PVC jacketed Bus **Drop Cable** is intended for use as drop cables from overhead busways and allows easy relocation of plant equipment. Resistant to oils, lubricants, acids, alkalies, ozone, water and abrasion. Individual grounds per conductor. Conductors, grounds and filler are cabled for flexibility then wrapped in a separator to aid strippability. Rated for use in wet or dry locations.

(iii) Unshielded Twisted Pair (UTP) cable contains 4 twisted pairs of wires, a total of 8 wires. The strands that constitute each wire will either be a single strand or multiple strands, usually referred to as solid or flex. Typically the solid is used to run through walls and ceilings and the flex is used to make drop cables (the cable from the wall plate to the desktop computer) and patch cables (the cable from the patch panel to the hub). Whether the exterior portion of the cable that contains the 4 twisted pairs, the jacket, is Plenum grade or Non-plenum grade is very important, it refers to the Fire Codes. The pairs of wires in UTP cable are colored so that one can identify the same wire at each end. Furthermore, they are usually color coded by pair so that the pairs can also be identified from end to end.

(iv) Fiber Optic Cables use light pulses to transmit information down fiber lines instead of using electronic pulses to transmit information in copper lines. Light pulses move easily down the fiber-optic line because of a principle known as total internal reflection. "This principle of total internal reflection states that when the angle of incidence exceeds a critical value, light cannot get out of the glass; instead, the light bounces back in. When this principle is applied to the construction of the fiber-optic strand, it is possible to transmit information down fiber lines in the form of light pulses.

(2) Security Threats

JUN2003, Q3(b), Page no.-170.

(3) CDMA

Refer to Q.No-10, Page No-128

Q2. (a) How do organisations ensure security in an Intranet? Explain the five security models used for chalking out the security plan and policy.

Refer to Q.No-3(b), Page No-170

(b) Explain ARP and UDP.

First Refer to Q.No-6(a)(i), Page No-231

Now Refer to Q.No-(b), Page No-218, 219

Q3. (a) "One solution for the protection of the computing infrastructure is to use digital certificate based solutions". Give Pros and Cons of implementing the statement.

Refer to Page No-43

(b) Explain the integrating Intranet and the single sign on Intranet.

Ans. First Refer to Page No-9

Single sign on Intranet is where Single sign-on (SSO) method of access control is used which enables a user to log in once and gain access to the resources of multiple software systems without being prompted to log in again. Single sign-off is the reverse process whereby a single action of signing out terminates access to multiple software systems.

Benefits of single sign-on Intranet includes :

- Reducing password fatigue from different user name and password combinations
- Reducing time spent re-entering passwords for the same identity
- Reducing IT costs due to lower number of IT help desk calls about passwords
- Security on all levels of entry/exit/access to systems without the inconvenience of re-prompting users
- Centralized reporting for compliance adherence.

SSO Intranet uses centralized authentication servers that all other applications and systems utilize for authentication purposes, and combines this with techniques to ensure that users do not actively have to enter their credentials more than once.

Q4. (a) Explain the terms "httpd" and "ISDN".

Refer to Page No-18

(b) Explain the need of Application Service Protocols in an Intranet. Describe any two Application Service Protocols of OSI Model.

Ans. For the sake of convenience, the Intranet protocols have been categorised into two sets, viz., the communication protocols and the application service protocols. Application Service Protocols are explained as follows. Many Internet users are familiar with the protocols such as TCP/IP to connect to the Internet. These include those protocols that permit the users to logon to remote computers, such as the following :

- World Wide Web's Hypertext Transfer Protocol (HTTP)
- File Transfer Protocol (FTP)
- Telnet (Telnet)
- User Datagram Protocol (UDP)
- Simple Mail Transfer Protocol (SMTP)

These and other protocols are often packaged together with TCP/IP as a "suite." Protocols related to TCP/IP include the User Datagram Protocol (UDP), which is used instead of TCP for special purposes. In combination with the IP, it is known as the UDP/IP suite.

Though not very well known otherwise, other protocols are used by network host computers for exchanging router information such as:

- Internet Control Message Protocol (ICMP)

• Interior Gateway Protocol (IGP)
• Exterior Gateway Protocol (EGP)
• Border Gateway Protocol (BGP)

One of several application service protocols defined at the application layer of OSI. The application service protocol defines an interface and sends the message from the application layer through layers of OSI. On the receiving side, it goes through the layers of OSI until the application layer. At the **application** level we find the **application protocols** that **need** to communicate with their counter parts at a remote machine. The user will mostly only see the 'front end'. E.g. HTTP is an "apllication protocol", the user will use a HTTP-client : a web browser.

Q5. Explain the following :

(a) SOCKS. Refer to Q.No-(b), Page No-156

(b) VPN. Refer to Page No-150

(c) POP. Refer to Page No-117

(d) Web based tools.

Ans. HTML, XML, CGI and other open standards. As is well known, the Web as well as Intranets speak and understand only one language i.e., the HTML, the browser at the client's end after downloading the pages from the server, interprets the language and converts it into human understandable format and the output would be what everyone actually sees on their computers. Until recently, HTML was available as an open standard, i.e., it was not under control of any vendor. Web application developers intending to release their product had to conform to this standard.

Web authoring tools : CGI was considered excellent in the beginning since it was also open standard. The only drawback it suffered was that it was slow. Major software developers virtually ignored the CGI and consequently CGI could not survive the competition.

The need arose for addressing various issues related to Web programming. Software were required for establishing connection to ensure security, connectivity to databases, conversion of the results to Web format, and a lot more. In response to the rising needs, numerous vendors have come up with numerous products. Some of them are given below.

• IntraLaunch, • CodeCharge, • Benefit Profiles Portal Suite, • Servicespace Suite consisting of Enterprise, Customer Portal, Partner Portal, • LiveHelp, • HTML/OS, • WebSiteManager.

(e) GPRS.

Refer to Q.No-14, Page No-133

CS-75 : Intranet Administration

June-2009

Note: Question number **1** is **compulsory**. Attempt **any three** from the rest.

Q1. (a) What are the salient features of general packet radio service.

Refer to Q.No.-14, Page-133

(b) Explain simple mail transfer protocol's functioning. For what purpose it is used.

Refer to Q.No.-(ii), Page-232

(c) List the salient characteristics of following types of server.

(i) iserver

Refer to Q.No.-5, Page-108

(ii) WN web server

Refer to Q.No.-6, Page-109

(iii) Samba server

Refer to Q.No.-7, Page-109

(iv) Internet Information Server

Refer to Q.No.-8, Page-110

(d) What is meant by firewall. Explain any three types of firewall architectures.

Refer to Q.No.-5(a) (i), Page-212 now refer to Q.No.-4 (a), Page-261

(e) Write a short note on SSL.

Refer to Page-171, 2nd Para.

Q2. (a) Explain various internal and external threats to intranet in context of security. How are they handled?

Refer to Q.No.-10, Page-50

(b) Explain intranet authoring tools. Also, list atleast two tools.

Refer to Q.No.-1, Page-100

Q3. Define following features of intranet management tools.

(a) multimedia capabilities

Refer to Page-102, 17th Point

(b) site map

Refer to Page-102, 12th Point

(c) Active X Data object support

Refer to Page-101, 9th Point

(d) clipart support

Refer to Page-102, 15th Point

(e) powerful search and replace facility

Refer to Page-102, 19th Point

Q4. (a) Explain ODBC with the help of a diagram.

Refer to Q.No.-2(a) 2nd Point, Page-201 and now refer to Page-256

(b) For what purpose post office protocol is used. Explain purpose of following commands in this content.

(i) STAT **(ii) RETR msg**

(iii) DELE msg **(iii) TOP msg**

Refer to Page-233

Q5. Write short notes on the following:

(a) Web master

Ans. Refer to Chapter-4, Q.No.-10, Page-84

An individual who manages a Web site. Depending on the size of the site, the Webmaster might be responsible for any of the following:

- Making sure that the Web server hardware and software is running properly
- Designing the Web site
- Creating and updating Web pages
- Replying to user feedback
- Creating CGI scripts
- Monitoring traffic through the site

The exponential growth of the World Wide Web has created an unprecedented demand for Webmasters.

(b) SQL / API

Refer to Q.No.-5 (b), Page-262

(c) Security configuration

Refer to Q.No.-C, Page-268

(d) Disk Quotas

Ans. A disk quota is a limit set by a system administrator that restricts certain aspects of file system usage on modern operating systems. The function of setting diskquota to disks, is to allocate limited diskspace in a reasonable way.

CS-75: INTRANET ADMINISTRATION
December, 2009

Note: Question number **1** is **compulsory**. Attempt **any three** from the rest.

Q1. (a) Define the following categories of intranet in brief:
(i) Bulletin board
Refer to Chapter-1, Q.No.-8, Page-9

(ii) Database management
Refer to Chapter-1, Q.No.-8, Page-9

(iii) Information access
Refer to Chapter-1, Q.No.-8, Page-9

(b) Explain the terms "Applet" and "Bookmark".
Refer Chapter-1, Q.No.-14, Page-17

(c) Explain JDBC with the help of a diagram.
Ans. Refer to Page-62, and Refer to Page-256

(d) What is meant by network environment? List various issues that are considered in network planning.
Ans. Refer to Chapter-3, Q.No.-5, Page-58
now refer www.gullybaba.com/ignou/bca/cs75.html

(e) Explain the concept of web graphics. List the salient characteristics of GIF and JPEG.
Refer to June-2005, Q.No.-1(d), Page-197

Q2. Write short notes on the following:
(a) Types of communication cables
Refer to Dec-2008, Q.No.-1(e), Page-271

(b) Security threats
Refer to Chapter-3, Q.No.-16, Page-74

(c) IP address
Refer to Dec-2006, Q.No.-3(a), Page-260

(d) Group ware
Refer to Chapter-3, Q.No.-7, Page-59

Q3. Define the purpose of following features that an intranet authoring tool should provide.

(a) auto coding

Refer to Chapter-5, Q.No.-1, Page-100

(b) object library

Refer to Chapter-5, Q.No.-1, Page-100

(c) WYSIWYG kind of output

Refer to Chapter-5, Q.No.-1, Page-100

(d) compatibility with other server architectures

Refer to Chapter-5, Q.No.-1, Page-100

Q4. (a) For what purpose the address resolution protocol is used. Explain it's functioning.

Refer to Chapter-6, Q.No.-1, Page-116

(b) What is meant by virtual private network? How they are different from normal LAN's?

Refer to Chapter-2, Page-47

A local network provides services like email, message boards, and access to company data that a worker needs to carry on. A VPN extends this network to almost anywhere, allowing employees to work at home, in the field, or even when travelling.

Q5. (a) Why network security is a critical issue? Explain public key encryption concept.

Refer to Chapter-1, Q.No.-10, Page-11

(b) Define following FTP services in brief:

(i) Simple drag and drop file transfers

Refer to Chapter-5, Q.No.-2, Page-102-105

(ii) Transfer queue and file transfer scheduling

Refer to Chapter-5, Q.No.-2, Page-102-105

(iii) File finder feature

Refer to Chapter-5, Q.No.-2, Page-102-105

CS-75: INTRANET ADMINISTRATION

June, 2010

Note: *Question number 1 is* ***compulsory****. Attempt any three questions from the rest.*

Q1. (a) List and explain any 10 benefits of Intranet to any organisation.

Ans. Refer to Page No.-5, Chapter-1, Q.No.-6

(b) Explain the roles played by Servers and Clients in an Intranet.

Ans. Refer to Page No.-56, Chapter-3, Q.No.-3

(c) Describe any two Intranet Authoring tools in detail.

Ans. Refer to Page No.-100, Chapter-5, Q.No.-1

Q2. (a) Explain the basis for any organization to decide that there is need for Intranet for it.

Ans. Refer to Page No.-3, Chapter-1, Q.No.-4

(b) Explain any two applications of Groupware.

Ans. Refer to Page No.-59, Chapter-3, Q.No.-7

Q3. (a) Explain any two ways of securing data on the Intranet.

Ans. Refer to Page No.-11, Chapter-1, Q.No.-10

(b) What is a Protocol? List any two protocols that are supported by Intranet.

Ans. A network protocol defines rules and conventions for communication between network devices. Protocols for computer networking all generally use packet switching techniques to send and receive messages in the form of packets.

Network protocols include mechanisms for devices to identify and make connections with each other, as well as formatting rules that specify how data is packaged into messages sent and received. Some protocols also support message acknowledgement and data compression designed for reliable and/or high-performance network communication. Hundreds of different computer network protocols have been developed each designed for specific purposes and environments.

Now Refer to Page No.-205, June-05, Q.No.-3(b)

Q4. (a) What is a centralized database? How does it differ from a distributed database?

Ans. Refer to Page No.-265, Q.No.-2(a) & Page No.-252, Q.No.-3(b)

(b) What is an IP address? Explain its significance.

Ans. Refer to Page No.-189

Q5. (a) What is Wireless Application Protocol (WAP)? Briefly explain its layered architecture.

Ans. Refer to Page No.-129, Chapter-6, Q.No.-11

(b) Explain the differences between two tier and three tier architectures.

In modern two-tier architecture, the server holds both the application and the data. The application resides on the server rather than the client, probably because the server will have more processing power and disk space than the PC.

In three-tier architecture, the data and applications are split onto separate servers, with the server-side distributed between a database server and an application server. The client is a front end, simply requesting and displaying data. Reason being that each server will be dedicated to processing either data or application requests, hence a more manageable system and less contention for resources will occur.

CS-75: INTRANET ADMINISTRATION
December, 2010

Note: *Question number 1 is* **compulsory***. Attempt any three questions from the rest.*

Q1. (a) What is an Internal Security threat? What is an External Security threat? Give an example of each.

Ans. Refer to Page No.-39, Chapter-2, Q.No.-2

(b) Mention the context where a database is required in the Internet Application. List any two DBMS which can be used as backed for the Intranet applications.

Ans. Refer to Page No.-254, Dec-06, Q.No.-2(b)

(c) Explain the process of creation of local and domain account types.

Ans. Refer to Page No.-250, June-06, Q.No.-1(e)

Q2. (a) Explain any two authentication mechanisms supported by WINDOWS 2000 Operating System.

Ans. Refer to Page No.-257, Dec-06, Q.No.-3(b)

(b) Explain the significance of Virtual Private Network (VPN). Also, write any one advantage of VPN.

Ans. Refer to Page No.-47 (Virtual Private Network)

Q3. (a) What is SSL? Explain any two features of it.

Ans. Refer to Page No.-171 (2nd Para) & Page No.-215, Q.No.-5(c)

(b) Explain the purpose of Kerberos v5.

Ans. Refer to Page No.-249, June-06, Q.No.-1(c)(i)

Q4. (a) What is IIS? What is IMAP? Briefly explain.

Ans. IIS: Refer to Page No.-215, June-05, Q.No.-5(b)(iii)

IMAP: Refer to Page No.-233, Dec-04, Q.No.-6(iv)

(b) What is a firewall? Explain its significance?

Ans. Refer to Page No.-182, Dec-02, Q.No.-5(a)

Q5. (a) Explain any two classes of IP addresses.

Ans. Refer to Page No.-196, June-05, Q.No.-1(c)

(b) What are Internet Authoring Tools? Briefly explain them.

Ans. Refer to Page No.-100, Chapter-5, Q.No.-1

●●●

CS-75: INTRANET ADMINISTRATION
June, 2011

Note: *Question number 1 is* ***compulsory****. Attempt any three question from the rest.*

Q1. (a) "Intranet is more than a LAN but less than Internet." Justify the statement with the help of a diagram.

Ans. Refer to Page No.-4, Chapter-1, Q.No.-5

(b) Explain the three security tools available in the market for securing the Intranet.

Ans. Refer to Page No.-62, Chapter-3, Q.No.-9

(c) Explain the use of databases in intranets. Explain the basic, ODBC, Distributed and Object Oriented Models of databases.

Ans. Refer Page No.-61, Chapter-3, Q.No.-8

A **distributed database** is a database in which storage devices are not all attached to a common CPU. It may be stored in multiple computers located in the same physical location, or may be dispersed over a network of interconnected computers. Collections of data (e.g. in a database) can be distributed across multiple physical locations. A distributed database can reside on network servers on the Internet, on corporate intranets or extranets, or on other company networks. The replication and distribution of databases improves database performance at end-user worksites.

An object database (also **object-oriented database** management system) is a database management system in which information is represented in the form of objects as used in object-oriented programming. Object databases are different from relational databases and belongs together to the broader database management system.

(d) What are IP Addresses? Explain the various components of an IP Address.

Ans. Refer to Page No.-189, Dec-2001, Q.No.-6(2)

(e) Explain, in detail, any two protocols used for E-Commerce.

Ans. Refer to Page No.-133, Chapter-6, Q.No.-15

Q2. (a) Explain the GIF and JPEG graphic formats supported by Web browsers today. When is each preferred?

Ans. Refer to Page No.-197, June-2005, Q.No.-1(d)

(b) What is Groupware? Explain its applications with the help of a diagram, depict the contents of the groupware?

Ans. Refer to Page No.-59, Chapter-3, Q.No.-7

Q3. Write short notes on the following:

(a) Hacking

Ans. Computer hacking always involves some degree of infringement on the privacy of others or damage to computer-based property such as files, web pages or software. The impact of computer hacking varies from simply being simply invasive and annoying to illegal. There is an aura of mystery that surrounds hacking,and a prestige that accompanies being part of a relatively "elite" group of individuals who possess technological savvy and are willing to take the risks required to become a true "hacker".

(b) VPN

Ans. Refer to Page No.-150 [Virtual private Network]

(c) Bulletin Boards

Ans. Refer to Page No.-9 [Bulletin board]

(d) TELNET and FTP

Ans. Refer to Page No.-93 [Remote login] & Page No.-94 [FTP]

(e) UDP

Ans. Refer to Page No.-124, Chapter-6, Q.No.-6

Q4. (a) Explain the CGI Protocol.

Ans. Refer to Page No.-125, Chapter-6, Q.No.-7

(b) What is WAP? Explain its advantages with the help of a diagram, explain the WAP Protocol stack.

Ans. Refer to Page No.-129, Chapter-6, Q.No.-11

Q5. (a) Explain the features of the Samba Server software.

Ans. Refer to Page No.-109, Chapter-5, Q.No.-7

(b) Mention any eight features an Editor tool should provide to qualify as an Intranet authority tool.

Ans. Refer to Page No.-100, Chapter-5, Q.No.-1

●●●

CS-75: INTRANET ADMINISTRATION
December, 2011

Note: *Question number 1 is* **compulsory**. *Attempt any three question from the rest.*

Q1. (a) What are Firewalls? Explain the three firewall architectures.

Ans. Refer to Page No.-44, Chapter-2, Q.No.-5

(b) Explain the statement "Intranet is a group of LANs interconnected (may be at different locations)", with the help of a diagram.

Ans. One major benefit of Intranets is that it could be used to enhance communication, which in turn could lead to improved linkages within the organisation.

This communication could happen between various workgroups, departments, or even within entire organisation, simply by hosting the contents on the Intranet server. E.g. Indian Oil Corporation, Bharat Petroleum Corporation, ICICI Bank.

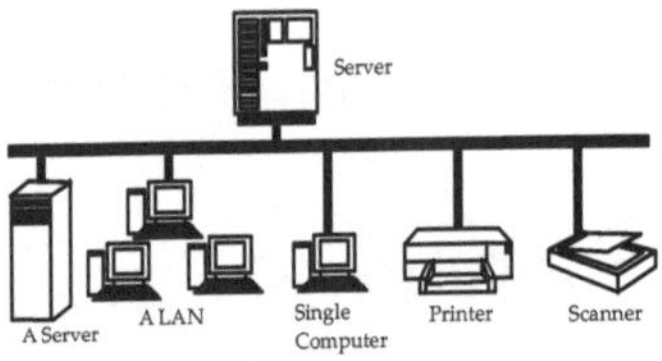

(c) Explain any four protocols supported by the intranet.

Ans. Refer to Page No.-156, June-2004, Q.No.-3(a)

(d) What are Disk Quotas? How are they managed on NTFS file system.

Ans. Refer to Page No.-276, June-2009, Q.No.-5(d)

Disk quotas are an integral part of the NTFS file system. When a file or a folder is created on a volume formatted with NTFS, that item is assigned an owner (typically the user who created the item). NTFS obtains the user ID of the file owner and stores that information in the file or folder's Standard Information attribute. This attribute tallies all the disk space allocated to the file or folder. NTFS then locates the quota entry for that user and determines whether the new allocation of disk space causes the user to exceed the assigned quota. If it does, NTFS then takes the appropriate steps, which can include logging an entry in the System event log or preventing the user from creating the file or folder. As the file or folder changes size, NTFS updates the quota control entry to reflect the total disk space used by the user. Disk quotas are not configured on a computer-wide basis, but are instead tied to individual NTFS volumes.

(e) Explain the SET protocol for E-Commerce.

Ans. Refer to Page No.-136, Chapter-6, Q.No.-16

Q2. (a) Explain the types of Intranets based on

(i) their functionality, (ii) application and architecture

Ans. Refer to Page No.-9, Chapter-1, Q.No.-8

(b) What do you understand by accounts? Explain the various types of accounts.

Ans. Refer to Page No.-250, June-2006, Q.No.-1(e

Q3. (a) What is ARP and why is it needed? Depict its message format and explain various fields.

Ans. Refer to Page No.- 116, Chapter-6, Q.No.-1 & Page No.-209, June-2005, Q.No.-4(b)

(b) Explain VPN as a Security tool on the Intranet.

Ans. Refer to Page No.-62, Q.No.-9, Chapter-3

Q4. (a) What are threats? Explain the internal and external threats.

Ans. Refer to Page No.-38, Q.No.-2, Chapter-2

(b) List and explain any five advantages of Intranets.

Ans. Refer to Page No.-6, Chapter-1, Q.No.-7

Q5. (a) What are User Profiles? Explain the types of profiles. Write steps for creating profiles.

Ans. A user profile (user profile, or simply profile when used in-context) is a collection of personal data associated to a specific user. A profile refers therefore to the explicit digital representation of a person's identity. A user profile can also be considered as the computer representation of a user model.

Types of user profiles include:

- **Local user profile:** Such type of profile is created when any authorized user logs on workstation or server for the first time.
- **Roaming user profile:** Such type of profile is created by administrator and stored on a server. This profile is available every time you log on to any computer on the network. Incase some changes are made to profile then profile on server is automatically updated.
- **Mandatory user profile:** Such type of profile is downloaded to the user's desktop each time the user logs on, and is created by an administrator and assigned to one or more users to create consistent or job-specific user profiles. Only members of the Administrators group can change profiles.
- **Temporary user profile:** Such type of profile is used as backup. If the roaming or mandatory profile is not available for some reason, a temporary user profile is automatically created for the user. The temporary profile is deleted when the user log out. so any changes that the user makes while using a temporary profile are lost at the end of the session.

Creating a roaming user profile: Creating a roaming user profile is a two-step process: creating a test user profile and then copying the test user profile to a network server.

Creating a test user profile: In this procedure, you create a test profile for the roaming user: (1) Create a user account to act as a test user account. For example, create an account named Sales Profile. (2) Log on as the test user account. A user profile is automatically created on the local computer in the c:\Winnt\Documents and Settings\username folder. (3) Configure the desktop environment, including appearance, shortcuts, and Start menu options. (4) Log off, and then log on as Administrator.

(b) Explain the POP and SMTP protocols.

Ans. Refer to Page No.-116, Chapter-6, Q.No.-1

●●●

CS-75: INTRANET ADMINISTRATION
June, 2012

Note: *Question number 1 is* **compulsory**. *Attempt any three questions from the rest.*

Q1. (a) What is an Intranet? How is it different from the internet? Explain the working of an Intranet with the help of a diagram.
Ans. Refer to Page No.-2 & 3, Chapter-1, Q.No.-1, Q.No.-2 & Q.No.-4

(b) Explain the five security models that can be referred to by organisations for chalking out their security plans and policies.
Ans. Refer to Page No.-272, Dec-2008, Q.No.-2(a)

(c) Name any four Editors that can be used for Web authoring. Explain any six features which are desirable in an Editor.
Ans. Refer to Page No.-100, Chapter-5, Q.No.-1

(d) Explain the working of Agora and SET as E- commerce based protocols.
Ans. Refer to Page No.-228, Dec-2004, Q.No.-4(i) & (iii)

(e) Define the following terms w.r.t. the Intranets:
(i) Daemon
(ii) Browser
(iii) URL
(iv) FAQs
Ans. Refer to Page No.- 17 & 19, Chapter-1, Q.No.-14

Q2. (a) What are Firewalls? Explain the three firewall architectures.
Ans. Refer to Page No.-44, Chapter-2, Q.No.-5

(b) Briefly describe the features of the AOL server.
Ans. Refer to Page No.-107, Chapter-5[AOL server]

Q3. Write short notes on the following:
(a) POP
Ans. Refer to Page No.-117, Chapter-6[POP]

(b) CGI
Ans. Refer to Page No.-125, Chapter-6, Q.No.-7

(c) GPRS

Ans. Refer to Page No.-133, Chapter-6, Q.No.-14

(d) ODBC

Ans. Refer to Page No.-62[ODBC]

Q4. (a) List and explain any six benefits that an organisation can draw from intranet applications.

Ans. Refer to Page No.-6, Chapter-1, Q.No.-7

(b) Explain how SOCKS can be used to construct a firewall on a TCP/IP based server.

Ans. Refer to Page No.-156, June-2004, Q.No.-2(b)

Q5. (a) What is GroupWare? List any five broad range of applications associated with them.

Ans. Refer to Page No.-59, Chapter-3, Q.No.-7

(b) Describe Address Resolution Protocol (ARP) as a communication protocol. Depict its message format and explain the various fields.

Ans. Refer to Page No.-116, Chapter-6, Q.No.-1 & Page No.-210, June-2005[Explanation of ARP message format.]

CS-75: INTRANET ADMINISTRATION
December, 2012

Note: *Question number 1 is* ***compulsory****. Attempt any three questions from the rest.*

Q1. (a) What is an Intranet? Explain the categories of the Intranets on the basis of their functionality and then on the basis of their application and architecture.

Ans. Refer to Page No.-2 & 9, Chapter-1, Q.No.-1 & 8

Some experts have taken a lead and categorised Intranet into four different categories based on their application or usage as well as its architecture. They are as follows:

- **The Communications Intranet:** Intranets of this type tend to feature in geographically dispersed organisations. The motivation for its implementation is greater efficiency and cost saving, through the reduction of fax and telephone calls. This Intranet is common with franchises or organisations that have a large number of sales people or agents in the field. Example, Maruti Udyog.
- **The Integrating Intranet:** These Intranets are designed to replace the complexity of in-house communications and processing systems that large organisations often use. Different interfaces commonly lack means of interconnection. Such Intranets offer organisations a common interface (through browser) that standardisation is paramount in an Integrating Internet. For example, IGNOU.
- **The Catalogue Intranet:** Intranets of this type are often more accurately described as Extranets. They are designed to give access to a large catalogue of information, like a multimedia catalogue. For example, a news agency or companies offering search engines like the Yahoo.
- **The Single Sign-On Internet:** This Intranet, if managed efficiently, allows maximum security by firewalling anyone from inappropriate sites automatically. For example, the Railways.

(b) What are Security Threats? Describe the Internal and External threats in an organisation.

Ans. Refer to Page No.-39, Chapter-2, Q.No.-2

(c) Describe databases as Intranet Management Tools.

Ans. The most prevalent tools are document management systems, search engines, and databases. And in some instances, combinations of all three tools. But before describing the tools, an issue that is becoming important is the lack of standards: "All of a sudden, with the rush to the Web, we all stepped back into the kind of application development we were doing in the '70's, as far as programming standards are concerned. Its all cut and paste from source code files all over again".

For now, the only real standard is International Standards Organisation (ISO) 8879:1986 which defines Standard Generalised Markup Language (SGML) of which HTML is a Document Type Definition (or more simply, a subset). But ISO 8879:1986 only addresses the markup of a Web Page (HTML Page) and not how to access that document. There are no standards on how a database is supposed to respond to a query generated by a CGI script.

Since product development seldom waits for standards to be defined, there are many tools available for managing Web Pages. One method is to rely on search engines that already commonly used by Internet users to search the World Wide Web. For instance, Open Text is a search engine capable of providing full text retrieval, which means Boolean searches are supported. Open Text is used by Caterpillar to manage data and search for information across stacks of CD ROMs located throughout Caterpillar's Wide Area Network. Seybold, 1995.

But search engines do not provide actual document management. Search engines can be used to located documents, but a search engine cannot determine if the document is outdated. But tools, called document management systems, can determine if a document is outdated.

"The union of the two technologies makes sense on a number of fronts. First, as Web sites become larger and filled with more critical business data, they fall prey to document management woes. That is, they need some way to track information for changes and edits, authenticate who has access and allow multiple formats". This article also points out that users are getting used to the idea of working with document management tools because data is changed much more often, from daily to weekly. And furthermore, the article states: "The opportunity for real-time distribution of wrong information is big".

And vendors are developing document management tools: "Universal access afforded by the Intranet is the main reason users are connecting document management systems to Web servers...Suddenly, the information stored and managed in their document management system is opened up to the entire corporation". The article also points out that internal documents are now being shared with customers, who are given access to segments of the Intranet. A set of statistics from the Gartner Group [research group that focuses on technology issues] included in the article states: "More than 95 percent of the information in enterprises is in the form of documents, and roughly 80 percent of those documents sit on desktop hard drives. An Intranet coupled with a document management system is an effective way to free those documents" Hibbard, 1996.

In addition to document management tools, many of which are really database applications with a specific purpose, another set of tools is the combination of databases and search engines. Oracle for instance, has licensed Open Text, and will incorporate the Open Text search engine into the database, which means in addition to performing traditional queries, you can now search text strings. Additionally many tools, such as Quicksite, Anonymous, 1996b, are touting the ability to access information from existing databases without creating CGI scripts and so forth.

(d) Explain the need of IP Addresses? Explain the various components of an IP Address. Also describe the four classes of IP Addresses with the help of a diagram.

Ans. Refer to Page No.-120, Chapter-6[Internet Protocol]

An IP address is a unique address used to locate and identify a device over a network. That device can be an electronic device, a computer, a server, a router or even an IP phone. It is the addressing used for the transmission of data packets over a network working with the IP protocol.

The IP Address Structure

All IP addresses are made up of four parts (quadrants) separated by dots, like this:

XXX.XXX.XXX.XXX

where each XXX can be any number between 0 and 255. If you know binary, you will understand that each of these numbers are stored in 8 bits (binary digits), and the number of possibilities you can have is 2 raised to the power of 8, which is 256 (0-255).

Examples of IP addresses are:

192.168.66.5

127.0.0.1

The second example above is the default IP address assign to any standalone machine. So, if your machine is not connected to any network, its address is 127.0.0.1. This is also called the localhost address.

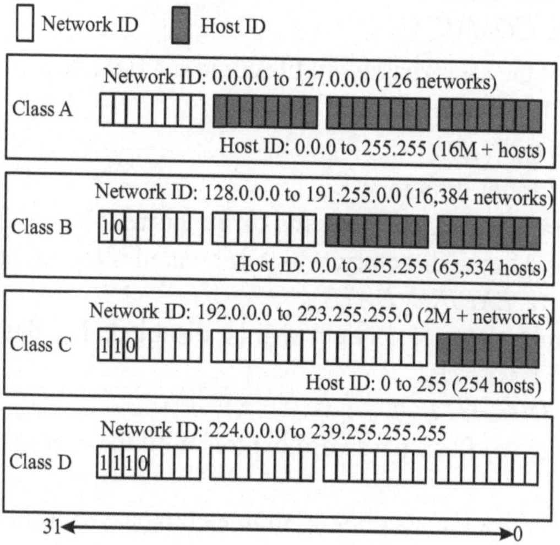

Q2. Define and briefly describe the following:

(a) Agora

Ans. Refer to Page No.-133, Chapter-6, Q.No.-15

(b) SMTP

Ans. Refer to Page No.-117, Chapter-6, Q.No.-1

(c) FTP

Ans. Refer to Page No.-123, Chapter-6, Q.No.-5

(d) HTTP

Ans. Refer to Page No.-122, Chapter-6, Q.No.-4

Q3. (a) What is Authentication? Explain any three types of authentication mechanisms supported by Windows 2000.

Ans. Refer to Page No.-257, Dec-2008, Q.No.-3(b)

(b) Write the steps for creation and modification of user accounts.

Ans. Refer to Page No.-250, June-2006, Q.No.-1(e)

usermod - modify a user account

The **usermod** command modifies the system account files to reflect the changes that are specified on the command line.

The options which apply to the **usermod** command are:

-a, —append

Add the user to the supplementary **group**(s). Use only with the **-G** option.

-c, —comment *COMMENT*

The new value of the user's password file comment field. It is normally modified using the **chfn**(1) utility.

-d, —home *HOME_DIR*

The user's new login directory.

If the **-m** option is given, the contents of the current home directory will be moved to the new home directory, which is created if it does not already exist.

-e, —expiredate *EXPIRE_DATE*

The date on which the user account will be disabled. The date is specified in the format *YYYY-MM-DD*.

-f, —inactive *INACTIVE*

The number of days after a password expires until the account is permanently disabled.

A value of 0 disables the account as soon as the password has expired, and a value of -1 disables the feature.

Q4. (a) Describe the working of any four protocols of the WAP stack.

Ans. Refer to Page No.-156, June-2004, Q.No.-3(a) & Page No.-131 [Figure Explanation]

(b) What is Encryption and Decryption? Explain their VPN and PKI implementations.

Ans. Refer to Page No.-11, Chapter-1, Q.No.-10 & Page No.-45, Chapter-2, Q.No.-6

Q5. (a) What is database connectivity? Explain the basic connectivity, middleware support, ODBC and JDBC technologies.

Ans. A database connection is a facility in computer science that allows client software to communicate with database server software, whether on the same machine or not. A connection is required to send commands and receive answers.

Now, Page No.-61, Chapter-3, Q.No.-8

(b) What is HTTP? Explain its utility and the various methods used by HTTP.

Ans. Refer to Page No.-122, Chapter-6, Q.No.-4